Inkscape 0.48 Essentials for Web Designers

Use the fascinating Inkscape graphics editor to create attractive layout designs, images, and icons for your website

Bethany Hiitola

[PACKT] open source *
PUBLISHING
community experience distilled

BIRMINGHAM - MUMBAI

Inkscape 0.48 Essentials for Web Designers

First published: November 2010

Production Reference: 1021110

Published by Packt Publishing Ltd.
32 Lincoln Road
Olton
Birmingham, B27 6PA, UK.

ISBN 978-1-849512-68-8

www.packtpub.com

Cover Image by John M. Quick (john.m.quick@gmail.com)

Credits

Author
Bethany Hiitola

Reviewers
Jack Armstrong
Richard Carter
Noreen McMahan
Vic Perez

Acquisition Editor
Dilip Venkatesh

Development Editor
Maitreya Bhakal

Technical Editor
Pallavi Kachare

Indexer
Hemangini Bari

Editorial Team Leader
Aanchal Kumar

Project Team Leader
Ashwin Shetty

Project Coordinator
Zainab Bagasrawala

Proofreader
Aaron Nash
Lynda Sliwoski

Production Coordinator
Kruthika Bangera

Cover Work
Kruthika Bangera

About the Author

Bethany Hiitola is a working writer. She's worked as a technical writer and multimedia developer for over 12 years and spends the rest of her time as a wife, mother, caretaker to pets, and Master of the household. She's written more user manuals than she can count, essays, short stories, academic papers, press releases, and feature articles. All between the day job, nap times, and diaper changes. More details are at her website: www.bethanyhiitola.com.

Without you Matt, this book wouldn't have been possible. Thanks for watching the kids for endless hours, late nights, and into the wee mornings.

About the Reviewers

Jack Armstrong spent over 40 years in the Silicon Valley computer industry as a researcher, programmer, analyst, designer, and network architect. At Stanford Research Institute he worked in a large scale scientific computing, artificial intelligence and robotics, and the development of ArpaNet, predecessor to the Internet. At Hewlett-Packard's Central Research Labs and Computer Division, he participated in the design of the HP3000 and the development of HTML, serving on HTML standards committees. After years of successfully operating a software and consulting partnership and 10 years with DHL as Manager of Infrastructure Research and Development and later as Principal Architect, he is now semi-retired, developing unique web sites for local and global clients and participating in development, testing, and standard groups to extend the use of XML and in particular, SVG on the Web. When away from computers, he can be found skiing in the Sierra Nevada mountains of California as often as possible.

Richard Carter is the Creative Director at Peacock Carter Ltd (`http://www.peacockcarter.co.uk`), a web design and development agency based in the North East of England, working with clients including Directgov, NHS Choices, and BusinessLink.

Richard is the author of *MediaWiki Skins Design*, *Magento 1.3 Themes Design*, and *Joomla! 1.5 Templates Cookbook*, and previously reviewed *MediaWiki 1.1 Beginner's Guide*.

He blogs at `http://www.earlgreyandbattenburg.co.uk` and tweets nonsense at `http://twitter.com/RichardCarter`.

I would like to thank the author of the book for dedicating time to Inkscape, which is fast becoming a better alternative to traditional graphic design software. As always, thanks to Alexandra and EJ.

Noreen McMahan lives in Austin, Texas, where she works for Freescale Semiconductor, Inc. as a member of their Single-Source Documentation System (SSDS) team. She is the SSDS training lead, providing both classroom and written instruction in the use of DITA XML, the Freescale component content management system (CCMS), and the tools required for SSDS content development, including Inkscape. She also participates in SSDS software regression testing and user acceptance testing, which are both activities that feed the training.

For several years, Noreen worked as an information developer and editor at Freescale Semiconductor. At one point, she supervised the work of an 8-person editing team. Noreen has over 20 years of experience drawing engineering diagrams for a variety of document types. She is among the early adopters charged with researching scalable vector graphics (SVG) and promulgating the use of Inkscape at Freescale Semiconductor.

Noreen has lived in Austin since she moved there as a graduate student to attend the University of Texas, where she earned her Ph.D. in English and taught technical writing. Noreen has a 25-year old son, Eric Garrison, and two cats, Xena and Gabrielle.

Vic Perez is a guy that loves art. His experience includes painting with oils and water colors, drawing with inks, pencils and prisma colors. He has created a few custom indoor and outdoor painted wall murals, numerous logos, and web designs.

Thanks to Zainab Bagasrawala, from Packt Publishing, the author of this book, and the Administrative Team at the Inkscape forum website.

Table of Contents

Preface

Do you think that your website could do with more visual appeal? Are you looking to spice it up with attractive designs and effects? Enter *Inkscape 0.48 Essentials for Web Designers* — the only book specifically tailored to using Inkscape for web design. This book will teach you how to effectively use the fascinating new Inkscape vector graphics editor, which, despite being in version 0.48 *and* having no dearth of competitors, has already separated itself from the competition. Learn everything you need to know about enhancing your website — from site layouts to templates and animations — whether you are looking for a new website design or just some eye candy.

The Inkscape graphics editor is powerful, but getting started is often difficult. *Inkscape 0.48 Essentials for Web Designers* walks you through the challenge of using Inkscape from a web design perspective in the easiest way possible.

The first book to unlock the potential of Inkscape for web design, it begins with an introduction to the basics of Inkscape and then journeys you through implementing them in your website one by one.

Learn to build your first website design using Inkscape. Create web page and desktop wallpapers with repeating pattern backgrounds and swirling designs. Incorporate icons and interactive maps on your website. Style and graphically manipulate text — from simple headings to shadowing, following paths, reflections, 3D effects, and more. Enhance your web pages using flowcharts, diagrams, and site maps and learn how to export them. Spruce it all up using animations.

This book will teach you all that and more, in a simple effective manner, and what's more — you'll have fun doing it.

What this book covers

Chapter 1, Inkscape 101: The Basics discusses vector graphics—what they are, how they differ from the rasterized images, what this means in terms of their creation, and how best to use them on the web. Then it gives simple instructions about using Inkscape including installation, details about all the menus and tools, and creating some simple and complex objects.

Chapter 2, Designing Site Layouts introduces design techniques that can make web pages move from good to great, describes a simple web page layout, and then shows how to make the site that has a header, navigation bar, and content areas.

Chapter 3, Working with Images teaches you everything you need to know about images—raster and vector—in Inkscape. From importing bitmap images, embedding images, rendering bitmap images as vector graphics, working a little with photographs and filters, importing clip art, and all the tips and tricks for "tracing" bitmap images to convert them into full vector graphics for both photographs and logos.

Chapter 4, Styling Text is about text editing and styling. Specifically about kerning, rotating, moving letters from the baseline, reflection, following paths, shadows, the perspective tool, and even some cool envelope effects.

Chapter 5, Creating Wallpapers and Pattern Backgrounds describes how to use the built-in patterns within Inkscape, create a new pattern, and use spirals and the Spiro effect, as well as how to manipulate the patterns to make them even more intricate and incorporate them into an example project.

Chapter 6, Building Icons, Buttons, and Logos starts by describing icon and button design principles. Then it explains new techniques like the glow effect and masking while creating buttons. There is also some discussion of logo design principles, how to best tackle that logo design project, and step-by-step directions on creating icons, buttons, and logos.

Chapter 7, Making Diagrams, Site Maps, and More teaches you how to use Inkscape to create diagrams, charts, and site maps—including the basics for what each type of diagram is, what it would be used for, and then how best to create each of them.

Chapter 8, Designing for Blogs and Storefronts is all about web design for blogs and online merchant stores. We walk through simple designs for each, defining common elements for each website type and even some sub-level pages to help keep the designs consistent. There is also a discussion about using grids and a CSS framework.

Chapter 9, Using the XML Editor is all about XML and SVG code. It teaches how to access the Inkscape XML editor in Inkscape and edit the code for a pleasant result in your graphical image.

Chapter 10, Creating Simple Animations discusses how Inkscape has limited capabilities for creating animations—but with a little help from another open source tool like Gimp, you can still create animations. We will break down an animation into individual animation frames and create each one that will then be brought together using Gimp to complete a full animation sequence.

Chapter 11, Plugins, Scripts, and Templates starts discussing the pre-installed templates in Inkscape. Then it describes how to install a new template, modify a standard template and save it as a custom, and how to start from scratch and save a custom template. Lastly, it discusses what plugins, scripts, and extensions are within Inkscape and how you can access them.

Appendix A, Keyboard Shortcuts mentions the basic keyboard shortcuts for Inkscape 0.48.

Appendix B, Glossary of Terms is a glossary of Inkscape and basic web design terms used throughout this book.

Appendix C, Fonts is an overview of how fonts are viewed in web browsers and in SVG files.

What you need for this book

You'll need the latest version of Inkscape 0.48 and the latest version of Gimp.

If you are using a Mac, then they also need the X11 app on your system to run Inkscape (this typically come pre-installed on Leopard OSX. More details in Chapter 1.)

Who this book is for

This book is written for web designers who want to add attractive visual elements to their website. It assumes no previous knowledge of Inkscape. General familiarity with vector graphics programming is recommended but not required. It will also be a useful guide for experienced Inkscape users who want to learn how to apply their skills to website design.

Conventions

In this book, you will find a number of styles of text that distinguish between different kinds of information. Here are some examples of these styles, and an explanation of their meaning.

Code words in text are shown as follows: "For any Windows device, an .EXE file is downloaded."

New terms and **important words** are shown in bold. Words that you see on the screen, in menus or dialog boxes for example, appear in the text like this: "Now find the **Inkscape** icon in the Application or Programs folders to open the program."

> Warnings or important notes appear in a box like this.

> Tips and tricks appear like this.

Reader feedback

Feedback from our readers is always welcome. Let us know what you think about this book—what you liked or may have disliked. Reader feedback is important for us to develop titles that you really get the most out of.

To send us general feedback, simply send an e-mail to feedback@packtpub.com, and mention the book title via the subject of your message.

If there is a book that you need and would like to see us publish, please send us a note in the **SUGGEST A TITLE** form on www.packtpub.com or e-mail suggest@packtpub.com.

If there is a topic that you have expertise in and you are interested in either writing or contributing to a book, see our author guide on www.packtpub.com/authors.

Customer support

Now that you are the proud owner of a Packt book, we have a number of things to help you to get the most from your purchase.

Errata

Although we have taken every care to ensure the accuracy of our content, mistakes do happen. If you find a mistake in one of our books—maybe a mistake in the text or the code—we would be grateful if you would report this to us. By doing so, you can save other readers from frustration and help us improve subsequent versions of this book. If you find any errata, please report them by visiting http://www.packtpub. com/support, selecting your book, clicking on the **errata submission form** link, and entering the details of your errata. Once your errata are verified, your submission will be accepted and the errata will be uploaded on our website, or added to any list of existing errata, under the Errata section of that title. Any existing errata can be viewed by selecting your title from http://www.packtpub.com/support.

Piracy

Piracy of copyright material on the Internet is an ongoing problem across all media. At Packt, we take the protection of our copyright and licenses very seriously. If you come across any illegal copies of our works, in any form, on the Internet, please provide us with the location address or website name immediately so that we can pursue a remedy.

Please contact us at copyright@packtpub.com with a link to the suspected pirated material.

We appreciate your help in protecting our authors, and our ability to bring you valuable content.

Questions

You can contact us at questions@packtpub.com if you are having a problem with any aspect of the book, and we will do our best to address it.

1
Inkscape 101: The Basics

Inkscape is an open source, free program that creates vector-based graphics that can be used in web, print, and screen design as well as interface and logo creation, and material cutting. Its capabilities are similar to those of commercial products such as Adobe Illustrator, Macromedia Freehand, and CorelDraw and can be used for any number of practical purposes—creating vector graphics for use in illustrations, business letterheads, computer and electronic wallpapers, designing logos, and—as is the focus of this book—designing web pages and the elements within web page design.

This book's purpose is to help you learn to use Inkscape to help develop web pages. We'll start at the beginning of design, the principles of web design, then move to wireframe and mockups development and then learn how to export all of your images and files for use in the HTML development. There will also be information about how to enhance your web page designs by learning the ins and outs of using Inkscape as a graphics tool for creating icons, backgrounds, buttons, blog designs, flowcharts, diagrams, site maps, banner advertisements, and more.

Specifically this book will teach you how to:

- Use Inkscape for web design
- Create graphics, logos, and icons
- Develop wireframes and web site mockups
- Learn about Scalable Vector Graphics (SVG)
- Integrate graphics into HTML, HTML5, and Cascading Style Sheets (CSS)

However, before learning the details on how to use Inkscape, let's take a step back and define **vector graphics**, how computer displays and vector graphics work together, and why we want to use them in web design.

Vector graphics

Vector graphics are made up of **paths**. Each path is basically a line with a start and end point, curves, angles, and points that are calculated with a mathematical equation. These paths are not limited to being straight—they can be of any shape, size, and even encompass any number of curves. When you combine them, they create drawings, diagrams, and can even help create certain fonts.

These characteristics make vector graphics very different than JPEGs, GIFs, or BMP images—all of which are considered **rasterized** or bitmap images made up of tiny squares which are called pixels or bits. If you magnify these images, you will see they are made up of a grid (bitmaps) and if you keep magnifying them, they will become blurry and grainy as each pixel with bitmap square's zoom level grows larger.

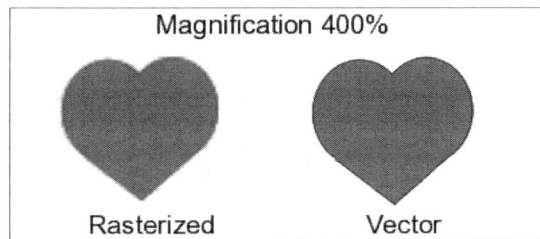

Computer monitors also use pixels in a grid. However, they use millions of them so that when you look at a display, your eyes see a picture. In high-resolution monitors, the pixels are smaller and closer together to give a crisper image.

How does this all relate to vector-based graphics? Vector-based graphics aren't made up of squares. Since they are based on paths, you can make them larger (by scaling) and the image quality stays the same, lines and edges stay clean, and the same images can be used on items as small as letterheads or business cards or blown up to be billboards or used in high definition animation sequences. This flexibility, often accompanied by smaller file sizes, makes vector graphics ideal—especially in the world of the Internet, varying computer displays, and hosting services for web spaces, which leads us nicely to Inkscape, a tool that can be invaluable for use in web design.

What is Inkscape and how can it be used?

Inkscape is a free, open source program developed by a group of volunteers under the GNU General Public License (GPL). You not only get a free download but can use the program to create items with it and freely distribute them, modify the program itself, and share that modified program with others.

Inkscape uses **Scalable Vector Graphics (SVG)**, a vector-based drawing language that uses some basic principles:

- A drawing can (and should) be scalable to any size without losing detail
- A drawing can use an unlimited number of smaller drawings used in any number of ways (and reused) and still be a part of a larger whole

SVG and **World Wide Web Consortium (W3C)** web standards are built into Inkscape which give it a number of features including a rich body of XML (eXtensible Markup Language) format with complete descriptions and animations. Inkscape drawings can be reused in other SVG-compliant drawing programs and can adapt to different presentation methods. It has support across most web browsers (Firefox, Chrome, Opera, Safari, Internet Explorer).

When you draw your objects (rectangles, circles, and so on.), arbitrary paths, and text in Inkscape, you also give them attributes such as color, gradient, or patterned fills. Inkscape automatically creates a web code (XML) for each of these objects and tags your images with this code. If need be, the graphics can then be transformed, cloned, and grouped in the code itself. Hyperlinks can even be added for use in web browsers, multi-lingual scripting (which isn't available in most commercial vector-based programs) and more—all within Inkscape or in a native programming language. It makes your vector graphics more versatile in the web space than a standard JPG or GIF graphic.

There are still some limitations in the Inkscape program, even though it aims to be fully SVG compliant. For example, as of version 0.48 it still does not support animation or SVG fonts—though there are plans to add these capabilities into future versions.

Installing Inkscape

Inkscape is available for download for Windows, Macintosh, Linux, or Solaris operating systems.

> To run on the Mac OS X operating system, it typically runs under X11—an implementation of the X Window System software that makes it possible to run X11-based applications in Mac OS X. The X11 application has shipped with the Mac OS X since version 10.5.
>
> When you open Inkscape on a Mac, it will first open X11 and run Inkscape within that program. Loss of some shortcut key options will occur but all functionality is present using menus and toolbars.

Let's briefly go over how to download and install Inkscape:

1. Go to the official Inkscape website at: `http://www.inkscape.org/` and download the appropriate version of the software for your computer.

2. For the Mac OS X Leopard software, you will also need to download an additional application. It is the X11 application package 2.4.0 or greater from this website: `http://xquartz.macosforge.org/trac/wiki/X112.4.0`.

   Once downloaded, double-click the X11-2.4.0.DMG package first. It will open another folder with the X11 application installer. Double-click that icon to be prompted through an installation wizard.

3. Double-click the downloaded Inkscape installation package to start the installation.

> For the Mac OS, a DMG file is downloaded. Double-click on it and then drag and drop the Inkscape package to the Application Folder. For any Windows device, an .EXE file is downloaded. Double-click that file to start and complete the installation. For Linux-based computers, there are a number of distributions available. Be sure to download and install the correct installation package for your system.

4. Now find the **Inkscape** icon in the Application or Programs folders to open the program.

Inkscape

5. Double-click the **Inkscape** icon and the program will automatically open to the main screen.

> In this book, the screen shots will be specific to the Mac OS X software. Don't be concerned if this is not the computer operating system of your choice; the software itself is very similar between them and notable differences in the Inkscape software screens will be noted.

The basics of the software

When you open Inkscape for the first time, you'll see that the main screen and a new blank document opened are ready to go.

> If you are using a Macintosh computer, Inkscape opens within the X11 application and may take slightly longer to load.

The Inkscape interface is based on the GNOME UI standard which uses visual cues and feedback for any icons. For example:

- Hovering your mouse over any icon displays a pop-up description of the icon.
- If an icon has a dark gray border, it is active and can be used.
- If an icon is grayed out, it is not currently available to use with the current selection.
- All icons that are in execution mode (or busy) are covered by a dark shadow. This signifies that the application is busy and won't respond to any edit request.
- There is a **Notification Display** on the main screen that displays dynamic help messages to key shortcuts and basic information on how to use the Inkscape software in its current state or based on what objects and tools are selected.

Main screen basics

Within the main screen there is the main menu, a command, snap and status bar, tool controls, and a palette bar.

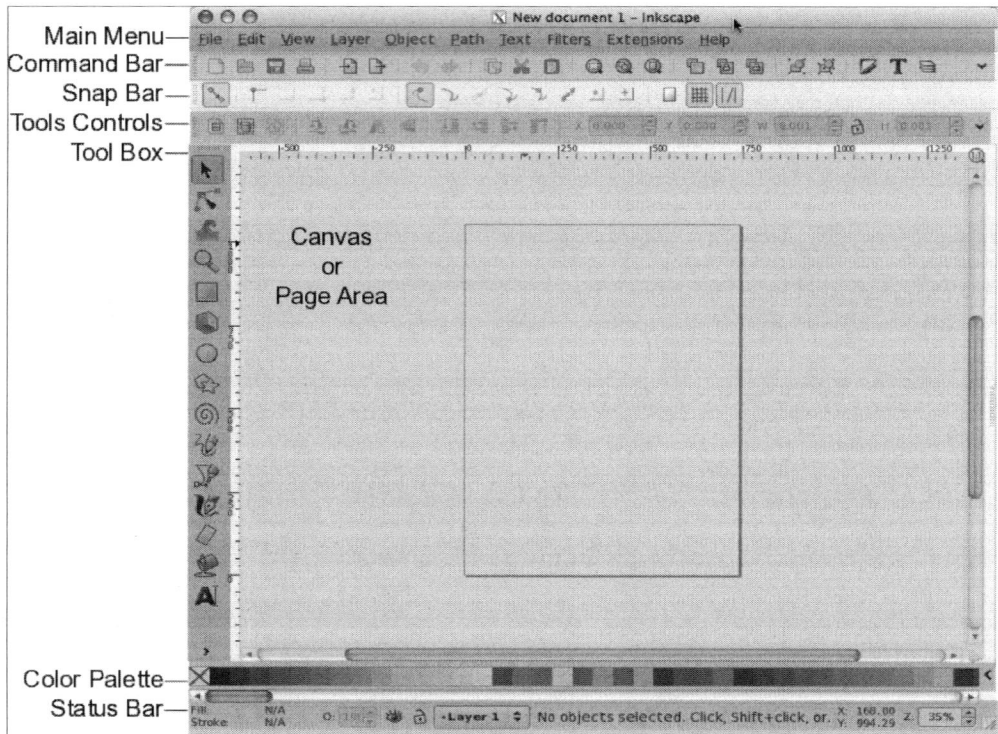

Main menu

You will use the **main menu** bar the most when working on your projects. This is the central location to find every tool and menu item in the program—even those found in the visual-based toolbars below it on the screen. When you select a main menu item the Inkscape dialog displays the icon, a text description, and shortcut key combination for the feature. This can be helpful while first learning the program—as it provides you with easier and often faster ways to use your most commonly used functions of the program.

Toolbars

Let's take a general tour of the tool bars seen on this main screen. We'll pay close attention to the tools we'll use most frequently.

If you don't like the location of any of the toolbars, you can also make them as floating windows on your screen. This lets you move them from their pre-defined locations and move them to a location of your liking. To move any of the toolbars, from their docking point on the left side, click and drag them out of the window. When you click the upper left button to close the toolbar window, it will be relocated back into the screen.

Command bar

This toolbar represents the common and most frequently used commands in Inkscape:

As seen in the previous screenshot you can create a new document, open an existing one, save, print, cut, paste, zoom, add text, and much more. Hover your mouse over each icon for details on its function. By default, when you open Inkscape, this toolbar is on the right side of the main screen.

Snap bar

Also found vertically on the right side of the main screen, this toolbar is designed to help with the **Snap to** features of Inkscape. It lets you easily align items (**snap to guides**), force objects to align to paths (**snap to paths**), or snap to bounding boxes and edges.

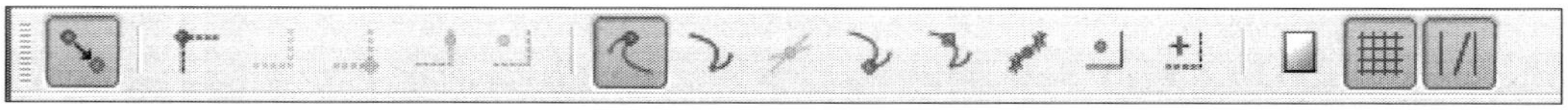

Tool controls

This toolbar's options change depending on which tool you have selected in the toolbox (described in the next section). When you are creating objects, it provides you all the detailed options — size, position, angles, and attributes specific to the tool you are currently using. By default, it looks like the following screenshot:

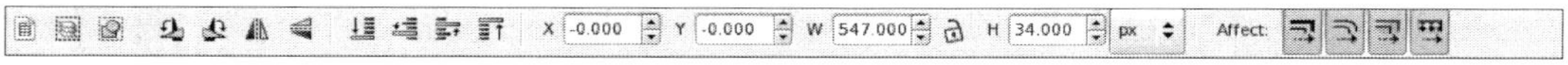

You have options to select/deselect objects within a layer, rotate or mirror objects, adjust object locations on the canvas, and scaling options and much more. Use it to define object properties when they are selected on the canvas.

Toolbox bar

You'll use the tool box frequently. It contains all of the main tools for creating objects, selecting and modifying objects, and drawing. To select a tool, click the icon. If you double-click a tool, you can see that tool's preferences (and change them).

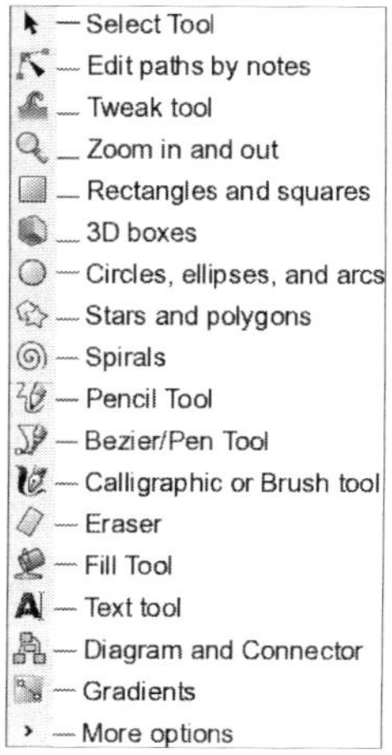

- Select Tool
- Edit paths by notes
- Tweak tool
- Zoom in and out
- Rectangles and squares
- 3D boxes
- Circles, ellipses, and arcs
- Stars and polygons
- Spirals
- Pencil Tool
- Bezier/Pen Tool
- Calligraphic or Brush tool
- Eraser
- Fill Tool
- Text tool
- Diagram and Connector
- Gradients
- More options

If you are new to Inkscape, there are a couple of hints about creating and editing text. The **Text tool** (**A** icon) in the **Tool Box** shown above is the only way of creating new text on the canvas. The **T** icon shown in the **Command Bar** is used only while editing text that already exists on the canvas.

Palette bar

This section of the Inkscape screen controls fill and stroke color options. **Fill** is the color that fills the object or shape. Alternatively, **stroke** is the outline around the object or shape.

There are a few ways you can set the fill and stroke in Inkscape:

- From the Palette bar, click a color and drag it from the palette onto objects to change their Fill. If you hold the *Shift* key and drag a color box onto an object, it will set the stroke color.
- Select an object on your canvas, and then right-click a color box in the palette. A pop-up menu appears with options to set the fill and stroke.
- Select the object on your canvas and then left-click a color box in the palette to immediately set the fill of an object. *Shift+Left-Click* a color box to immediately set the stroke color.

There are a large number of color boxes to choose from. Use the Palette bar scroll bar along the bottom to see more choices to the right of those displaying on the screen.

Status bar

This toolbar contains information relating to a selected object within the canvas or page of your document.

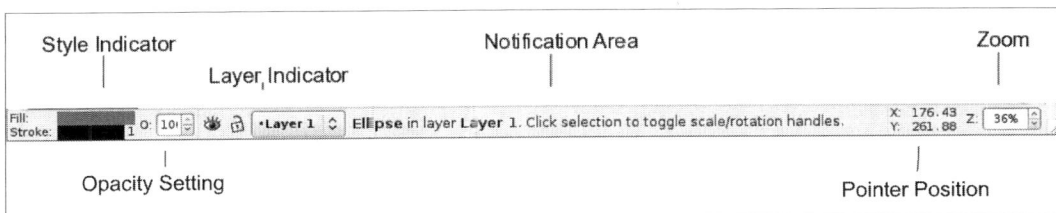

You can also use it to modify canvas settings. Here are the details:

- **Style Indicator**: This focuses a bit more on the selected object. If you choose any object in your canvas, you can change its **fill** (overall color of the object) or **stroke** (border color). Drag a color from the palette to this section for easy color changes. Right-clicking the Style Indicators provides a pop-up menu letting you make quick and easy coloring edits. Double-clicking the Style Indicators will launch the Fill & Stroke Menu. If you right-click the number next to the Stroke Style Indicator, you get a choice of Stroke thicknesses to choose from.

- **Opacity Setting**: This is the drop down box near the Style Indicators. Right-click the drop down box to change the opacity percentage (%) value (the default is 100%). A pop-up menu displays a set of preset values to choose from.

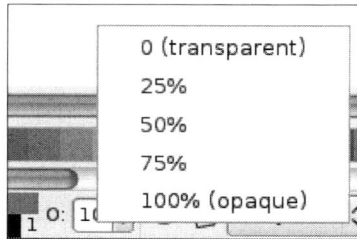

- **Layer Indicator**: Within Inkscape when you create documents you can have many **layers** of objects. This gives great flexibility when creating web layouts. You can move groups of objects at once (placing a group of them on a layer), separate objects by layer to manipulate and play with how they interact with one another when stacked, re-ordered, or hidden. You can also set certain settings by layer. You can even create drafts or different versions of mockups and keep all of this in one file.

  The The Layer Indicator drop down menu lets you choose which layer you are currently using and placing objects to—this is called the **drawing layer**. You can then set whether this layer is visible or locked. Sometimes you can use your documents as a "working draft" and decide to hide certain layers while developing others. You might also **lock** layers when you have specified the exact positioning determined and you don't want it accidentally changed while manipulating other layers.

- **Notification Area**: This contains hints or tricks about the objects or area you currently have selected in your document. Keep an eye on this area because it guides you with helpful information as you work within the layer. This feature is unique to Inkscape and the help messages change and update as you work with objects to reflect your available options.

- **Pointer or Cursor Position**: When designing any space—print or web—it is often important to get precise placement of objects. To help do this, sometimes you want to see when/where your cursor or pointer is placed on the screen. This is the area on the Inkscape main screen where you can always see the exact x (horizontal) and y (vertical) placement of your cursor within the document.

- **Zoom**: Use the zoom tools to magnify your canvas for super close-up work or zoom out to see the whole canvas in one shot. If you right-click the zoom field a pop-up menu with commonly used preset zoom levels is displayed and you can select one to immediately adjust the canvas to. It's nice because you can customize your viewable magnification at any time, and to whatever level you would like.

- **Window resize**: By default, Inkscape opens to a default window size. With the resize window option in the lower right side of this area you can click, hold, and drag the window to an appropriate size for your computer screen. Or you can choose to make the window full screen by going to the main menu and choosing **View** and then **Full Screen** (press *F11* on a Windows or Linux-based system).

Canvas

Let's open a new document in Inkscape and discuss this portion of the screen.

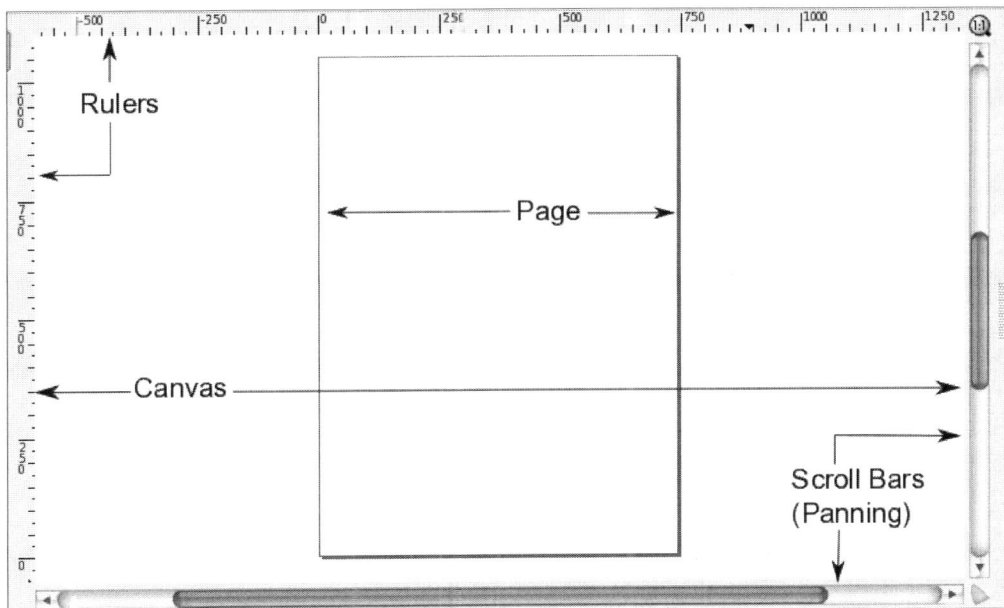

The terms **canvas** and page are used interchangeably within the Inkscape interface. For simplicity, we'll refer to the canvas as the entire portion of the open document screen. A page is the portion of the canvas that is contained within the printable area—seen as a black bordered box in the previous screenshot.

You can always adjust the page—or printable area—size. Go to the main menu and select **File** and then **Document Properties**. In **Document Properties** window **Page** tab, look in the **Format** field. You can select any number of pre-defined sizes, or change the **Custom Size** field measurements to your liking.

The pre-defined sizes are specific to print media, while those found in the main menu, **File | New** path give common web design, logo, or web banner sized templates.

As soon as you make changes to these properties, you can see them reflected on your screen.

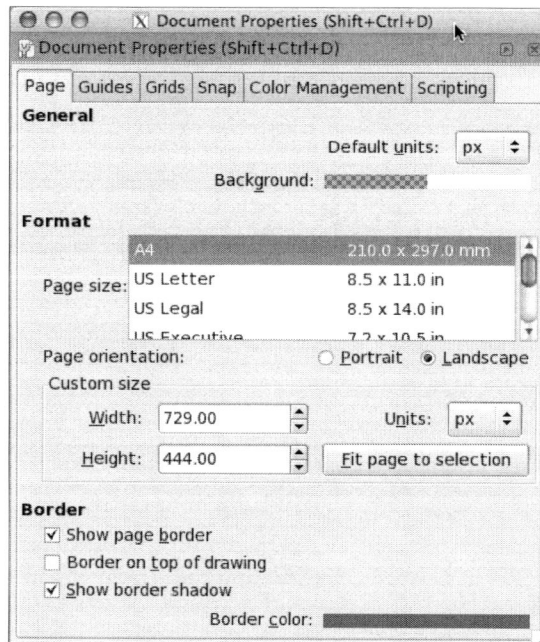

Dockable Dialogs

Dockable Dialogs are a great feature in Inkscape 0.48. They give you more freedom in your screen layout. You can Show (or Hide) dialog boxes on the right side of your screen or move to the top of your screen.

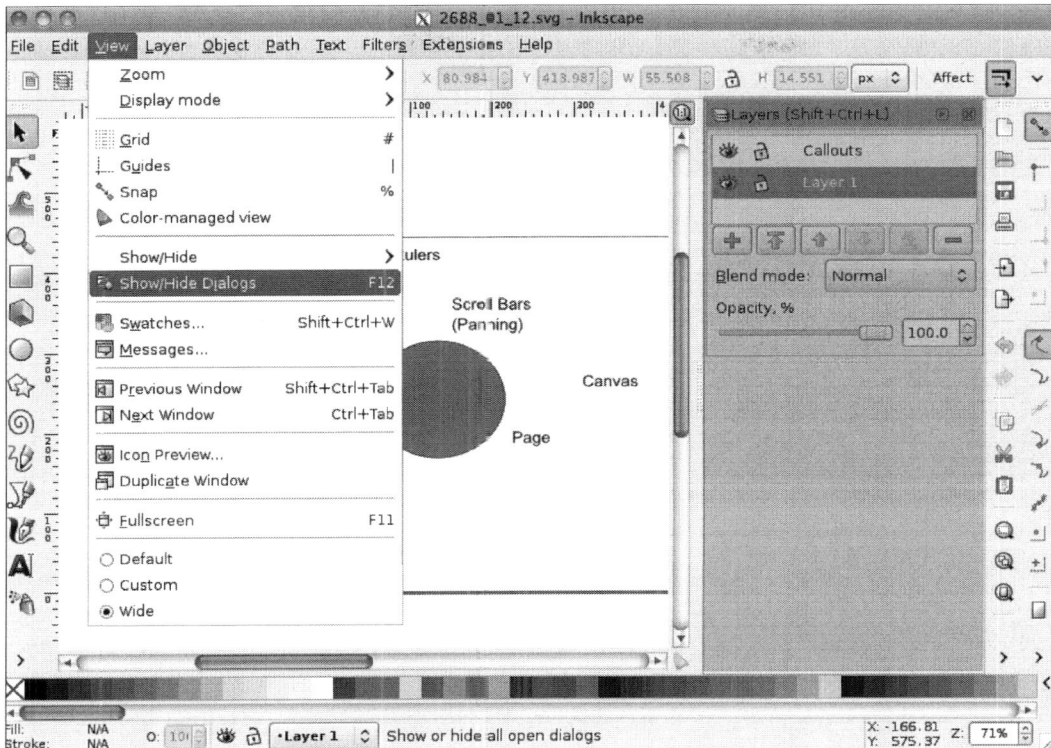

Useful dialogs to be shown here are:

- Layers
- Transform
- Path Effect
- SVG Font Editor
- Filter Editor

The docked dialogs can be minimized, rearranged, stacked, and pulled into a separate window on your desktop. Here's how to do some of the basics:

- **Showing dialog boxes**: To show these dialog boxes, on the main menu select **View** and select **Show/Hide Dialogs**. Then go to the **Layer, Object, Path**, or **Text** menus and choose the **Editor, Layer**, or **Property** options to show the correlating dialog box.

- **Displaying more than one dialog box**: If you open more than one dialog box, they **stack** in the order they were opened in the **Dialog** area of the main screen. Use the scroll bar to see those below the first viewable.

- **Minimizing dialog boxes**: To minimize a dialog, press the right arrow button, along the right side of the title bar of each dialog box. This places a shortcut along the left side of the Inkscape screen. To re-open it, just click the text/icon and the dialog re-opens to the large state on the screen.

- **Floating dialog boxes**: Dialogs can also be dragged off of the main window into their own window. Each dialog can have its own window or they can be grouped in floating docks.

- **Closing dialog boxes**: To close the dialog window, you can click the **X** on title bar for that box. It immediately closes.

For initial web design using these docks can be extremely useful. Particularly useful is having the Layers Dock visible, as it lets you re-order and select layers and the items in each layer quickly. To determine which dialog you have opened, there is a visual cue—the layer's menu title will be a darker in title.

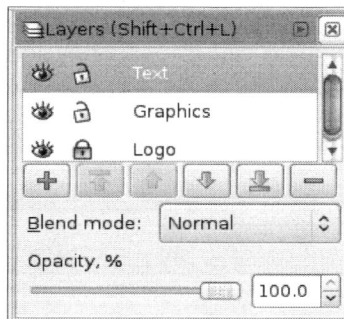

Panning and zooming

There are several ways to view your canvas or page in an open document. **Panning** means moving left, right, or up and down on the main screen.

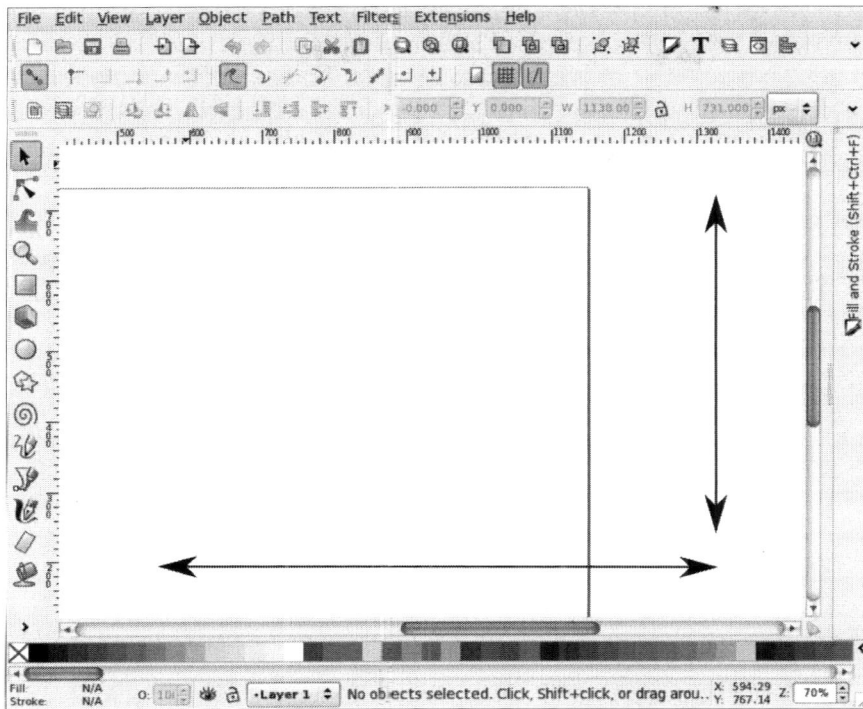

The easiest way to pan to the left and right is to use the horizontal scroll bar along the bottom of your Inkscape screen. Panning up and down can be done with the vertical scroll bar on the right side of the screen. But, if you own a mouse with a scroll wheel you can use it to pan as well. Just scrolling with the wheel moves the canvas up and down, pressing *Shift* on the keyboard and then using the scroll wheel moves it sideways.

As discussed in the Status bar overview, you can use the **Zoom** tool to magnify your canvas so that you can see a lot of detail (zoomed in) or the entire canvas at a glance (zoomed out). By default, Inkscape opens documents at about 35%. You can also use the **Zoom** tool on the **Tool** box, a mouse with a scroll wheel, or use your keypad (= or + zoom in and – zooms out).

> For easy access to the Zoom to fit selection, Zoom to fit drawing, and Zoom to fit page in the window options, see the options in the command bar.

Creating and managing files

As stated when you first open Inkscape, a new document is opened and ready to start. However, it uses a default canvas sizes as 8.5in x 11in (standard letter size) and you likely need orientations and sizes for web design elements.

Creating web sized documents

You'll love that if you choose **File** and then **New** from the main menu, Inkscape has many pre-defined sizes for you already generated. For web design, you can choose from:

- Desktops with sizes: 1024 x 768, 1600 x 1200, 640 x 480, 800 x 600
- Web Banners 468 x 60 or 728 x 90
- Icon sizes: ranging from 16 x 16, 32 x 32, and 48 x 48

If you want to manually change your document properties just go to the main menu and select **File** and then **Document Properties**. You'll see the **Document Properties** window displayed with a number of options for customizing your canvas and "printable" page.

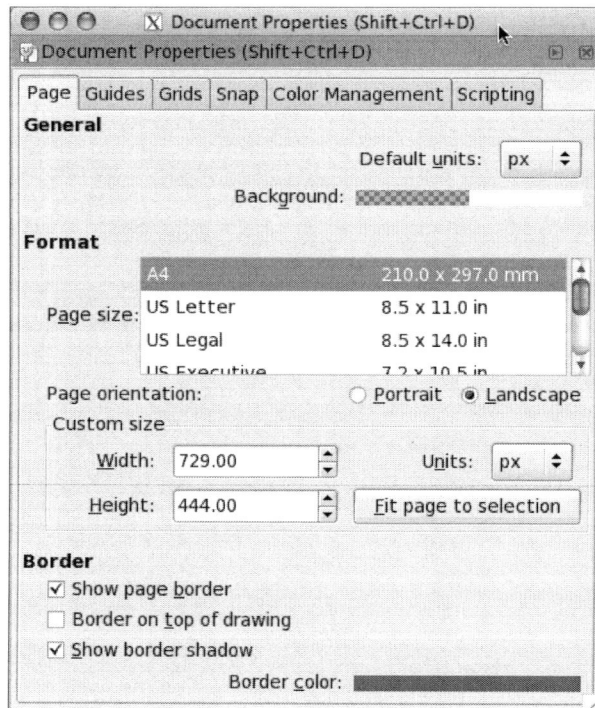

Some of the web-based elements are also listed in the pre-define **Format** list on this screen. You can select any item in that field (i.e. **Banner 468 X 60** or **Icon 48 X 48**) and return to the Inkscape main screen to begin.

To open an existing file, go to the main menu and choose **File,** then **Open** (or **Open Recent**).

Inkscape supports a number of graphic formats. Particularly it can import or open a number of vector and bitmap based graphic formats, PDFs, and even text files. Some require additional plug-ins to be installed. See this version of the Inkscape manual for the fully supported formats and the caveats of importing each: `http://tavmjong.free.fr/INKSCAPE/MANUAL/html/File-Import.html`.

Remember, if you import and open a non-native Inkscape file, you may not be able edit all of the elements. Inkscape imports non-native files as flattened graphic files, so you can't edit anything within the graphic, but can manipulate or use the flattened image within Inkscape.

> The recommended format for transferring non-native Inkscape files is to use the original source program and files to create a PDF. Then open the PDF in Inkscape.

Saving Inkscape files

You'll notice when you are ready to save the document, Inkscape suggests saving in the Inkscape SVG format. Always save a version of your file in this format to allow editing at a later time. If file size is a concern, you can also save in the Inkscape compressed format of SVGZ.

For web design, it is possible that you can use the SVG files directly in the HTML/XML code. However, work with your programming team to confirm that they can use the SVG format (not all browsers or platforms support this). Using a file in any other non-Inkscape-SVG-format won't be editable to the extent of the original. So, always save the native Inkscape document and then export bitmaps and other graphics and or use **File | Save Copy As** to save in another format.

Exporting an entire canvas in PNG format is useful in web design when the client wants to see the graphical layout of the web design (a mockup) without having a need to interact with a live web site. Details on how to perform this export will be given in *Chapter 2, Designing Site Layouts*.

Managing multiple file projects

Since you can export objects themselves or entire "pages" of content, you will need to create a directory—or folder—where you store all of the files for one project.

Just create a project folder on your computer in an easy to access location. Whenever you create a new file in Inkscape, you can save those source Inkscape files in a folder named `Source`. Then you can also create a Deployment folder (or another intuitive name) where you export all files in the various formats you need to hand off to a developer for web site integration.

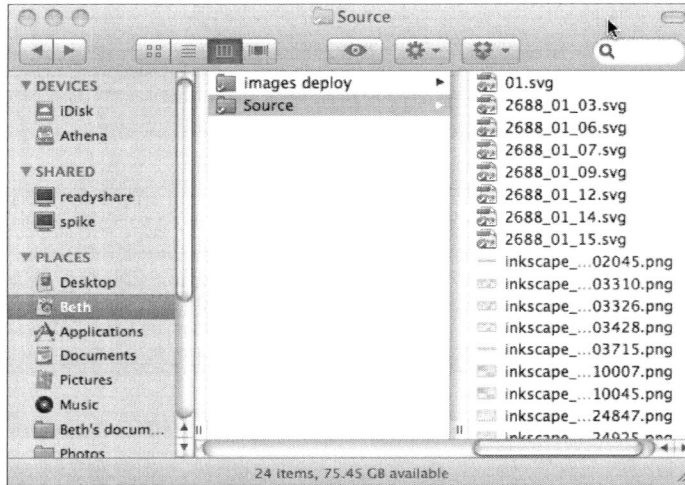

Paths

Paths have no pre-defined lengths or widths. They are arbitrary in nature and come in three basic types: open paths (have two ends), closed paths (have no ends, like a circle), or compound paths (uses a combination of two open and/or closed paths).

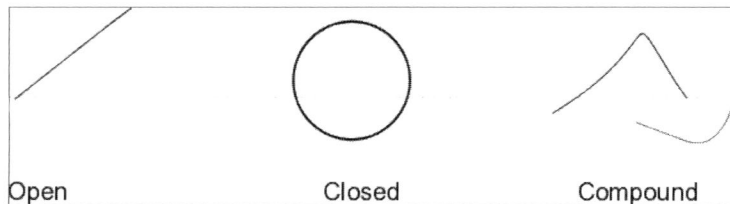

In Inkscape there are a few ways we can make paths: the Pencil (Freehand), Bezier (Pen), and Calligraphy tools—all of which are found in the tool box.
They can also be created by converting a regular shape or text object into paths.

Paths are used in web design to create unique text styling (discussed in *Chapter 4, Styling Text*), when tracing other images like photographs (examples shown in *Chapter 3, Working with Images*) and when building icons, buttons, and logos (*Chapter 6, Building Icons, Buttons, and Logos*).

In general, we use paths to build unique objects that aren't part of the SVG standard shapes in Inkscape discussed in the next section. Since we can combine paths and make them closed objects—they again can be resized, manipulated, and then exported as web graphics.

Creating shapes

Different from paths, Inkscape can also create shapes that are part of the SVG standard. These are:

- Rectangles and squares 3D boxes
- Circles, ellipses, and arcs
- Stars
- Polygons
- Spirals

To create any of these shapes, see the following screenshot. Select (click) the shape tool icon in the tool box and then draw the shape on the canvas by clicking, holding, and then dragging the shape to the size you want on the canvas.

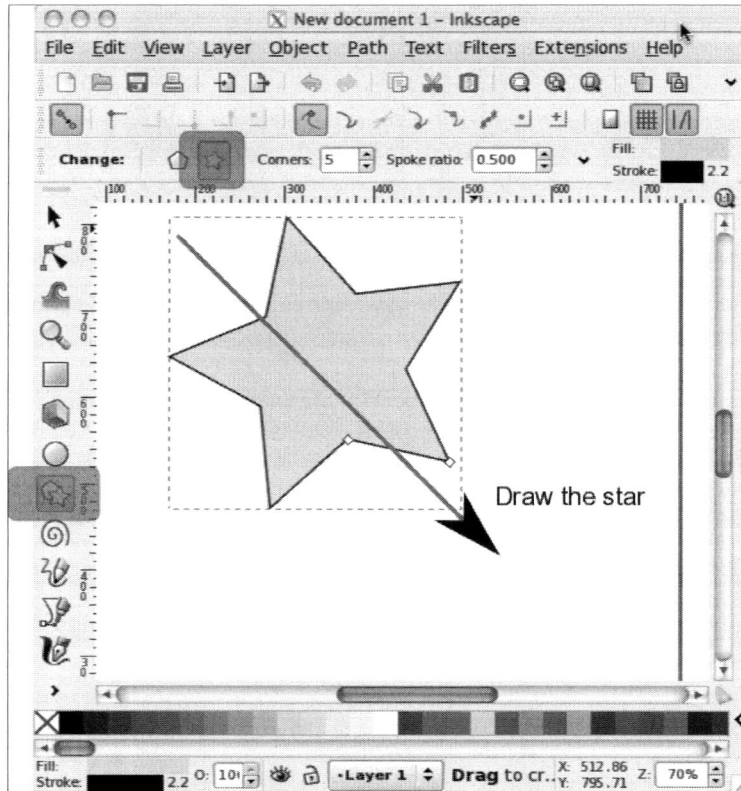

To switch between creating stars and polygons, select that star/polygon icon in the tool box on the left hand side of your screen, and then select either the polygon or the star icon in the Tool controls (just above the canvas).

Once the shape is drawn you can:

- Change the **fill** color of the shape by selecting a color in the color palette
- Change the **stroke** or border color by pressing and holding the *Shift* key and then selecting that color from the color palette
- Change the **position** of the shape on the canvas by choosing the **Select** tool in the tool box, clicking and holding the shape and moving it where you need it to be

- Change the **size** of the shape by also choosing the **Select** tool from the tool box, clicking and holding the edge of the shape at the **node** (small square or circles at edges) and dragging it outward to grow larger or inward to shrink until the shape is of the desired size.

When creating the circle-based shapes you can get fancier. Just as with any other shape, you select the circle or ellipse tool and then click, hold, and drag on the canvas to create the initial shape. The shape now has a set of nodes (small white squares, circles, or diamonds) that you can move to change the size (if you want a perfect circle, press the *Ctrl* key while resizing).

For more help when transforming a shape with the nodes, watch the Notification Display along the bottom of the Inkscape screen. Descriptions of next steps and combination keys are in bold text.

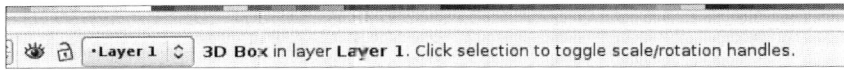

Here's how to convert an ellipse into an arc:

1. Make sure that the **Circle/Ellipse tool** is still selected and you can see the nodes on the shape on the canvas.

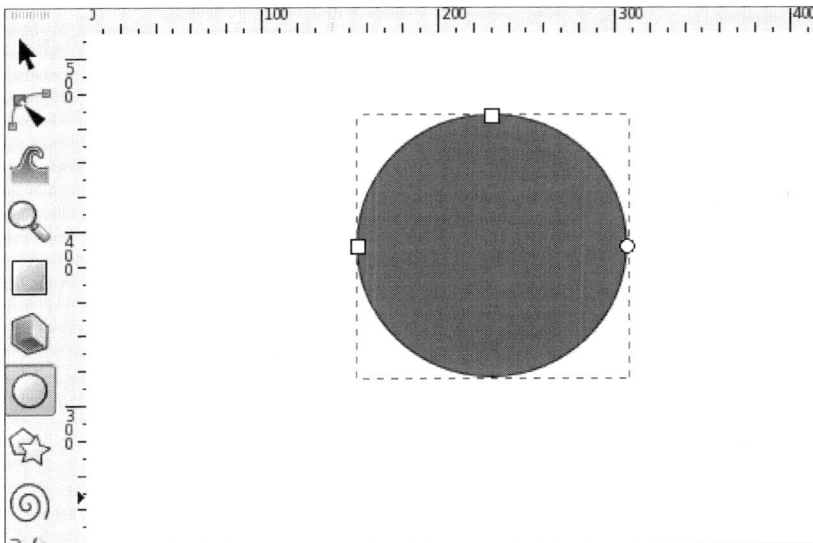

2. Drag an arc node (the circle one) to set one end of the arc.

   Once you "pull" or drag one of the arc nodes, you will see that there were actually two overlapping arc nodes for you to manipulate.

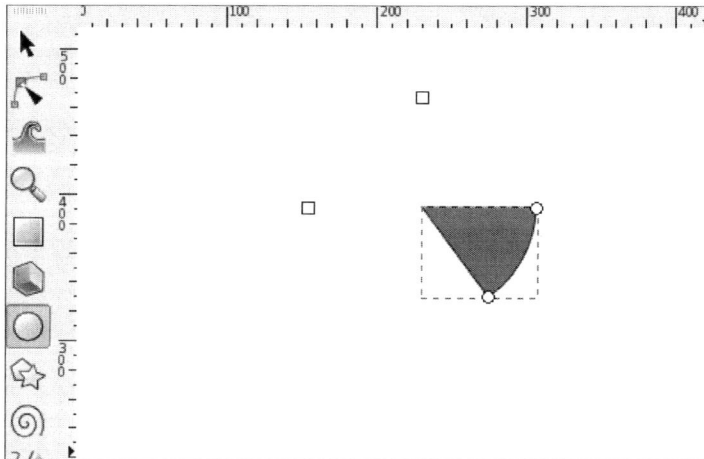

3. Drag the second arc node (in the original position) to the other end of the arc.

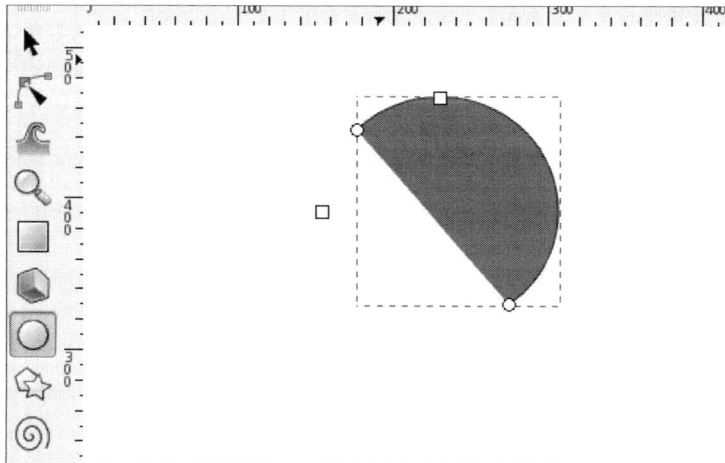

4. Hold the *Ctrl* key while dragging an arc node, to force the angle of the arc to begin or end at a multiple of the Rotation snap angle (15 degrees by default). To precisely place objects on the canvas, an object is made to snap to a target that is an object, guide, grid, or in this case an angle. Drag one of the arc nodes outside the curve of original ellipse (outside the dashed box); the arc node icon turns blue and a wedge is created at the center of the shape.

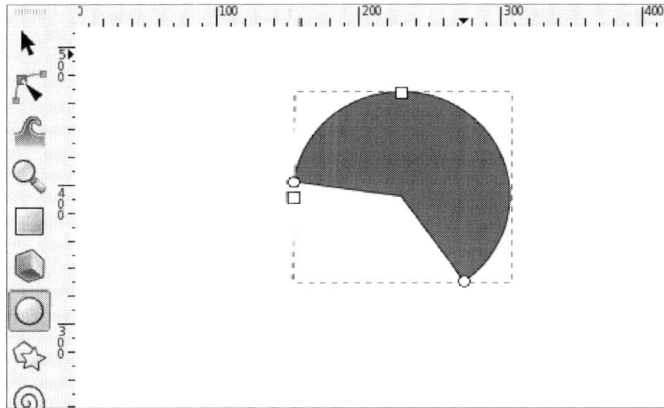

5. If the arc node is dragged with the cursor inside the curve, the segment defining the arc starts and stops at the two arc nodes, as shown below:

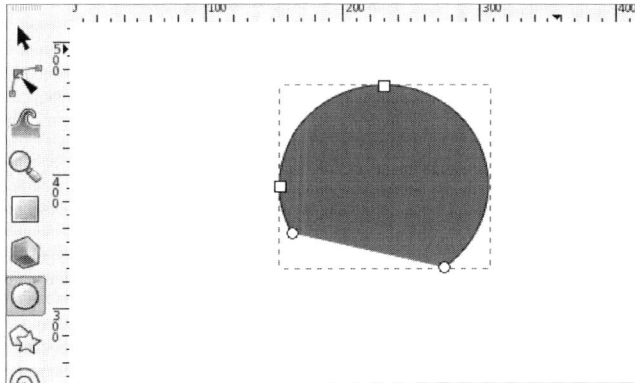

6. Once the arc is created and selected on the canvas, you can use the Tool Control bar to set specific locations for the start and stop arc nodes.

Complex shapes

Sometimes as a designer you are asked to create logos or shapes that are outside the standard ones provided in the software. Since Inkscape is vector-based, you can combine simple shapes, masking, hiding, and layering them to create these more complex shapes. Let's perform a couple of examples to see how this can be done.

Combing shapes

So the simplest way to create more complex shapes is to combine others into one—or merge the shapes. Let's show how we can do this by creating a heart with two circles and a polygon shape.

1. Open a new document (any size will do, since we are just practicing).
2. Select the **Circle/Ellipse tool** in the tool box.
3. Create a circle shape.

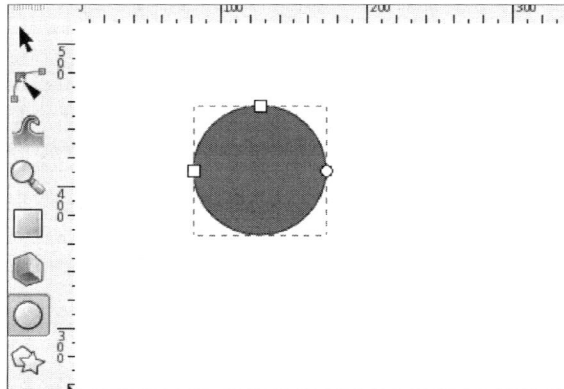

4. On the main menu and choose **Edit** and then **Duplicate**.

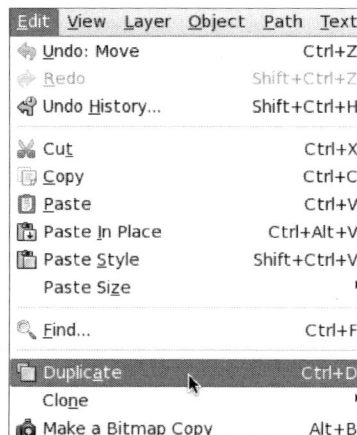

5. From the tool box, choose the **Select tool** and then select the topmost circle object (the duplicate) and move that circle to the right side of the first, to make the crest of the heart. Press and hold the *Ctrl* key while you drag the circle to lock the horizontal axis of both circles.

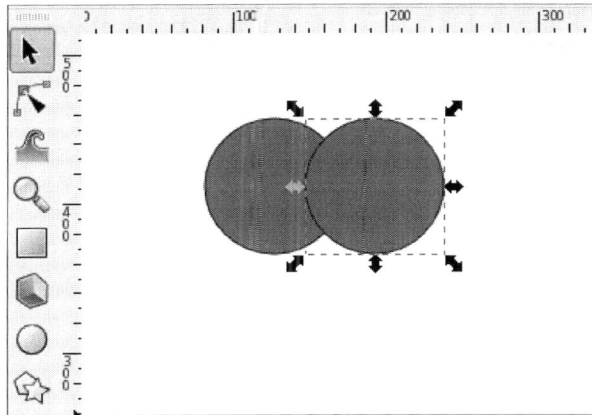

6. From the tool box, choose the **Star/Polygon tool**.

7. In the Tool Control bar, make sure that the **Polygon tool** is selected.

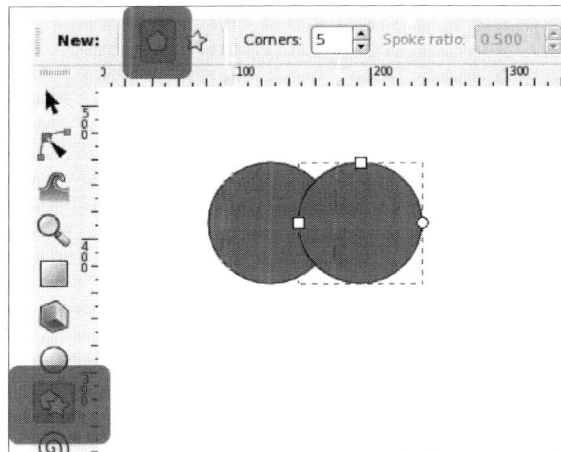

8. Draw a polygon just below the circles on the canvas, with a point facing downward.

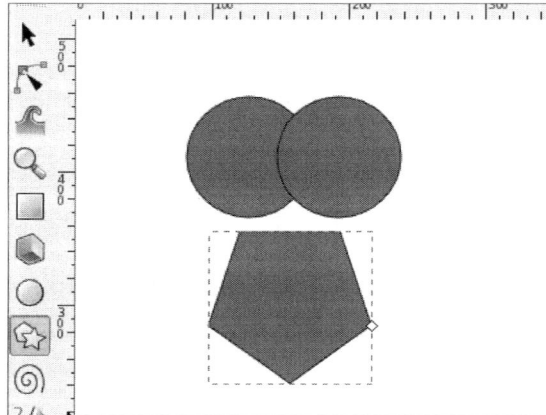

Rotating an object

While drawing the polygon on the canvas, you can swivel it up, down, left, and right to position it with a point downward (for the bottom of the heart).

It is okay if you don't do this while drawing it initially, you can always choose the **Select tool** from the tool box, and click the polygon until the nodes turn to arrows with curves (this might require you to click the polygon object a couple of times). When you see the curved arrow nodes, click and drag on a corner node to rotate the object until it is positioned correctly.

9. Now choose the **Select tool** from the tool box, and drag the polygon so it creates bottom point of the heart.

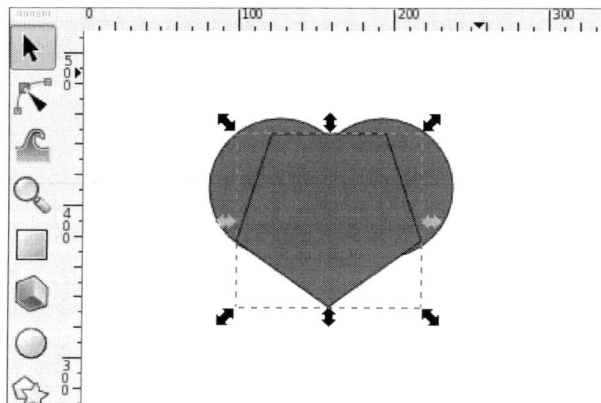

10. To readjust the size of the polygon so that the "top" doesn't ruin the crest of the heart and so that side points align with the sides of the circles just make sure the **Select tool** is active, and click the polygon. The resize nodes appear.

11. Click the node on a side that needs to be adjusted and resize. Repeat this as necessary until the polygon "fits" within the circles correctly.

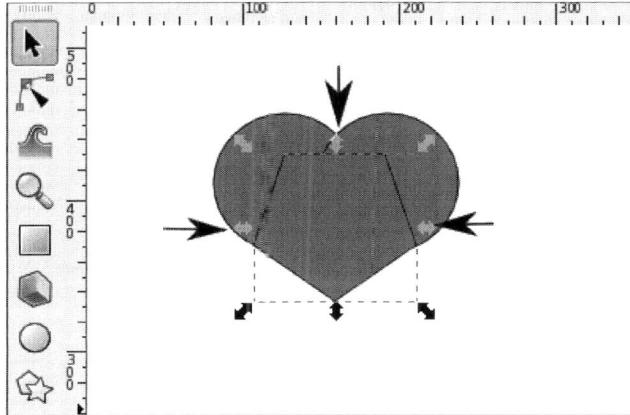

12. With the polygon still selected, press and hold the *Shift* key, while you select each circle so all objects are selected.

13. On the main menu select **Path** and then **Union**.

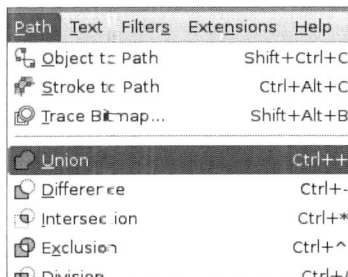

This merges all three shapes into one... and voila, it's a heart!

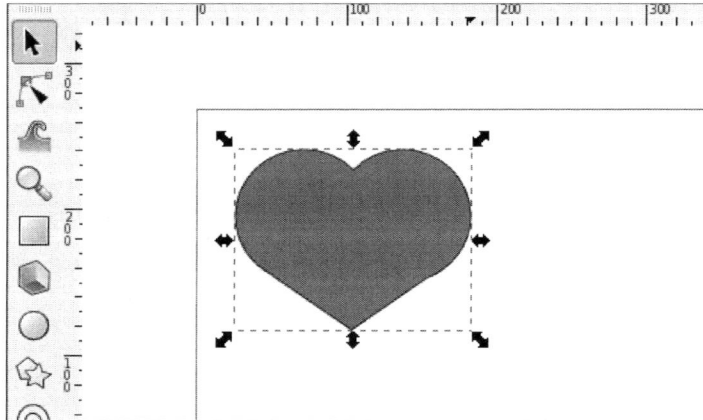

Freehand objects (Paths)

You can also use the **Bezier (Pen) Tool** to create objects in a bit more freehand form. This tool allows you to create straight lines and curves and connect them to create a freehand object. Here's an example of how to create a lightening bolt:

1. From a new document, choose the **Bezier Pen tool** from the tool box.

2. Click somewhere on the canvas to start drawing a straight line on the canvas, click to establish a node. Click again to change the direction of the straight line to create an angle in our lightening bolt.

    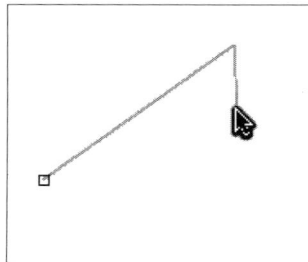

3. Continue to create the lightening bolt object by joining line segments.

Don't worry if you stop a line and realize you need to extend its length. Just drag a straight line to add on to the original to make it as long as you need. Click again when you are ready to change directions.

Also, if you made a mistake, there's no need to start over. Press the *Backspace* or *Delete* key and it removes the last line segment.

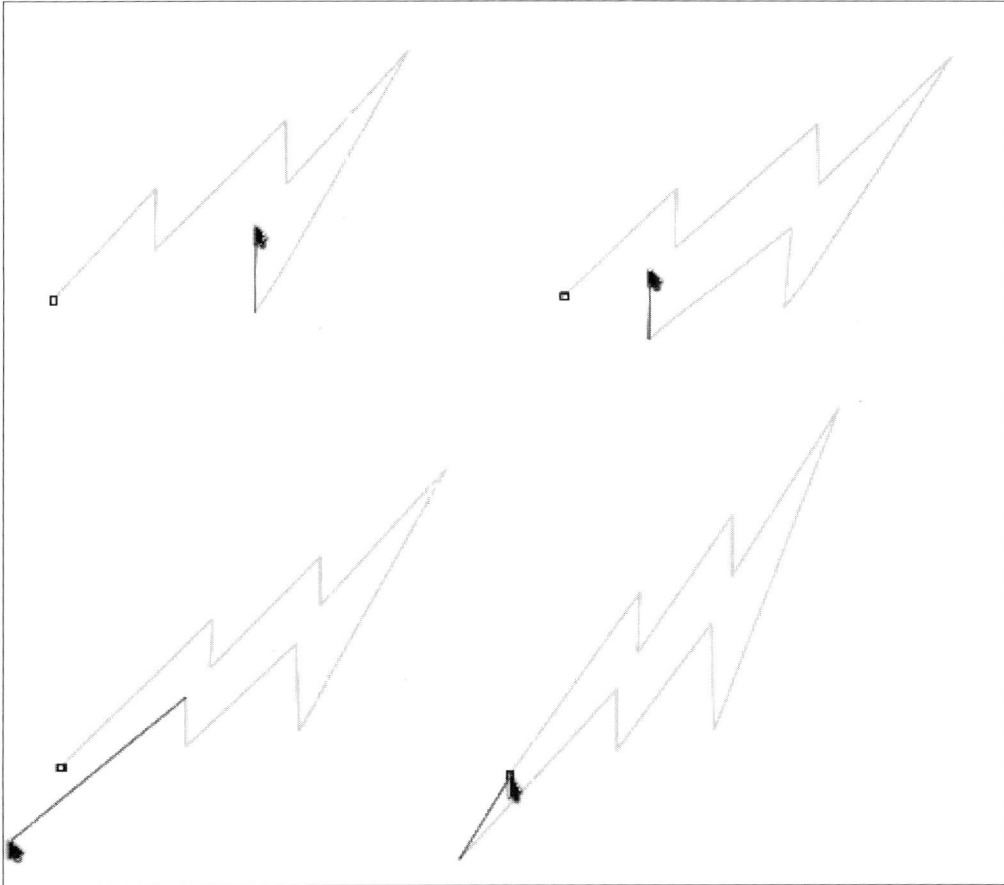

4. To "close" the lightening bolt, just create a line segment and join it to the starting point with a final click. You'll see that all of the lines are combined into one continuous closed path—a lightning bolt.

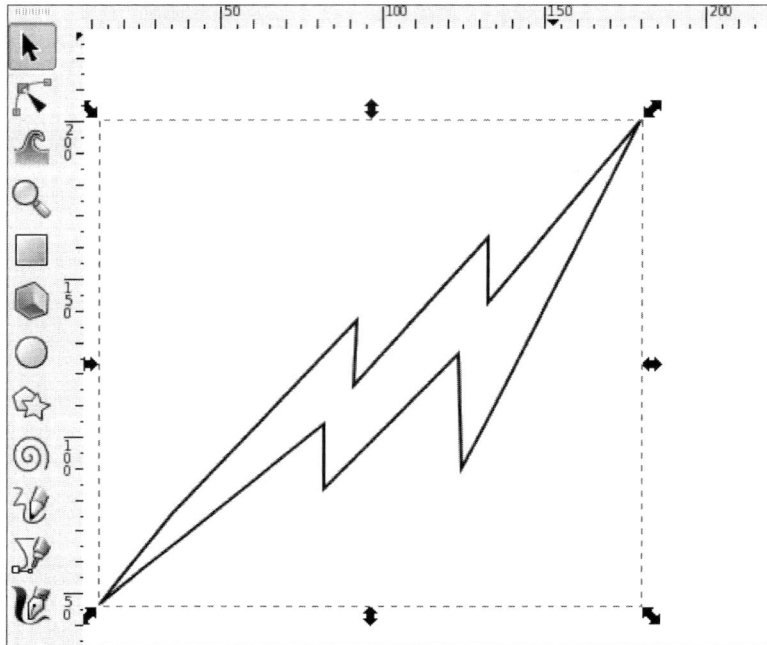

When you select the lightning bolt, the entire object is selected. You can resize it, fill it with a color (select it and choose a color from the color palette), and move it to another location on the canvas. It's become a unique object for you to work with.

The **Bezier Pen tool** also allows you to create controlled curves to create even more complex and unique objects. Try creating objects on your own and experimenting. These complex objects can be used for icons, banners, and for unique logo designs.

Summary

We spent much of this chapter understanding vector graphics—what they are, how they differ from the rasterized images, what this means in terms of their creation, and how best to use them on the web.

Then we dove right into the basics about Inkscape, what the program is about, what it can do for you, installation, and then the details about all the menus, tools, and using the basics in the software. We even created some simple and complex objects to reacquaint ourselves with the Inkscape software and its capabilities. All of this should be a great foundation (or a review for those of you who have been using the software for a while) to start building web page designs. Which we'll be starting in the next chapter with our first site design mock up!

2
Designing Site Layouts

Designing a web page layout is one of many steps in making a website. How involved you are in each part of this process depends on whether you are creating a website for yourself or a client (you do it all) or for a company in which you work. In this book, we'll take the stance of a web designer who is a part of a team of people that will help creating the web site. We focus primarily on the design and graphical elements of a web page and assume that other members of the team are working on the back-end tasks.

In this chapter, we will focus on:

- How to create the overall front or main page design of a web site
- Defining some basic design elements
- Options for using grids and guidelines for alignment
- Common screen sizes
- Creating a basic example layout and then learning how to export the page as images for final integration into a web site

Architecting a web site

Although as a web designer you will usually be regarded as the "look and feel" person for a web site, you are also a key partner in determining the site architecture. As you design, you often define how the site will be navigated. Is this web site one page or will an end-user "click around" the site to other areas or sub-pages and explore? Where will each page inter-link or link out to other websites? What is the main navigational element: a navigation bar? Where will it reside on all the pages? Is this site content or search driven? All these questions (and many more) require the entire team's involvement (and a client's opinion) to make the appropriate decisions. As the web designer, it is your job to work with all of these elements at a visual level — navigation bars, search fields, buttons, title bars, footers, and more — and fit them into the overall web site design.

Web layout—principles and basics

Designing for the web and for print are similar in that they have the same principles and goals for an end-viewer: appealing content that works together in the space. You may find it helpful to review these four basic design techniques as written in the *The Non-Designer's Design Book: Design and Typographic Principles for the Visual Novice* by Robin Williams. Although the principles are basic, they represent guidelines that improve any web page design. Here are the techniques:

- **Proximity** or grouping similar information together on a web page. You can get creative in how you group this information by using alignment, icons, and even just white space, but regardless, the technique and principles are the same. Information that belongs together should be together.

- **Alignment** is the simple idea of making sure all of the elements line up on the screen. If you have everything left aligned, keep it that way on the page. Use natural alignments within an entire web space when you use more than one graphical element such as photos, graphics, and/or text. Throughout our examples, we'll use grids and guides in Inkscape to help us achieve this technique.

- **Repetition** can help unify a web page. Repeating elements such as buttons, shapes (graphical or just placement), or colors can really make an impact and keep the design simple and clean, thus, easier for a viewer to navigate.

- **Contrast** can have a huge and favorable impact in web design, as long as it is used effectively. Contrast is achieved with size, colors, direction, shapes, and fonts (mixing modern with old style). Even font weight can help create contrast. Just make sure that all of these elements still work well with the content on the web page itself—not for the sake of contrast.

In fact these principles can be used for design in any medium. We'll use these techniques in our example layouts and full web designs in this book. As well as explaining how we create certain web page elements in Inkscape, the elements could help to adhere (and strengthen) these techniques.

The basic design

Before designing the layout in Inkscape, it can help to plan the placement of the main areas of a web page—in essence to help with the design's overall alignment of items and proximity of similar items. For our purposes, we'll create a simple main web page for a small business. This main page will have these areas:

- Header
- Footer
- Sidebar
- Content
- Navigation

Each web page project is different and you may have to add more page elements to this list or delete some so that the final list of elements fits the needs of the overall design. For the purposes of getting agreement from a team working on this project, a good practice is to create a basic layout showing where each of the areas will be placed on the screen—and is often referred to as the web page wireframe. Typically, wireframes are completed before any graphics are created. The following screenshot illustrates a basic layout or wireframe:

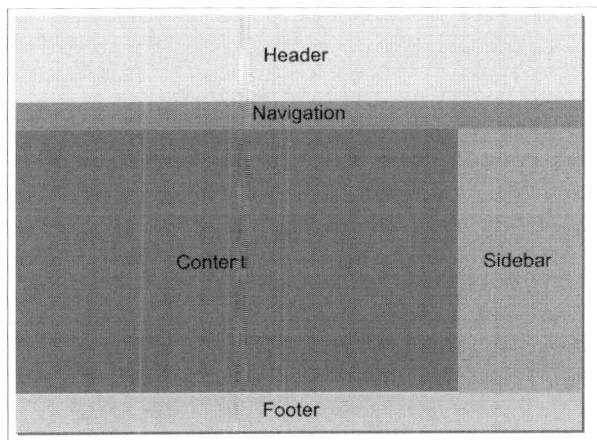

This high-level approach is a great start to actually building the page design. It gives us general placements of each area of the design and then we can set up grids and guidelines.

Starting a new design project

When you open Inkscape, it opens to a new document. However, we want to ensure that we have a page size that is the right size for our web page, so we create a new document based on predefined desktop sizes, which are common web page sizes, as follows:

1. From the main menu select **File** and then **New**. A pop-up menu appears showing a number of default page sizes to choose from.

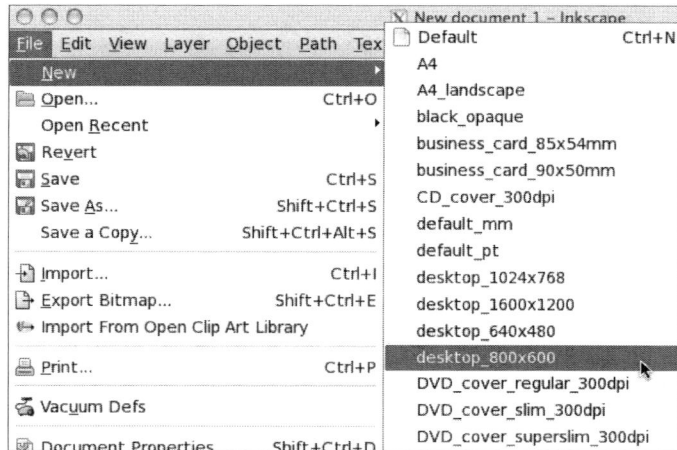

Choose a template size based on the browser standards or specifications.

Most of the templates in this menu are based on web designs. If you want to view the print media template sizes, go to the main menu and select **File** and **Document Properties** and view the **Format** section.

2. We'll choose **desktop_800x600**. However, the dimensions should be specified by how your target viewer will view the site, whether it is via a computer, or via a mobile device. Also, sometimes your client or company will specify a specific size your web pages need to be.

   A new document opens in Inkscape and you are ready to begin.

Let's set a few more preferences and then save the file with your project name before we start designing.

Using grids and guidelines

When designing any space on the web keep the page clean and — as stated in the design principles and techniques — aligned. So let's make the canvas grid viewable on the screen and set up some guidelines based on our wireframes.

Viewing the grid

With your new document still open on your computer, on the Inkscape main menu select **View** and then **Grid**.

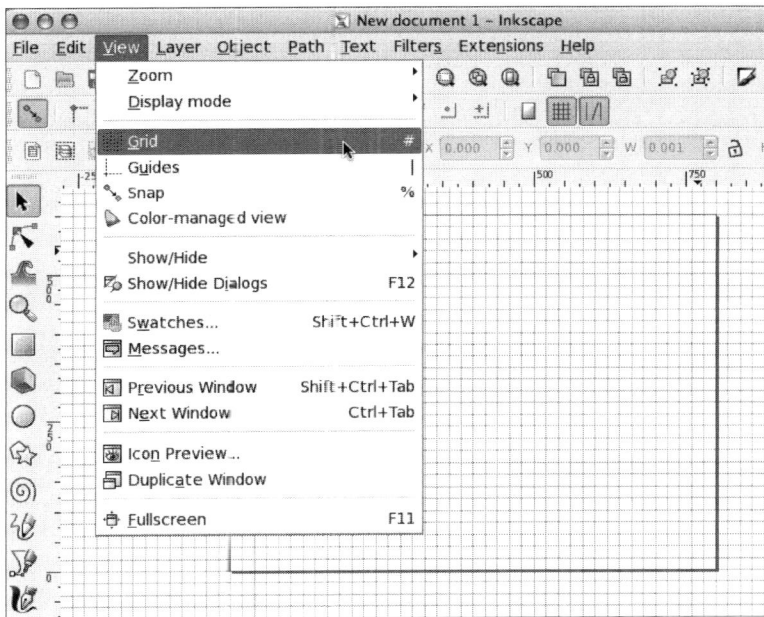

You'll see that a blue grid will appear across the entire canvas area. We'll use these grids to create basic areas of our layout and then create guides to begin creating our actual layout elements.

Making guides

Guides are lines on the screen that you will use for aligning i.e. *guiding* objects. These lines are only seen while you are working in Inkscape and we can set objects to "snap to" them when we are designing. Both of these simple tools (guides and the Snap to feature) will give you automatic alignment for the basic areas of your web page layout — which in turn will help your web page have the best design.

To create a guide in any open document, make sure the **Select** tool is selected and drag from the left side or top of the screen towards your page as shown in the following screenshot. A red line represents the guide until you 'let go' of the guide and place it on the page. Then the line turns blue.

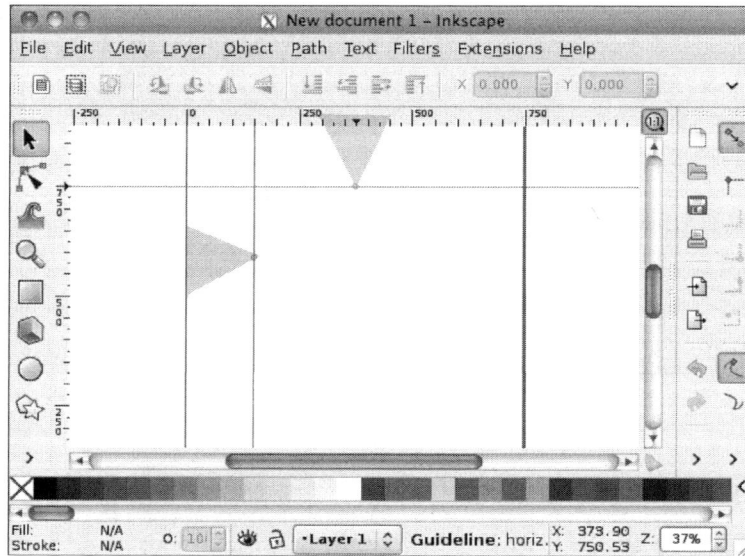

You can move the guides after placing them on the page, by using the select tool and clicking and dragging the circle node on the guide.

Now let's discuss how to use wireframes and create guides based on those web page layout elements.

Creating a new layer

When you create documents within Inskcape, you can have **layers** of objects. This gives great flexibility when creating web layouts. You can move groups of objects on a layer, separate objects by layer, and 'stack', re-ordered, or hide layers. Settings can be set by layer, so you can save drafts or different versions of mockups and keep all of this in one file.

The layer you are currently using is called the **drawing layer**. It is selected in the **Layer Dialog** and is shown in a darker color. In your open document with viewable grids let's make the layers viewable and create a layer called **Basic Layout**.

1. To make the Layers Dockable Dialog viewable, from the main menu select **Layer** and then **Layers**. On the right side of your screen the Layers Dialog is displayed.

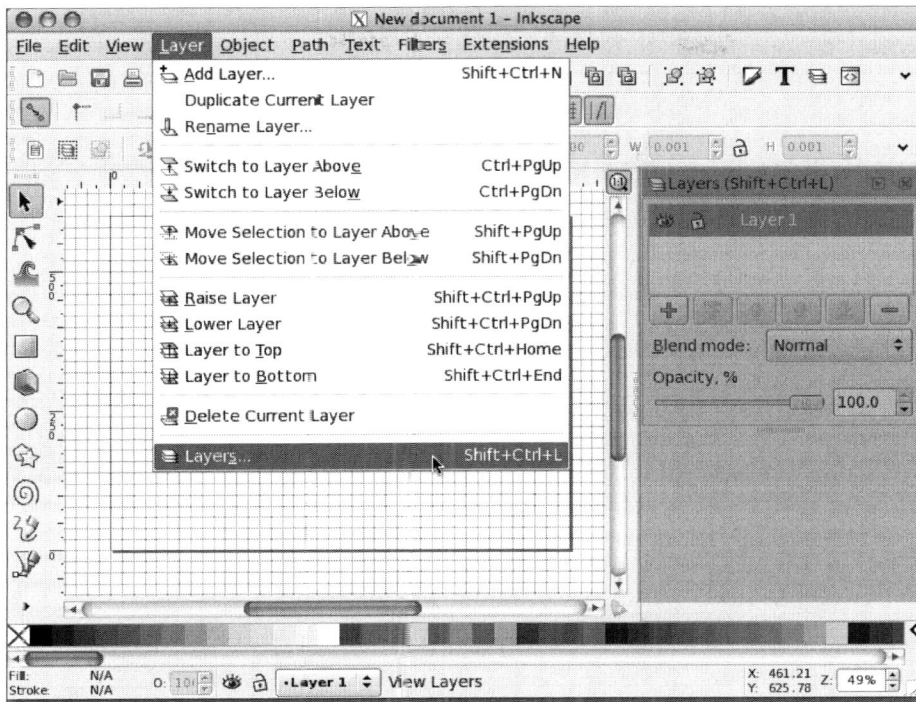

You can also press *Shift* + *Ctrl* + *L* on your
keyboard to display the Layers Dialogue.

2. In the Layers Dialog, press the **+** button to create a new layer.

3. In the **Layer Name** field type the name: **Basic Layout** and click **Add**. You will
notice the new layer is added above the existing one in the Layers Dialog.

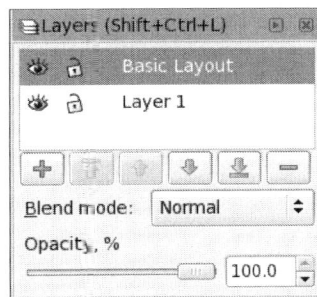

Creating basic design areas in Inkscape

Here's where we begin to transfer our wireframes into Inkscape so we can start the design process. To start:

1. Use the **Rectangle Tool** to draw rectangles for each of your layout areas in your basic design.

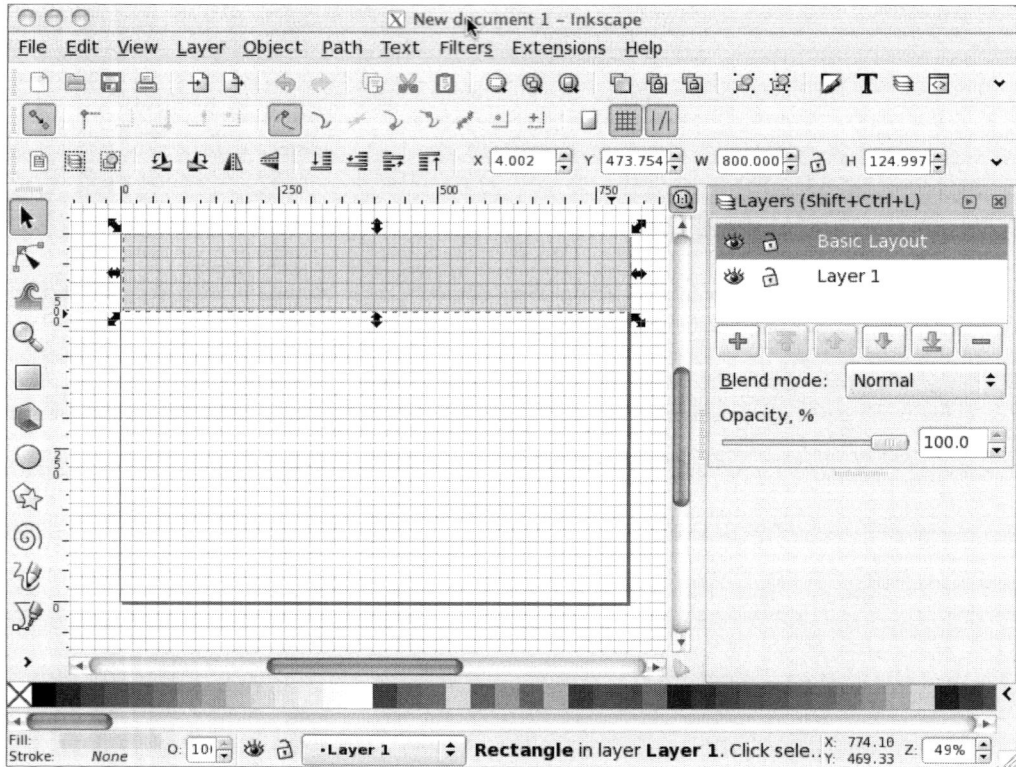

2. For now, use different shades of gray for each area so you can easily distinguish between them at a glance. To change the fill color of a particular rectangle, left click the rectangle and choose a gray shade for the rectangle. Or drag the gray shade from the color palette onto the rectangle.

3. Use sharp edged (not rounded) rectangles. If you need to change to sharp, click the **Make Corners Sharp** button in the Tool Controls Bar.

4. Make sure your rectangle shapes do not have an outline or stroke. Use the *Shift + Left* click keypad shortcut to open the **Stroke** dialog and choose **No Color** (the icon with an **X**) to delete the stroke.

5. Position the rectangles so there are no white spaces in between them.

6. From the main menu choose **Object** and then **Align and Distribute**. In the **Remove Overlaps** section, click the icon. This makes sure that the bounding boxes around each object don't overlap each other and place the objects tangent to each other.

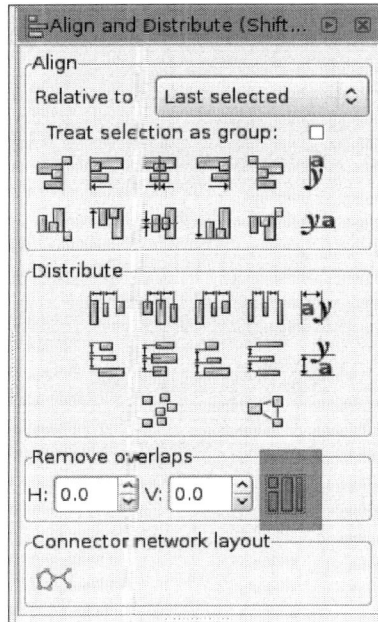

7. Use the Tool Controls Bar **W** (width): number field to apply a setting of 800.0 px. The X:0.0 and Y:0.0 fields reference the bottom left corner of your page border.

Here's roughly what your canvas should look like:

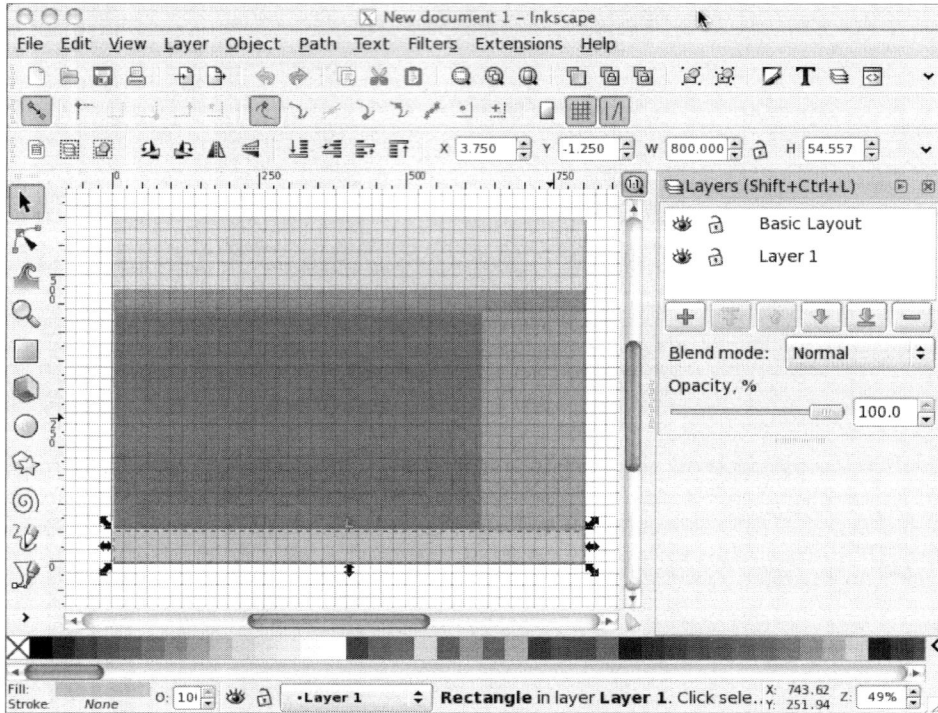

Converting shapes to guides

Once all of your areas are blocked out on the canvas, we'll need to convert the current rectangles into guides so we can use the guides when creating our web page layout graphics in the next chapter.

1. We can easily keep the Basic Layout Export layer intact; we need to copy all of the rectangles in this layer. On the main menu, select **Edit** and then **Select All** (or use the keyboard shortcut keys *Ctrl + A*).

2. Then select **Edit** and **Duplicate** (or use the keyboard shortcut *Ctrl + D*) to duplicate all of the elements in this layer.

3. Now you are ready to convert these current shapes into guides. First, select all the rectangles in the top (duplicate) layout. Do this by clicking a rectangle and then hold the *Shift* key on your keypad. Then click/select the next rectangle.

4. When you have all five rectangles selected, from the main menu select **Object** and then **Object to Guide**. Your duplicate rectangles will be removed from the canvas and replaced with blue guides. To better see the guides, turn off the grid (from the main menu choose **View** and **Grid**).

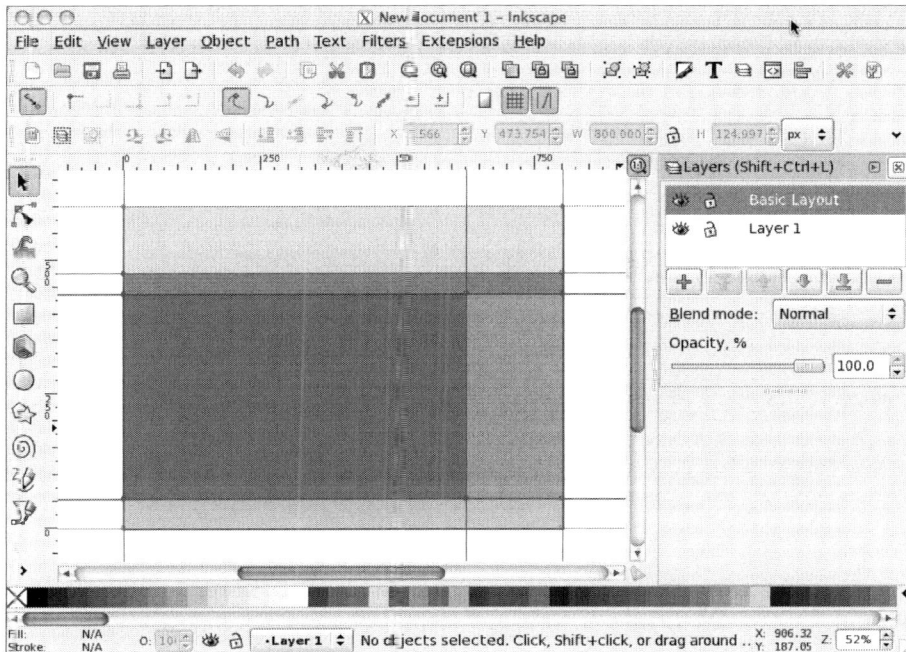

5. You'll also notice your originally created basic layout areas defined on the screen. We'll use these shapes later on to help export our design into workable graphics for the HTML programmers.

6. Now it is time to save this new document before you start the details of the design. From the main menu select **File** and then **Save As**. Choose an appropriate file name for your project and save it.

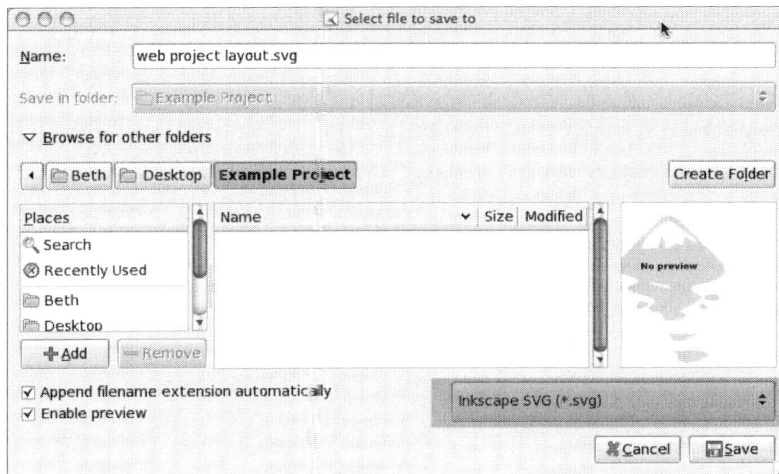

7. Make sure you save this document in the native Inkscape format of SVG to retain its editable features and layers.

Project file management

To keep all files for this project in an easy-to-find location, it might make sense to create a project folder on your computer and save this design file within that folder. As you export designs for use within web pages and HTML, you will need a number of files. Using a directory or folder to house all project files makes them easier to find.

Creating a layout example

Now it's time for the fun part—creating your web page layout! This part of web development allows the most creative expression for web designers. It's creating a mock up of how the web page will look when complete. Mock ups are graphic images of the web page, so we don't worry about all the technical details in making the web page work, just how it looks.

For this layout example, we'll continue our simple web page design for a small business. We'll be using very basic shapes and limited effects. But don't worry, the next chapters will show how we can make these very simple elements into something much more polished and elegant.

Let's get started!

Designing the background

In Inkscape, since your canvas is white, it looks like your web page might have a white background. It does not, without creating a background image, currently it would be transparent or 0 percent opacity. So we need to start by determining which colors to use for the background.

You can get really creative here, as you don't need to use just one color! Create a header background color, one for the main body, and then another for the footer area. Let's start by creating a simple background based on our Basic Layout layer.

Making the header background

To start, we're going to create a simple header background—a rectangle with a simple divider line and drop shadow. Here are the detailed steps to make this header background:

1. With your new document open and the newly created guides viewable, first lock the Basic Layout layer (click the lock icon) and hide its elements (click the Eye icon).

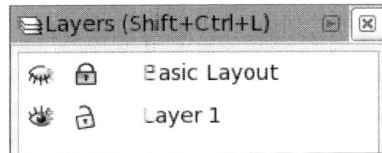

2. Now create a **Background** Layer.

3. Draw a rectangle that fills the header and navigational areas. We're going to create only one background for both of these, as the navigation will be in the same color and area as the header.

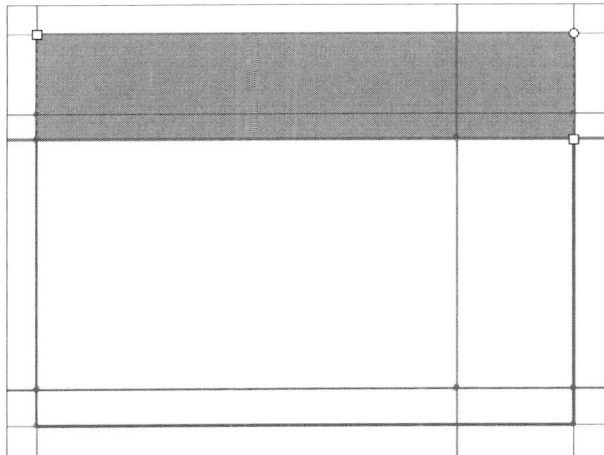

4. Choose a fill color and no stroke (border). If you decide you want to change either of the option, open the fill and stroke dialog box (from the main menu select **File** and then **Fill and Stroke** or the keypad shortcut *Shift + Ctrl + F*) and adjust colors accordingly.

5. Want to add in a gradient? Click the Gradient icon, and adjust how you want your gradient to appear.

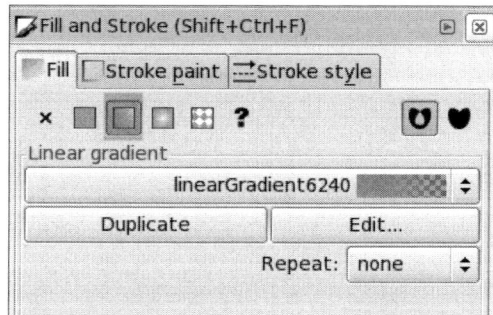

6. By default the Inkscape gradient applies an alpha setting of 0 to the stop gradient, which will be fully transparent. This means, in the above settings, the right side of the gradient would be transparent. Click **Edit** to change this setting.

7. From the **Linear gradient** field, choose the **Add stop**.

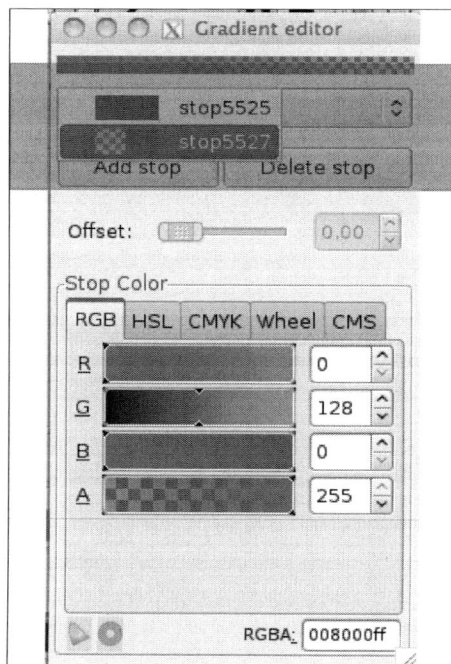

8. Change the alpha opacity setting (**A**) to a solid color—either move the slider to the left side of the screen or change the value to 255.

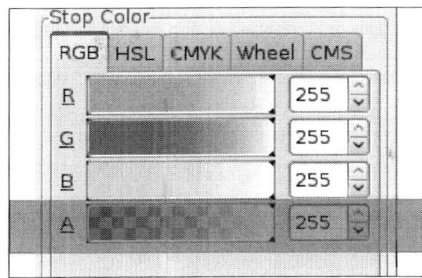

9. Next change the solid color value. In this example, we used white and changed the **R, G, B** values to achieve the results.

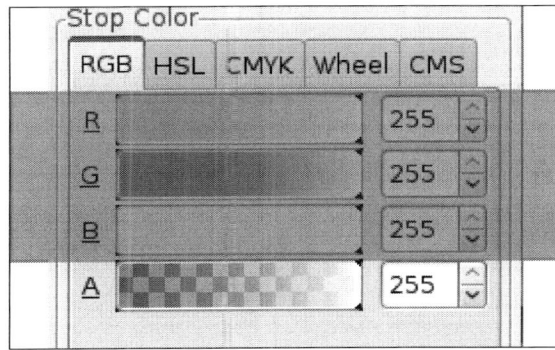

10. For this example, the gradient goes from a bit darker green on the left to a lighter shade on the right side.

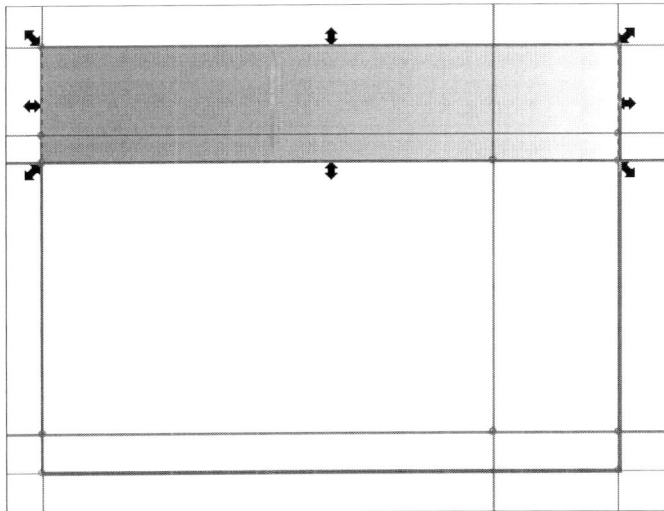

11. Next, let's add a simple drop shadow. From the main menu select **Filters**, **Shadows and Glows**, and then **Drop Shadow**. For this example, the Blur Radius px 10, Opacity, 20% and a vertical offset px of 5 and click **Apply**.

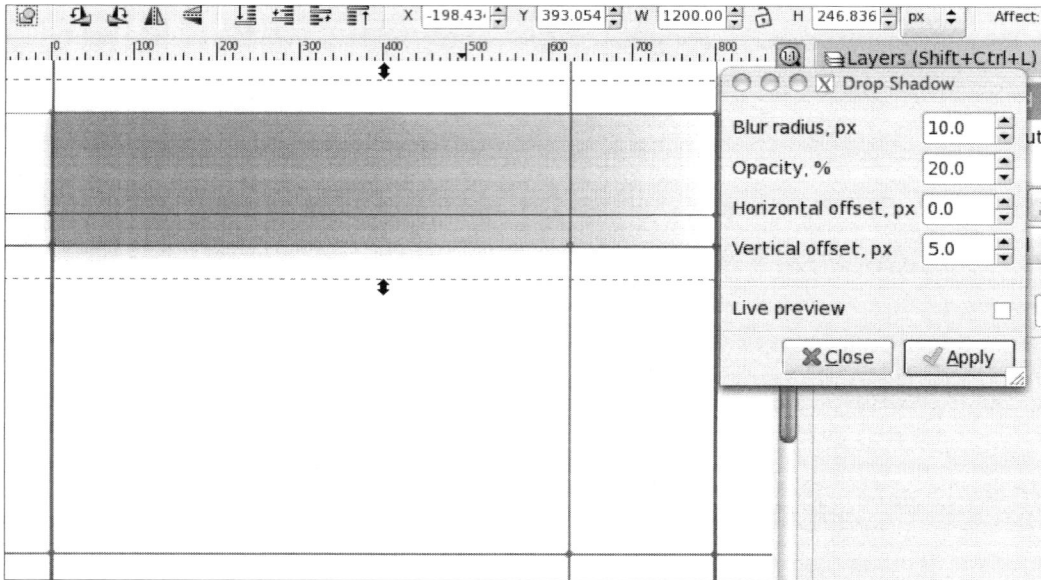

12. Close the drop shadow box and then save your file.

13. Your header is complete! Now let's add to this to create the main content background.

> To change the gradient orientation, you can drag the outer two gradient stop nodes indicated by the square and circle handles on the object. You can also add more gradient stops and edit their transparency (**A**) values and colors to adjust to your liking.

Building the main body background

For the main part of the web page sample, we're using a white box as a background with a similar drop shadow. Here's how to add this to your **Background** layer:

1. Draw a rectangle that fills the entire content, main content area. This includes the entire middle portion of your web page, and covers all the 'sections' between the header and the footer in the basic layout.

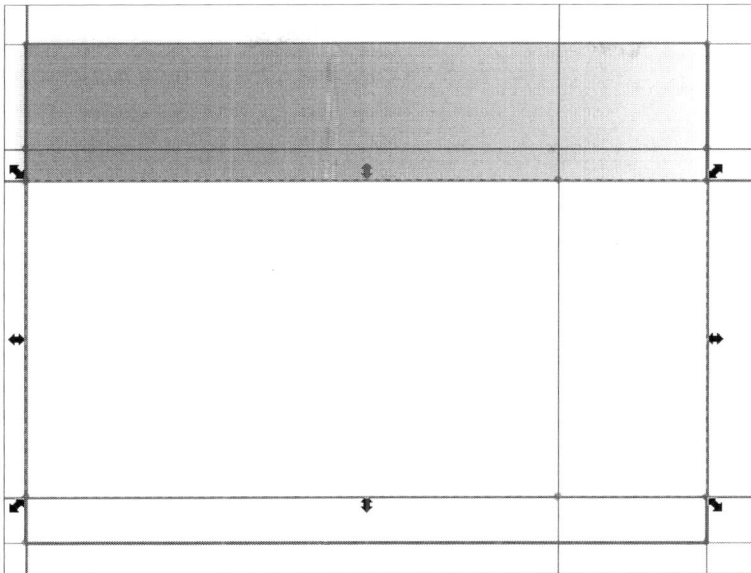

The example above shows white as the fill color and no stroke (border).

2. Let's also put a drop shadow on this box as well. From the main menu select **Filters, Shadows and Glows,** and then **Drop Shadow**. Adjust the settings to be the same as the previous drop shadow so they match (Blur Radius px 10, Opacity, 20% and a vertical offset px of 5) and click **Apply**.

3. Close the drop shadow box and then save your file.

4. The main content background is complete. Lastly, we need to create the footer background.

Creating the footer background

Creating a footer background is the last step to this process. Very much like the header, we'll follow these steps:

1. Duplicate the header background. Select the header and from the main menu, choose **Edit** and then **Duplicate**.

2. Drag the duplicate rectangle down to the footer area of the page and adjust the size so it fits within the footer defined area.

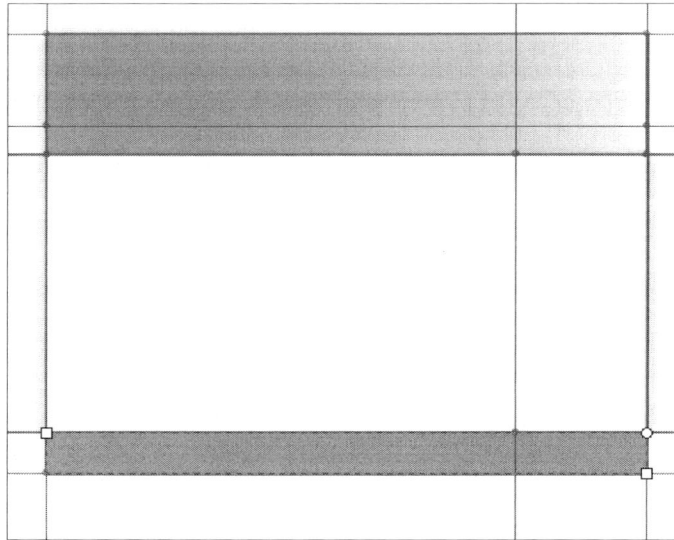

3. Notice, since the object was duplicated all formatting—gradients and drop shadows—were maintained.

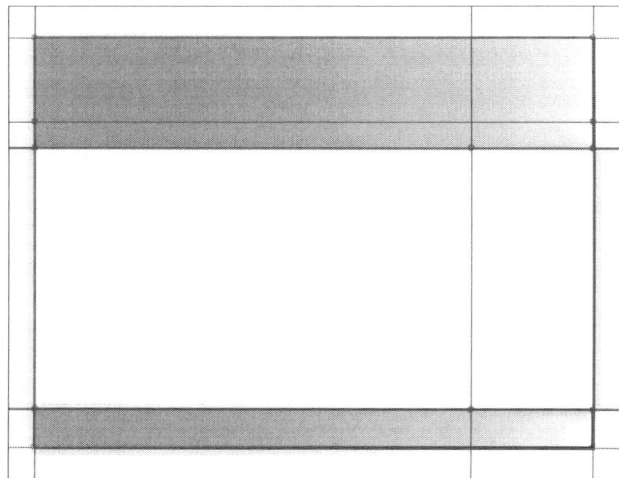

4. Save your file.

Now that your footer background is complete, so is the entire web page background. Let's move on to details.

Designing the header

Now that we have the entire background already created, it's time to add details to the header area like a logo and company name. Here are the steps to add in these basic details to our example design:

1. Before any more work is done, it makes sense to 'lock' the background layer. We don't want any items shifting, or any elements being selected accidentally when we are working on other layers. To lock the background layer, click the lock icon in the **Background** layer dialog box.

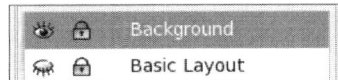

2. Create a new layer and name it **Logo**.

[💡 To create a new layer, you can use the *Shift+Ctrl+N* keyboard shortcut.]

3. Within the **Logo** layer, create and/or import the logo and place it on the header background. If you are importing a graphic that has already been created, it's as simple as clicking **File** and selecting **Import**. Find the logo file and use the selection tool to place it correctly in the header area.

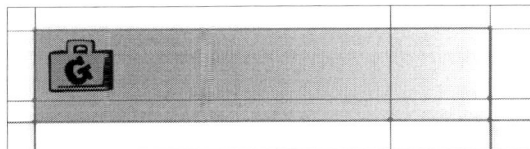

4. Lock the logo layer, and then create a new layer and name it **Title**.

5. Within this layer, use the **Create and Edit Text** tool and type in the business name and then place it on the header background.

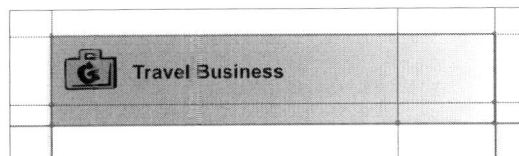

6. Save your file.

Next up, is to create the Navigation tool bar.

Navigational elements

This portion of the website is essential to most web pages, as it is the common element (like the header) on all pages of this website. For our example, we are only creating one web page, but typically web sites include a number of pages. This is the menu that allows a user to move between the pages in the web site.

We'll create a simple bar of rectangular buttons along the bottom of the header area for this element. Here are the details:

1. Create a new layer called **Navigation**.

2. Draw a long rectangle along the bottom of the header area.

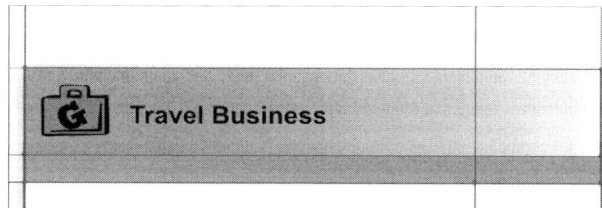

3. Change the fill color of the navigation rectangle by left clicking a color box in the **Palette** bar and set the fill.

4. Since we know the width of our entire page all we need to do is a little math to determine the width of each of the buttons. Take the page width (800) and divide it by the number of buttons (4). 800/4=200. This means each of the buttons will be 200 pixels wide.

5. From the left side of the navigational bar, draw a vertical path at 200 pixels. Using the *Ctrl* key will snap the path's angle, on top of the navigation bar, and this will make the first button.

6. Tap the *Space* bar to quickly change to the Selector tool, and then set the X position in Tool Controls Bar at 200.0.

7. Select the line you just created and duplicate it. From the main menu choose **Edit** and then **Duplicate** or use the *Ctrl + D* keyboard shortcut.

8. Again, press the *Space* bar to toggle to the Selector tool and change the X position to 400 pixels.

9. Repeat Steps 6 through 8, but position X will be at 600. Now we have four evenly spaced buttons for the design.

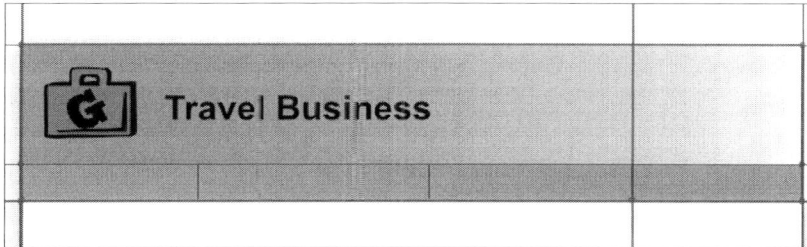

10. Label each button with the appropriate page or menu item.

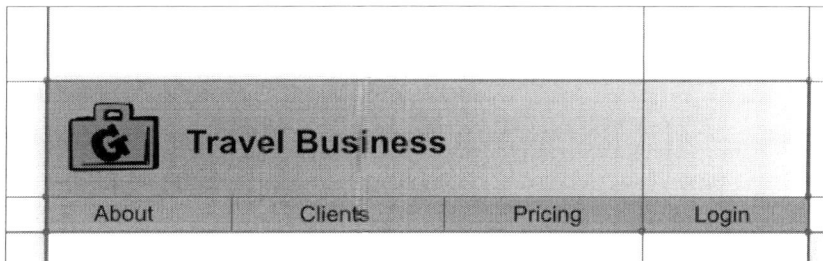

11. When complete, save your file.

Creating a footer

This is a very simple item to frame the web page from a design perspective. In this example, we are just going to add a simple legal disclaimer for this webpage.

1. Create a new layer named **Footer**.

2. Use the Create and Edit Text tool and type the disclaimer information along the footer area.

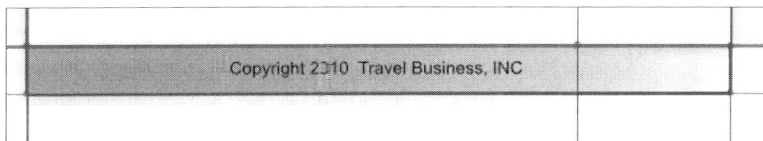

3. To ensure correct positioning, select the text first and then the rectangle background object last using the *Shift* + Left click combination.

4. From the main menu, select **Object** and then **Align & Distribute**.

5. In the **Relative to** drop down box, select **Last Selected**.

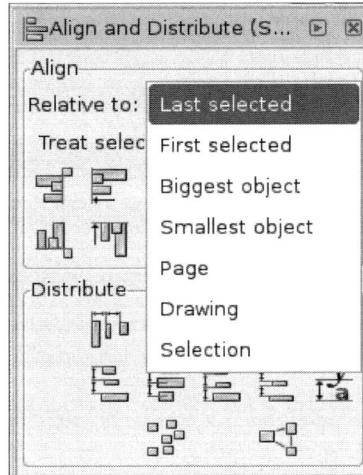

6. In the **Align** section, click the Align Objects Equidistantly Horizontally icon and in the **Distribute** section, click the Center on Horizontal Axis icon as shown in the following screenshot:

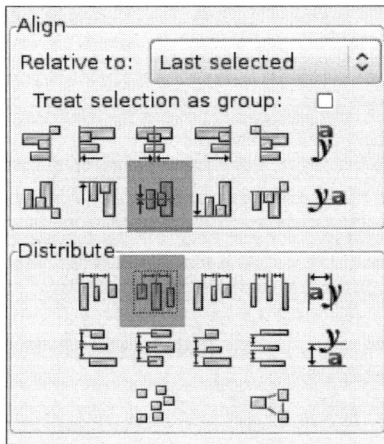

7. Then save the file to make sure your work is not lost.

Making a sidebar

Now we are moving to create some content within the main content areas of the web page. Sidebar information is not always needed in a design. Or some designs might call for navigational elements to be shown here. For our example, this will include some information about the company and links to other articles relevant for this small business.

1. Again, lock all layers you are not using, and create a new layer using the *Shift + Ctrl + N* keyboard shortcut. Call this layer **Sidebar**.

2. Then select the Create and Edit Text tool. This time, type a title for this section of the site. For our example, we will name this sidebar **About Us**.

3. Using the Tool Controls bar, adjust the font size and leading so that it is appropriate for a heading.

4. Next select the Create and Edit Text tool and drag your mouse to create a flowed text bounding box (a 'text box' that will automatically wrap larger amounts of text).

5. Let's generate some dummy content for this small paragraph of text.

6. In the Tools Control bar, set your font size.

7. From the main menu, select **Extensions** and then **Text** and **Lorem Ipsum**. Once you adjust the settings press **Generate**, you'll have some placeholder text that you can place on the screen.

> It's possible that your Inkscape installation did not come with the Lorem Ipsum extension pre-installed. Don't worry! You can download and install it from `http://cheeseshop.python.org/pypi/lxml/`. It is called the fantastic `lxml` wrapper for `libxml2`.

8. Next we're going to create another part of this sidebar. So we'll create another heading called **Articles** and then create some dummy text for visual placement.

> Inkscape does not currently support bulleted lists. In order to create the look of bullets use a dash/minus sign to mimic a list.

9. Once everything is complete, again save the file.

Lastly, we're going to place some dummy text in the main area of the website to pose as our content.

Creating content areas

In our simple design example we are going to create a grid of content in this area. As it will only be dummy text, we'll just be creating headings and then using the Loren Ipsum extension to fill the rest of the area. With proper alignment and placement it will give a great look at the design of the site. Let's get started:

1. Use the *Shift + Ctrl + N* keyboard shortcut to make a new layer called **Content**.

2. Use the Create and Edit Text tool and create a heading for the first of two "articles" of content we are going to create.

3. Then add the dummy text in any fashion you like. To show off some simple design options, we created two columns of dummy text.

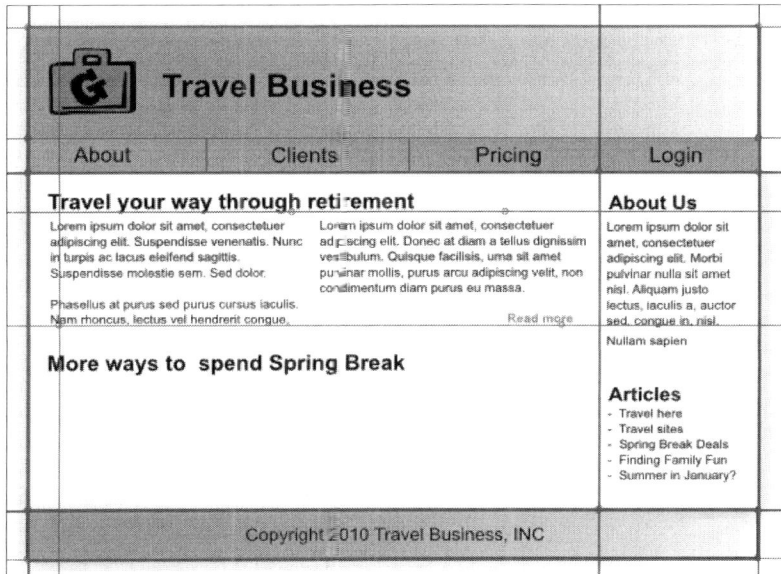

4. Repeat creating another header and some text as shown below.

5. Once all is created, and you have no more final touches to your design, your mock up is complete. Save your file.

Your web page mock up is ready to go out for approval! That's right, you can now export this to a PNG file (**File | Export Bitmap**) or save a copy as a PDF file (**File | Save a Copy**) and send it via email for others to approve.

> Remember, you always want to keep the source Inkscape SVG file intact as it saves all of your layers and editing functionality so you can adjust the design based on feedback from the client or others on your team.

It is likely you will have a number of review cycles before the design is indeed approved. But once it is complete we're ready to save this design for use by a programming team.

Also, we used dummy text for our design mock up. It's likely your client will want real content inserted into the content area space. It can be static content—content that doesn't change or dynamic content that changes frequently (like a blog or through a content management system). The following section will explain how to export this design in a way that will allow a software programming team to work within your design and add in the code that will allow those dynamic posts to work. Essentially it means we export the header, navigation, a small portion of the content area, the sidebar, and footer.

Exporting design mock-ups

Once the design in final, it is time to export our design. We'll do this in two general steps—slicing the web page into separate images (via a layer we'll name slice) and then exporting all of **sliced** images into an appropriate directory.

Creating a slice layer

What is slicing? It is a term used to describe breaking of an image created in a graphics program apart so that it can be re-assembled in HTML to create a web page. To do this, we'll use Web Slicer Extension.

1. From the main menu select **Extensions | Web | Slicer | Create a slicer rectangle**.

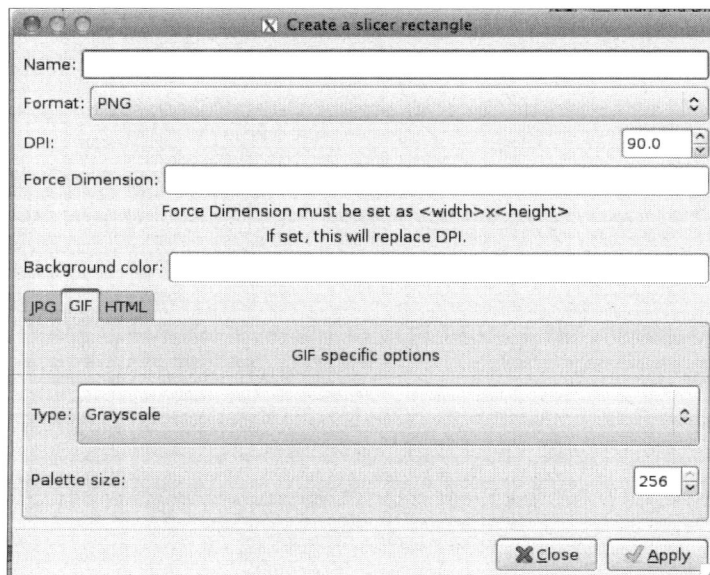

2. Type an appropriate name for this 'slice'. Ideally it would be a recognizable name like Header, so that when exporting all the slices of the image, the files will be named in a way that is intuitive to place it all back together into the specified design.

3. Specify the format for this slice. The default PNG format works best.

4. You can force the slicer to a certain size by entering it in the **Force Dimension** field.

5. Choose all other appropriate settings and click **Apply**. A rectangle is displayed on the screen.

6. Place the rectangle in an appropriate location, based on its name.

7. Repeat Steps 1 through 6 until your entire design is 'covered' with slicer rectangles—as follows:

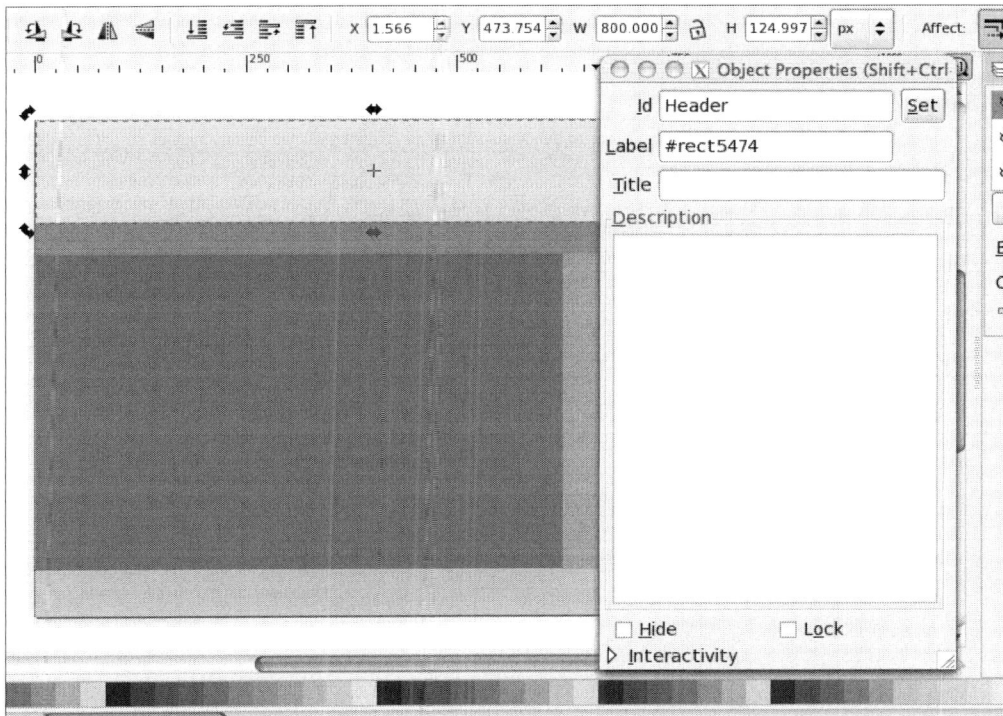

8. Save your file again to keep all of the changes you have done so far. Now, you're ready to export the images for the web!

Exporting slices

In Inkscape 0.48 there is a batch export layout pieces and HTML + CSS Code option. This means you can export all your layout slicer rectangles and more all at once. Here's how it's done.

1. From the main menu select **Extensions | Web | Slicer | Export layout pieces and HTML+CSS code**.

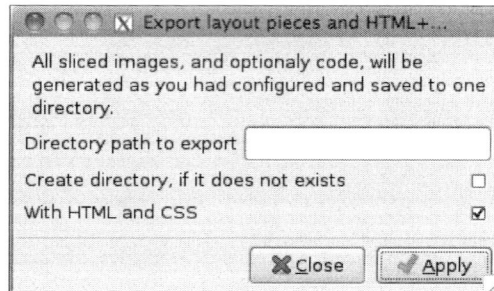

2. Choose a directory or folder to save all of the slicer rectangles (PNG image files) and the HTML/CSS code.

3. Check the **Create directory, if it does not exist** and **With HTML and CSS** checkboxes.

4. Click **Apply**.

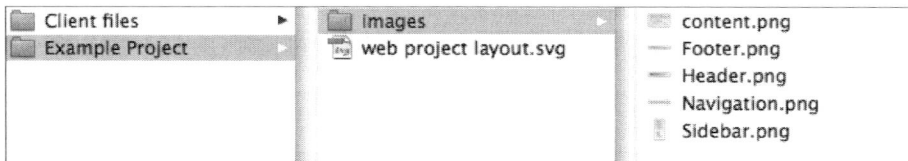

5. Inkscape will automatically save the slicer rectangle areas—as you have defined in the **Name** fields—as PNG image files in the export location in the Filename field.

> **Issues finding your exported files?**
> Make sure, before you perform an export you have saved you source Inkscape SVG file in the main directory (folder) where you want the sliced files to be exported.

Now you're ready to hand off your files to the team that will complete the HTML for the web pages.

Working with programmers

You've done a lot of work to create the look and feel for this website, and even built what essentially will be the interface for this website—at least from a graphical standpoint. Now it is time for programmers to take your images, and make them work together on a web site. At a basic level they will take each graphic image you exported and then piece them back together—but not from within a graphics program. They will use HTML code to make this happen.

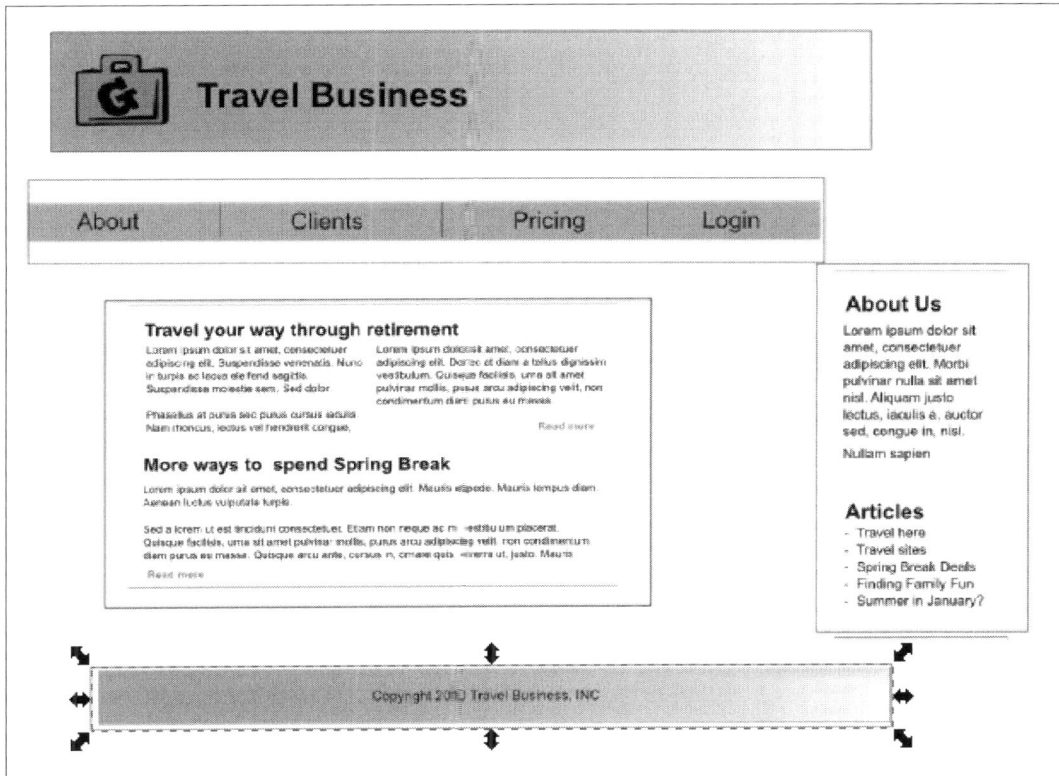

Then the hard part starts—they start coding links, dynamic content plugins that will pull content into the content areas and more. As a designer, you might also be asked to help do the layout for some sub-pages within this website (if the header, footer or sidebar changes). Or you might also be asked to help make the graphics for dynamic menus that might 'drop down' from the navigation bar we created in the example web page.

So what do you provide to the programming team?

- The PNG image files you exported from your design (likely within a folder called **images**)
- The source Inkscape SVG file of your design mock up

Why do you give them the source files? As stated in *Chapter 1, Inkscape 101: The Basics*, Inkscape creates SVG files that are more and more commonly able to be read in web browsers as they are. Want to try it out?

Take the SVG source file you just created, and then drag it over a browser window. Did it open a 'page' that looks almost like the one you created? There might be some black boxes or alignment issues. But the code can *almost* work for the programmers. At the very least it gives them already created IDs and parameters to start working with to create the web pages.

Our example in this chapter was focused on designing a web page for computer viewing. But, with the increasing use of mobile handheld devices, you might be asked to design a mobile website.

Summary

From architecting a web site to exporting image files for inclusion in a web pages code—we've done it all in this chapter. We discussed design techniques that can make web pages move from good to great, and then started designing a sample web page project. Using many layers we created a header, navigation bar, content areas, and footer for our site, and then worked to slice it into images and export for final integration into a web site.

This is only the beginning. In the next chapter, we're going to look at how we can manipulate images (photographs, drawings, and more) and use these skills in our sample web project to enhance and expand the basic elements even further.

3
Working with Images

We talked a lot in the first chapter about rasterized versus vectorized images and how Inkscape is best used for vector graphics. But what if you only have rasterized images? Can you import them into Inkscape, manipulate them, or even save them as vector images? Of course you can. There are some minor limitations on how you export rasterized images, but this feature is often used to import the image and then manipulate it a bit for the vector use you need it for.

This chapter will focus on:

- Importing bitmap images
- Embedding images
- Rendering bitmap images as vector graphics
- Working with photographs and filters
- Tracing bitmap images to convert them into full vector graphics
- How to export images for best use in the web page

Importing images in Inkscape

Inkscape can import almost any image type—from the main menu select **File** and then **Import**. You can select common image file types and bring them into the open document.

Or you can:

- Copy an open image and paste into the open document
- Drag an image into the Inkscape canvas
- Click the **Import** icon in the Command Bar

Any way you choose to import the images, they are only "linked" or referenced in the open document. Meaning, if you move the original file from its current location, the Inkscape file won't be able to find the image and will give you an error. But you can also embed these images into your document. Here's how:

Embedding images

Most imported images are only linked to the original file. If you want to embed them you need to do the following:

1. In an open Inkscape document, select the image(s) you want to embed into the document.

2. From the main menu select **Extensions**, then **Images**, and **Embed Images...**

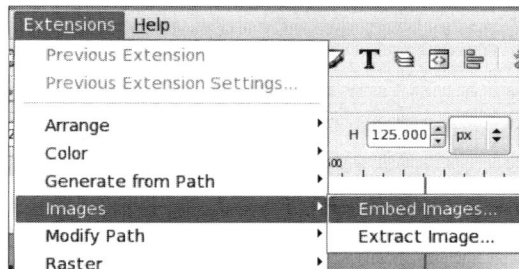

3. Check the **Embed only selected images** box.

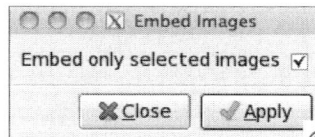

[✐ If you want to embed all images in the document, then don't check this box.]

4. Click **Apply**.

Now all images will be included within the Inkscape SVG file. This is useful if you want one all-inclusive file that can be sent or posted individually without worry for additional source files or directory structures.

Please note, however, there are some limitations to embedding images into the Inkscape SVG files:

- An increase in file size. Most of the times, it can be increased by a third. (For SVG files used directly on the web, this increases bandwidth usage on the server or host).

- You can't share images across documents. For example, if you do one PNG image as a background file, you can't share it across SVG files.

- Sharing copyrighted fonts or images in a document could be illegal (depending on how extensive the rights you have purchased to use these items are to begin with). This is particularly important when working on commercial or widely used projects.

- If there is extensive text-editing done with the SVG files themselves, then this can be complicated and time-intensive.

Importing from the Open Clip Library (Mac users)

The Open Clip Art Library is an open source, free clip art image library that you can search directly from Inkscape.

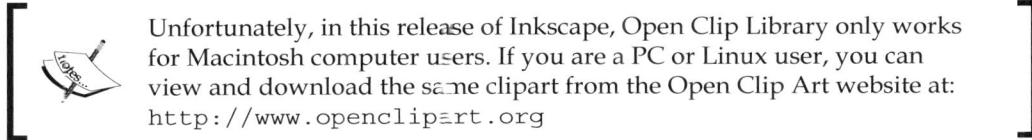

> Unfortunately, in this release of Inkscape, Open Clip Library only works for Macintosh computer users. If you are a PC or Linux user, you can view and download the same clipart from the Open Clip Art website at: http://www.openclipart.org

Here's how it works:

1. In an open Inkscape project, from the main menu choose **File** and then **Import From Open Clip Art Library**.

2. In the **Import From Open Clip Art Library** dialog box, **Search for:** field enter a keyword to describe the clip art you want to place in the document and click **Search**.

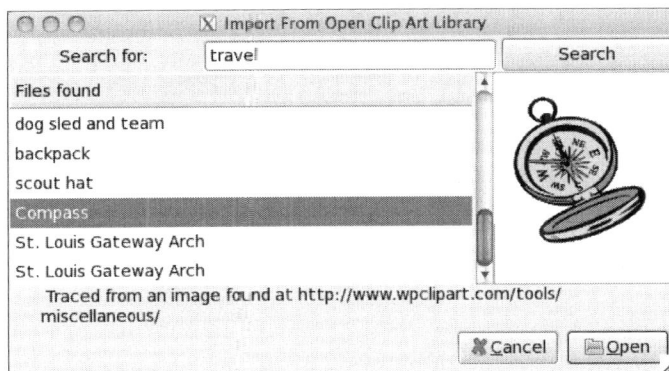

3. Inkscape then connects to the Open Clip Art Library website and previews of files are shown in a window on the right side of the dialog.

4. Try other keyword searches until you find one you like and then double-click the name of the image to place it in the document.

Using the clip art library can be useful in a number of ways:

*   It allows for free-use of a number of images that you may like to use in a web design mock up—for placement or for end-use.

*   You can also ungroup the pieces of the image and adjust colors, remove items, edit the overall image, and use it in your own design.

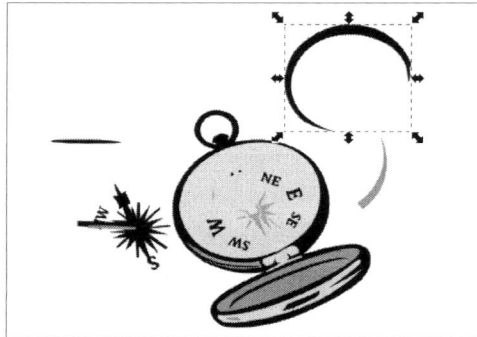

Importing clip art and images can give you a starting point for your own designs—as well as give great layout perspective when web site mock ups are created.

Rendering a Bitmap image

In the last chapter we talked about exporting a simple web design into PNG files that can be used by programmers when creating a website. Essentially, when we did that process, we rendered an image in Inkscape. It has its own renderer library that can render images up to 25600% zoom with anti-aliasing. You can export the entire document or page or just the current selection. Let's try this again on a simple image to refresh our memory.

1. With the new clip art image open from the previous section, from the main menu select **File** and then **Export Bitmap**.

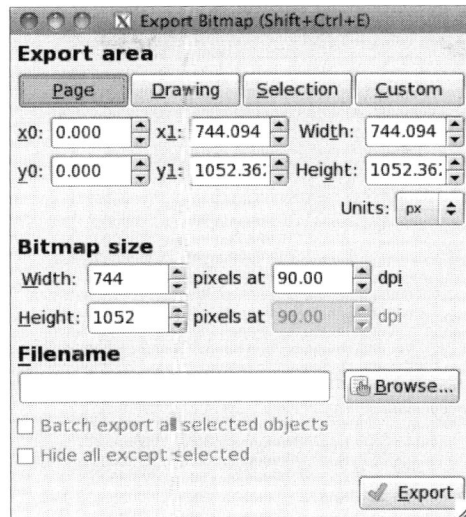

2. If you want to export the entire document, as shown, in one bitmap image, then select **Page**.

3. You can also choose **Selection**; if you have selected the item you want to export individually.

4. Change the **Bitmap size** and **DPI** format, if needed.

> Dots per Inch or DPI refer to an images resolution. The ideal resolution varies across print and web. For print, typically images are suggested to be 300 DPI. For the web 72 DPI is more common as it is the number of pixels across one inch of most monitors.

5. Click **Browse**, to change the default filename and/or the location of where you want the file saved.

6. Then click **Export**.

7. Your new PNG file is saved. These new images pieces won't be editable in Inkscape, or the layers will not be intact, but you should be able to import it for use in another SVG file.

> Inkscape currently only supports rendering exported images in PNG format. If you need a file in another format, you can use the **Save As** or **Save a Copy** function for other format types.

Basics about photo manipulation

Inkscape doesn't allow for extensive photo manipulation, but some filters within the program are best used for photographs or non-vector based images. These are the basics and fun effects for your photographic images. Filters that are photo- and bitmap-friendly are:

- Blurs
- Bumps
- Color
- Distort
- Image Effects
- Image Effects, Transparent
- Transparency Utilities
- Overlay filters—For some fun try Scatter and Texture filters and Clip with photographs as well

Let's walk through using one of these filters as an example. Keeping in mind the theme for our travel web site design, we'll work with a photograph of a local lake and see if we can enhance it for use within our design.

1. Open a new Inkscape document and import a bitmap. From the main menu select **File** and then **Import**.

2. Select the correct bitmap file and click **Open**. Make sure your imported bitmap is selected, and then select **File** and then **Document Properties**. In the **Custom Size** section, click **Resize page to content**.

3. Click **Resize page to drawing or selection**.

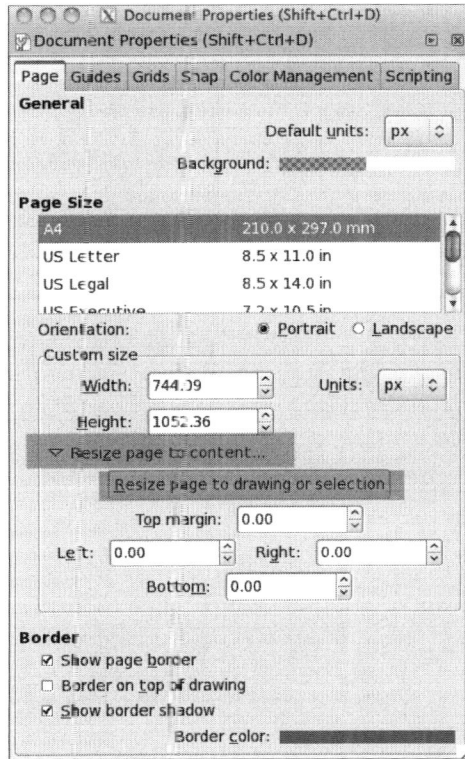

4. Your document page size will now be adjusted to match that of your imported bitmap image as shown in the following screenshot:

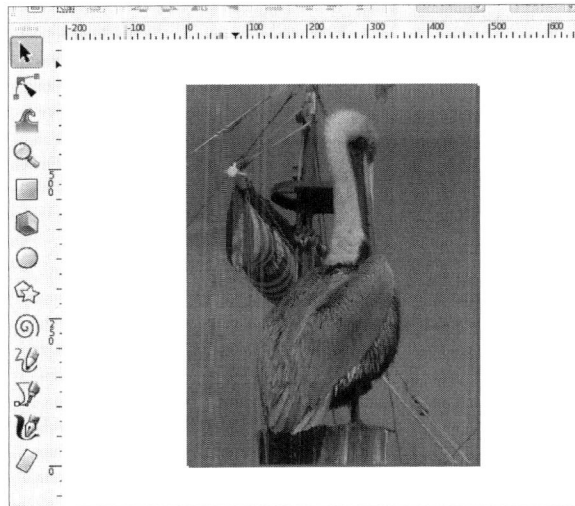

5. Select the image and then from the main menu, select **Filters** and then **Image Effects** and **Soft Focus Lens**. This will create a "soft" image and give a dreamy effect.

6. Next, we will create a 'torn edge' effect around the photo by making sure the photo is selected and then from the main menu choose **Filters** and then **Distort** and **Torn Edges**.

7. Now the photo can be saved as a PNG and placed in our overall design of the site to enhance it a bit. To save this file, from the main menu select **File** and then **Export**. Give it a file name and save it within the project file folders.

We'll import this new photo into the design mock up later on in this chapter. Let's first learn how to trace images—or convert them into vector graphics.

Tracing images

Tracing essentially creates paths (and nodes) it identifies within a bitmap image and then uses those paths to create a vector-based image from the bitmap. In Inkscape there are two pre-installed add-ins that you can use to do this: Protrace and SIOX.

The results of this tracing process depend heavily on the quality of the original images. Protrace works best for black-and-white line drawing or black and white pictures with high contrast. It can be used for screened color prints and color photography as well, but it can require a bit more careful detail work to make it happen. SIOX is primarily used with Protrace to separate a foreground from a background. Using both tools requires some practice and finesse to make them work best, but it is well worth it if you want the scalability of vector graphics within your design. Let's go through a couple of examples.

Using Protrace

1. Open up the bitmap image you want to trace in Inkscape.

2. Make sure the image is selected and then from the main menu choose **Path** and then **Trace Bitmap**. The Trace Bitmap dialog box appears.

3. The **Mode** tab defines characteristics of the tracing mode.

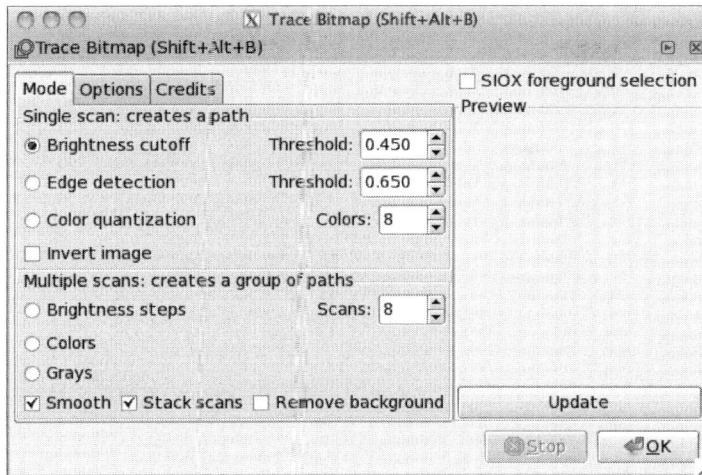

4. There are two sections: **Single Scan** and **Multiple scan** settings. Let's define each of these scan setting and their respective options so you can determine what is best for your picture.

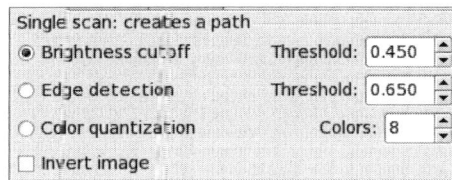

5. **Single scans**, as the name suggests, is done with a single pass (or scan) and it creates a path from the bitmap images.

6. **Brightness Cutoff**: Every pixel has a red, green, and blue value. Brightness, then, is the sum of all those values for a pixel. For grayscale images this value is the sum of the black and white value. So, when this option is selected, a path is created by containing all pixels that are darker than the **Threshold** setting. This option works well for black-and-white line art.

7. **Edge Detection**: This setting is based on the brightness differences between adjacent pixels. The path is created *between* pixels with changes that are above the **Threshold** setting.

8. **Color Quantization**: It depends on changes in color between adjacent pixels. The **Colors** field gives the number of different colors used to look for edges. Again, only one path is created, but it is based on whether the index of the color is even or odd (All odd indexes are grouped together or all even).

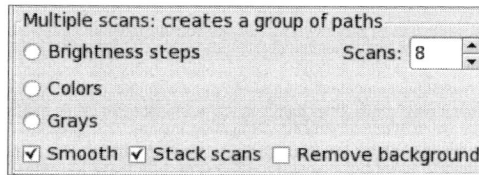

```
Multiple scans: creates a group of paths
○ Brightness steps          Scans: 8  ▲▼
○ Colors
○ Grays
☑ Smooth ☑ Stack scans □ Remove background
```

9. **Multiple scans** scan the image multiple times, using a different setting each time. One path is created with each scan and the paths are stored in a group. The settings used at each scan are Brightness, Colors, and Grays. For all three of the settings, the Scans field determines how many times an image is scanned. Since we're starting from a 0 (zero) count it is actually the Scan number + 1.

10. **Brightness steps**: The darkest scan is always done at a brightness threshold of 0.2 and the lightest scan is done at a threshold of 0.9. The rest of the scans are at evenly spaced positions in between. If the **Remove** background box is checked, the 90% region is ignored.

11. **Colors**: Once a value is entered in the **Scans** field, the number of colors in the bitmap is reduced via the Octree Quantization method. This means that an optimal set of colors is chosen based on a mathematical calculation. Based on that a black-and-white image is created for each color and then that is used to create the trace.

12. **Grays**: The process is the same as what is used for the **Colors** method, but using gray color values instead.

There are three other settings for multiple scans that apply no matter what mode is chosen:

   ° **Smooth**: This setting when turned on (checked) forces a Gaussian Blur effect to be applied to the image before performing a trace. It smoothens out the difference between adjacent pixels and is very useful when working with screened prints.

   ° **Stack scans**: This determines how paths are defined. Leaving the **Stack scans** box unchecked (or off), the paths won't overlap. If you turn this setting on (checked), each path includes the area of the paths above it. The one advantage of using stacked paths is that there are no 'holes' between the paths.

    ◦ **Remove background**: The background, by default is the lowest object in the stacking order or drawings. Thus, this is the lowest path when tracing objects as well. So, when the **Stack scans** option is checked, the background path that corresponds to a rectangle the size of the scanned image will be ignored.

13. For this picture we will set the following:

    ◦ **Single Scan**

    ◦ **Brightness Cutoff**: **Threshold 0.450**

14. Click the **Options** tab, to set some additional options.

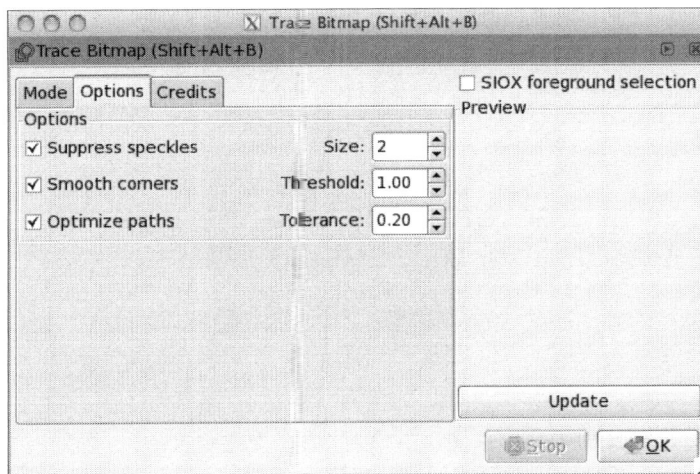

15. These options are used across either the single or multiple scan modes.

    ◦ **Suppress speckles**: If you check this box, it will remove all paths that have a size less than the amount specified.

    ◦ **Smooth corners**: This will force all nodes on a path to have round corners. The smaller the value, the sharper the corner (and a value of 0 means there will be no smoothing). This setting will require some testing to see if it works for your image.

    ◦ **Optimize paths**: Using this option tries to reduce the number of nodes used in the paths. The tolerance value determines how many errors are allowed in the resulting curve from the merging. The higher the tolerance, the more likely two curves can be merged into one. The **Smooth corners** option must be used for this option to work.

16. For this sample, we'll select the checkboxes for all options (essentially turning them on) with these settings:
    ◦ **Suppress speckles: Size 2**
    ◦ **Smoother Corners: Threshold 1.00**
    ◦ **Optimize paths Tolerance 0.20**

17. When all settings are in place, click **OK** to perform the conversion.

18. Within a few moments, you will be able to see the results.

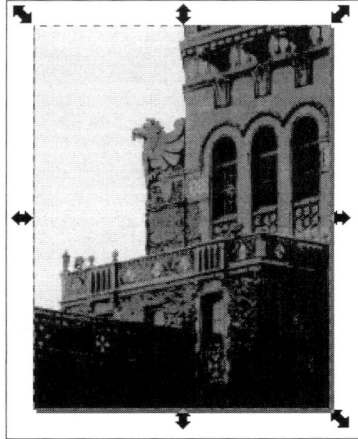

19. You'll notice your original image will still be viewable on the canvas. From the main menu, select **Object** and then **Lower** — to "lower" the new image below the original.

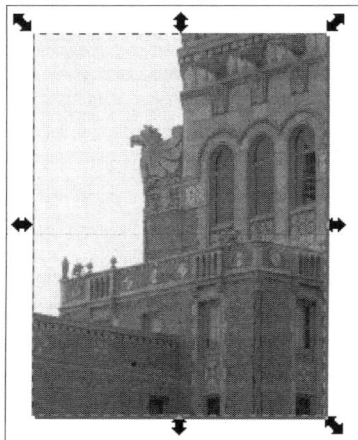

20. Select the original image and then press the *Delete* key on your keyboard. Your new vector image should be viewable.

21. Save this new file (Choose **File** and then **Save As...**), with a new descriptive file name and be sure that the file type in the bottom right is **Inkscape SVG**.

In this example, we kept the background in place and just tried to create a vector image from an entire photograph. However, another scenario is that you want to take one object from the picture and create a vector object from that one object. That is where using SIOX comes into play. Let's learn how to use it in the next section.

Using SIOX

SIOX means **Simple Interactive Object Extraction**. It let's you separate an object from the background in a bitmap image. If you have paid close attention in the steps performed to do a trace in the previous section, you'll notice that the option to use this feature is within the Tracing Bitmap dialog box.

Using SIOX depends on the characteristics of the bitmap image. If you have a photograph where an object is clearly distinguished in color from the background—you have a great chance for success in "re-creating" it with a trace using this feature. Here's how it's done.

1. Open up the bitmap image you want to trace in Inkscape.

2. Make sure the image is selected and then from the main menu choose **Path** and then **Trace Bitmap**. The Trace dialog box appears.

3. Check the **SIOX foreground selection** box to turn it on.

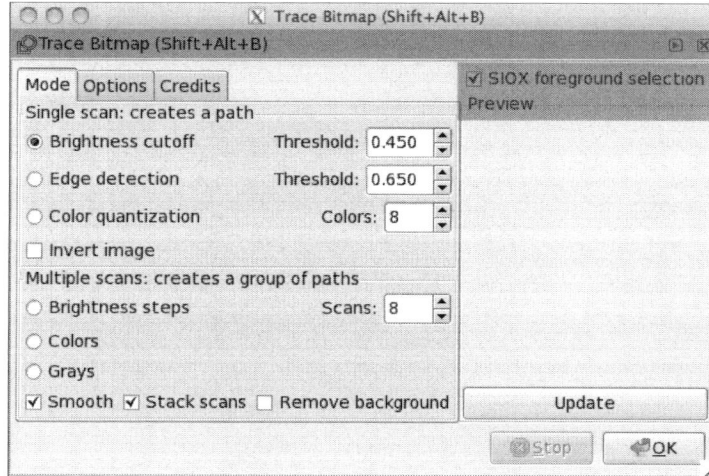

4. Now, use the freehand tool or a box, circle, or another object, and select an area of the image that includes the entire object you want to extract and some of the background.

5. Give the path an opaque fill if it doesn't already have one.

6. Select both the bitmap image and the path and then perform a trace by clicking **OK** in the Tracing Bitmap dialog box.

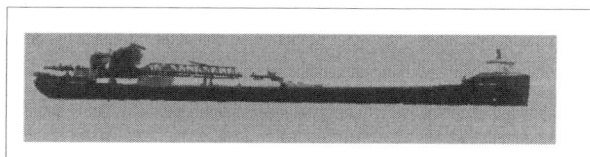

7. Within a few moments, you'll see the background "disappear" from the canvas. Select the opaque object used in the process and delete it to show your final image.

8. Save your new image in SVG format—it's now a vector graphic!

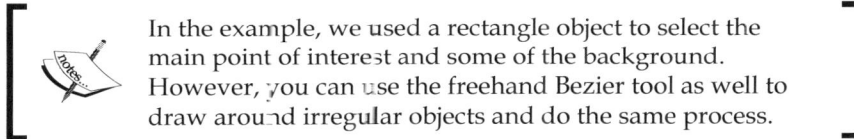

> In the example, we used a rectangle object to select the main point of interest and some of the background. However, you can use the freehand Bezier tool as well to draw around irregular objects and do the same process.

Ultimately, tracing bitmap images so that they can be turned into vector graphics takes some practice and trial-and-error. However, if you can do this well, you will use it in a variety of projects—anywhere from the web design, to helping create and **clean up** logos and more.

Converting raster logos to vector-based logos

Many clients might only have their logo images in raster or bitmap formats—JPG, GIF, PNG, or BMP. These, as we defined in *Chapter 1, Inkscape 101: The Basics*, are a grid of pixels that are set to certain colors. When these logos are made larger there's a loss of quality (remember the boxey, pixilated look?). And often, you might need to scale a logo larger so it fits in your new design. And, of course, you want it to maintain smooth edges.

Here's how you use Inkscape to convert a raster image logo into a SVG image in vector graphic format (that will be scalable!):

1. Open the logo you want to convert in Inkscape. In this example, I opened the logo file we used in our initial web site example. You can see from the enlarged screenshot that the edges are not smooth.

2. Select the entire image (**Edit** and then **Select All**) and then perform a trace by choosing **Path** and then **Trace Bitmap**.

3. In the Trace Bitmap dialog box, select **Multiscan Colors** as the mode and be sure that **Smooth** is **unchecked**. The **Scans** can be set to 15.

4. Click **OK** to start the conversion.

5. Next you need to delete your original image. From the main menu, select **Object** and then **Lower**. You will now see that your new vector image was "lowered" beneath the original jagged edged image.

6. Select it and then press the *Delete* key on your keyboard. Your new vector image should be viewable.

7. Save this new file (choose **File** and then **Save As...**), with a new descriptive file name and be sure that the file type in the bottom right is Inkscape SVG.

Now it's time to learn how to pass along and incorporate all of these new images we've created in this chapter into our design mock up.

Using individual images as design elements

Throughout this chapter we've created five new images that can enhance our initial web page design:

- Clip art
- Manipulated photo

- Line art drawing
- Individual picture
- Vector image

Let's import each of these into our design to make it better.

1. Open the SVG project file in Inkscape.

2. From the main menu, select **File** and then **Import**. Select the Compass Clip Art PNG file and place it in the design where it fits.

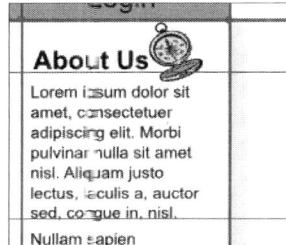

3. Next perform the same process to import the manipulated photo.

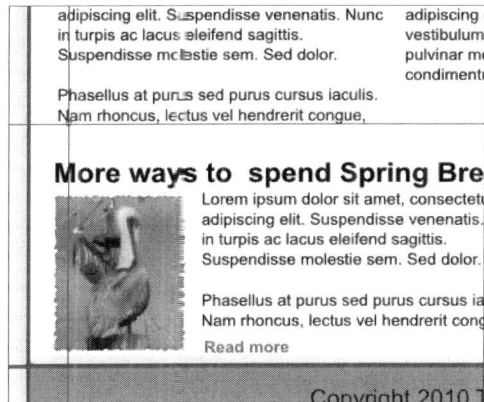

4. Then do the same for the line art drawing, object picture, and logo—but with these SVG files, you can resize the images (even making them very large and opaque) and notice you won't lose any quality since they are now vector graphics.

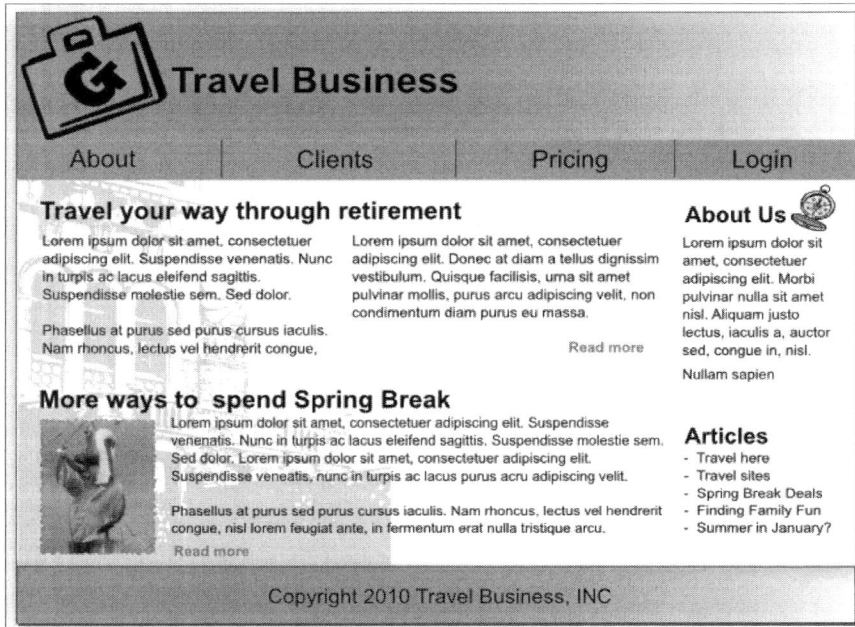

5. When you've enhanced the design to your liking, save the SVG file again to maintain all of your edits.

Again, if you want to send updates to the web programmers, you need to perform the export process as explained in *Chapter 2, Working with Programmers* and send them the following:

*   The PNG image files you exported from your design (likely within a folder called images)

*   And the source Inkscape SVG file of your design mock up with all images used in the creation of it (including the five we just made)

Summary

In this chapter, we learned a lot about working with images—raster and vector—in Inkscape. From importing bitmap images, embedding images, rendering bitmap images as vector graphics, working a bit with photographs and filters, importing clip art and all the tips and tricks for "tracing" bitmap images to convert them into full vector graphics for both photographs and logos.

Now we can re-create all of those non-editable images and make them resizable and enhance them in our current web design project. In the next chapter we're going to learn all about text: how to style it, make it unique, and wrap it around images.

4
Styling Text

The idea of text styling is manipulating text so that it creates a certain feel when seen in an overall design. By study, text styling is called typography and a form of typesetting. Compare the look and feel (or design) of your local newspaper with that of a children's magazine. Or start comparing web designs of the same—a newspaper site, or a children's television network and then compare it to a sport's web site.

As seen in all of the mentioned web site types—text is an important element in web design. It is the means by which the web site viewers see the content on the site. It is also a key element within headings, banners, and logos. In these areas it can be even more critical to get creative and try any number of text styling elements so that the simple content of the business or web site name stand out among the other content elements.

This chapter will cover:

- Basics about text editing tools within Inkscape—using reflection, following paths, shadows, the perspective tool, and even the envelope effect.
- Creating a killer header bar—this can make or break a web page design (and how you can take that banner and make it the centerpiece of your next web page design).
- Best practice for exporting images for use by a web programmer and as an individual element is to use it in an already created web design.

Creating and editing text tools

As seen in previous chapters, creating text in a project is simple—select the Create and Edit Text tool in the tool box, click at the insertion point within an open project, and start typing.

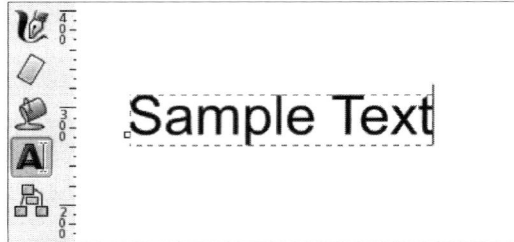

The text is immediately displayed on the canvas.

> The text tool (**A** icon) in the tool box shown above is the only way of creating new text on the canvas. The **T** icon shown in the Command Bar is used only when editing the text that already exists on the canvas.

You can use the Text and Font Menu to change everything from the font, style, size, and alignment. To open this window, from the main menu select **Text** and then **Text and Font** (or use the shortcut keys and press *Shift+Ctrl+T*).

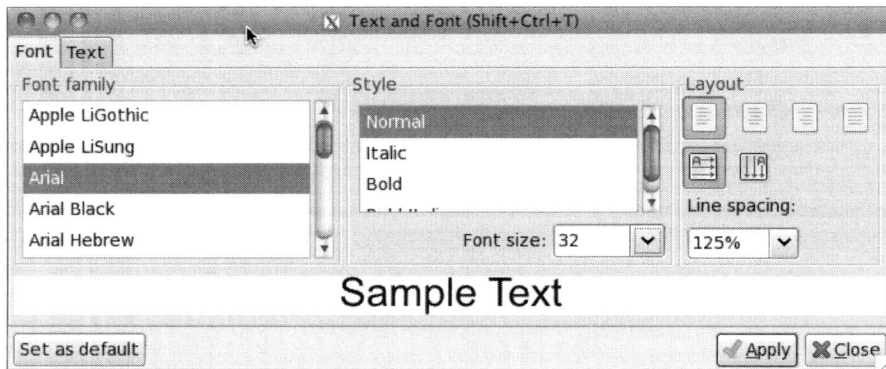

This window dialog also has a unique (and often useful) feature where you can edit your text directly. Click the **Text** tab and select the text you want to change, or add/delete text.

Back in the **Font** tab you can change the font itself, the point size, alignment, line spacing, and even change from horizontal to vertical text layout. But note, even with options for Bold, Italics, or Bold Italics there is no option for Underline.

Spacing shortcut keys

You can also change the spacing of a selected text by using shortcut keys. Use the *Alt* + > or *Alt* + < keys to try it out. See the following information box about limitations of these shortcuts with Mac and Linux OS versions. For more information about keyboard shortcuts, see Appendix A, *Keyboard Shortcuts*.

One of the more important items in typography and working with text that you will want to learn is **kerning** — or the ability to adjust the spacing between letters.

$$\boxed{\text{S.am..ple Text}}$$

There is no menu path to perform this in Inkscape. Instead you use handy shortcut keys. For more information about keyboard shortcuts, see Appendix A, *Keyboard Shortcuts*.

Unfortunately, there are issues with the current version (0.48) of the Inkscape software and how it is run within Mac OS and Linux. They both require an additional 'shell' application in order for Inkscape to operate (X11). That being said, the *ALT* key which is required for the following steps does not always work correctly. Here are some work around steps to get the LEFT *ALT* key on your keyboard to work correctly (based in instructions found at the link below):

On your computer open the terminal application. (From the main Mac OS screen select **Go, Applications**, and then **Utilities**. Then the **Terminal** application and double-click it to open).

At the main prompt type, you'll be typing a number of commands to create a new text file, and then map your *Option/Alt* key on your keyboard to work as expected in the X11 application.

To start, type: cd ~

Next type: touch .xmodmap. This command creates a new text file called .xmodmap in your home directory.

Now type: open .xmodmap to open the text file.

Then type: keycode 66 = Alt_L at the prompt. This maps the *Options* key to work as the *Alt* key in the X11 application.

If you had X11 open during this process, exit it and restart to have the changes take affect.

For more issues on possible solutions to this problem you can see this website for possible work around: http://wiki.inkscape.org/wiki/index.php/FAQ#How_to_make_the_Alt_key_work_.3F

If these workarounds do not work, there are no alternative steps for kerning options.

Here's how to kern text that already exists on your canvas:

1. First, double-click some text that you have already entered in an open project. This will take you into the Create and Edit Text tool allowing you to edit the text letter by letter.

2. Using the arrow keys, move the cursor between the two letters you want to add or diminish the space between.

3. Then, press the *Alt + Right Arrow Key* to add space between the letters. Or alternatively, press the *Alt + Left Arrow Key* to lessen the space between those two letters. Each time you press the arrow key, the space increases or decreases by one pixel.

4. Alternatively, if you want to move individual characters (or multiple) up and down, then just move your cursor near the letter (or letters) which you want to move vertically.

5. Select the letter(s) by using the *Shift* key and the Right/Left Arrows or drag your mouse over the character(s) you want to edit.

6. Then press *Alt + Up Key* to move the letter(s) up from the horizontal baseline.

7. Or use the *Alt + Down* Key combination to move a letter down from the horizontal baseline.

8. You can even rotate letters. Select a letter you want to rotate left or right and then use the *Alt + [or [keys* to start moving it.

9. Feel free to save the file now if you think you might want to use this going forward.

It is convenient to leave these letters as text—instead of the alternative of converting the text to paths—as the text remains editable. You can easily switch fonts, change font sizes and styles all without removing the kerning and spacing information that you have already set. One small disadvantage to this approach, is that when you re-open (or deliver) an SVG file, you must have the original font used in this creation on that computer. Just remember when providing and saving the SVG file, keep all graphics and fonts used in the creation of the web design or graphic together and available for any future use.

> You can also create a duplicate layer (**File | Layer | Duplicate**) and then hide it to preserve text styling for future re-work of the document and text information.

Text styling keyboard shortcuts

Since not all text styling options are available via a menu item, here's an overview of all the text options via keyboard shortcuts. Also refer to Appendix A for all key combination shortcuts available for Inkscape.

Remember: See the previous information box about the limitations of using shortcuts that contain the *Alt* key with Mac and Linux operating systems.

Text selection shortcut keys	
Ctrl + Left/Right Arrows	Cursor moves word by word
Shift + Left/Right Arrows	Selects/Deselects letter by letter
Ctrl + Shift + Left/Right Arrows	Selects/Deselects word by word
Double click on letters	Selects the word
Triple click	Selects the entire line of text
Shift + Home For Mac OS: *Shift + Fn + Left* Arrow	Selects from the beginning of the line until the cursor position
Shift + End For Mac OS: *Shift + Fn + Right* Arrow	Selects from cursor to the end of the line
Ctrl + Shift + Home For Mac OS: *Ctrl + Shift + Fn + Left* Arrow	Selects from the beginning of the text until the cursor position
Ctrl + Shift + End For Mac OS: *Ctrl + Shift + Fn + Right* Arrow	Selects from the cursor position until the end of the text
Hot keys	
Ctrl + B	Applies bold style to the selected text
Ctrl + I	Applies italic style to the selected text
Alt + Right or Left Arrows	Increase or decrease the space between characters (kerning)
Alt + > or < keys	Changes the overall letter spacing within that text box
Alt + [or [keys	Rotates letters
Alt + Up or Down Arrows	Change the vertical position of the selected text relatively to the baseline.
Alt + Shift + Arrows	Moves position by 10 pixel steps
Ctrl + [or [	Rotates 90°

Text effects

Sometimes when using text within web design you'll need to "reserve" a portion of the screen real estate for text that isn't written yet, or replace one word with another throughout a large amount of text, or change capitalization rules. To do this there are some effects that can help do some of the process automatically.

Using the Lorem Ipsum effect

In the first chapter, we used the Lorem Ipsum effect to create or design layout mockup. It's a pseudo-Latin form of text that is commonly used as "placeholder" text because when seen in a larger context of a design it gives the feel for real sentences and paragraphs of text at a visual level. Let's review how to use it:

1. In an open project, choose the Create and Edit Text tool and create a text box.

2. From the main menu, select **Extensions** and then **Text** and **Lorem Ipsum**.

3. In the Lorem Ipsum window, choose some settings and then press **Generate**.

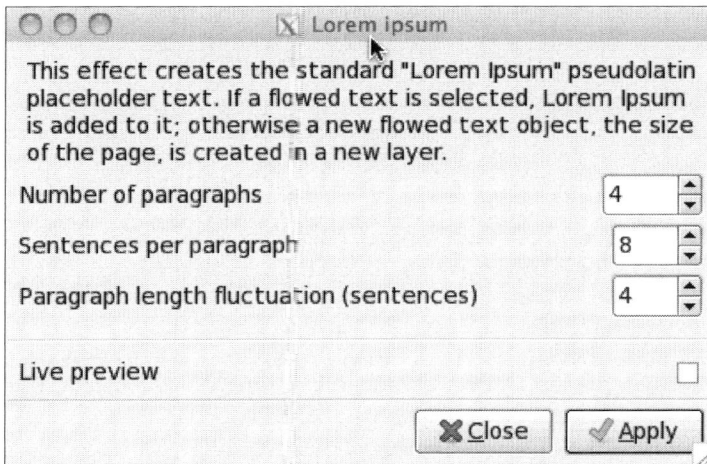

4. Within a few moments, you'll have some text which you can place on the screen as follows:

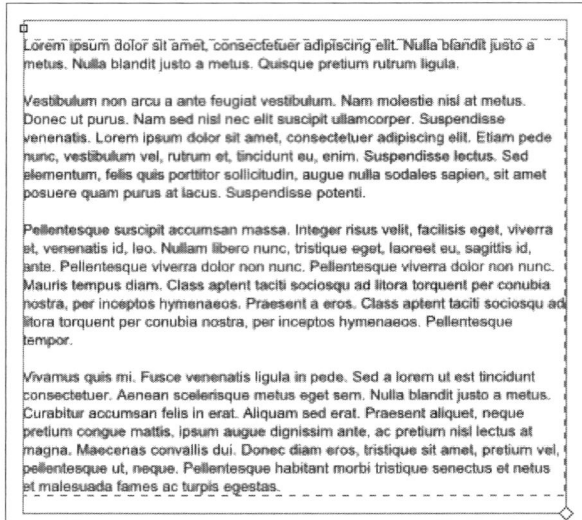

Lorem ipsum dolor sit amet, consectetuer adipiscing elit. Nulla blandit justo a metus. Nulla blandit justo a metus. Quisque pretium rutrum ligula.

Vestibulum non arcu a ante feugiat vestibulum. Nam molestie nisl at metus. Donec ut purus. Nam sed nisl nec elit suscipit ullamcorper. Suspendisse venenatis. Lorem ipsum dolor sit amet, consectetuer adipiscing elit. Etiam pede nunc, vestibulum vel, rutrum et, tincidunt eu, enim. Suspendisse lectus. Sed elementum, felis quis porttitor sollicitudin, augue nulla sodales sapien, sit amet posuere quam purus at lacus. Suspendisse potenti.

Pellentesque suscipit accumsan massa. Integer risus velit, facilisis eget, viverra et, venenatis id, leo. Nullam libero nunc, tristique eget, laoreet eu, sagittis id, ante. Pellentesque viverra dolor non nunc. Pellentesque viverra dolor non nunc. Mauris tempus diam. Class aptent taciti sociosqu ad litora torquent per conubia nostra, per inceptos hymenaeos. Praesent a eros. Class aptent taciti sociosqu ad litora torquent per conubia nostra, per inceptos hymenaeos. Pellentesque tempor.

Vivamus quis mi. Fusce venenatis ligula in pede. Sed a lorem ut est tincidunt consectetuer. Aenean scelerisque metus eget sem. Nulla blandit justo a metus. Curabitur accumsan felis in erat. Aliquam sed erat. Praesent aliquet, neque pretium congue mattis, ipsum augue dignissim ante, ac pretium nisl lectus at magna. Maecenas convallis dui. Donec diam eros, tristique sit amet, pretium vel, pellentesque ut, neque. Pellentesque habitant morbi tristique senectus et netus et malesuada fames ac turpis egestas.

Find and replace

Just like in a word processing program, you can find and replace a word (or term) in the text box of an Inkscape document. To do this:

1. In an open project, choose the Create and Edit Text tool and select an already created text box with content residing in it.

2. From the main menu, select **Extensions** and then **Text** and **Replace Text**.

3. In the **Replace** text dialog box, place the word you want to replace in the first field and the new word in the second field.

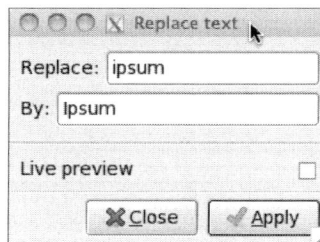

Replace text

Replace: ipsum

By: Ipsum

Live preview ☐

✖ Close   ✓ Apply

4. Click **Apply** and every instance of the old word will be replaced within the selected text box.

Remember, using this process will replace every single instance of a word in the selected text. If you only want to replace certain instances of the word, this process might be superseded by some careful proofreading of the content.

Sentence case

Sentence case simply means, using capital letters as you would in sentences — it replaces lower case characters by capitals in the beginning of every sentence.

The quick brown fcx jumps over the lazy dog.

To use this in Inkscape:

1. In an open project, choose the Create and Edit Text tool and select an already created text box with content residing in it.

2. From the main menu, select **Extensions** and then **Text** and **Sentence Case**. All capitalization rules will change to sentence case.

Title case

Instead of capitalizing the first word in ever sentence like the previous example, this text effect capitalizes the first letter of every word in the text box.

1. In an open project, choose the Create and Edit Text tool and select an already created text box with content residing in it.

2. From the main menu, select **Extensions** and then **Text** and **Title Case.** All capitalization rules will change to be title case.

The Quick Brown Fox Jumps Over The Lazy Dog.

Uppercase and lowercase

These effects simply change the case of each letter in the text box. The uppercase effect makes each letter a capital, whereas the lowercase effect changes all letters to their lowercase form.

THE QUICK BROWN FOX JUMPS OVER THE LAZY DOG.
the quick brown fox jumps over the lazy dog.

As with the other effects you do this in the following way:

1. In an open project, choose the text tool and select an already created text box with content residing in it.

2. From the main menu, select **Extensions**, **Text** and then **Uppercase** or **Lowercase**. All capitalization rules will change as specified.

Flipcase

This is a fun effect for text. It reverses the written letter case. So all capitals will become lower case, and all lower case letters become upper case letters. It looks like this:

The Quick Brown Fox Jumps Over The Lazy Dog.
tHE qUICK bROWN fOX jUMPS oVER tHE lAZY dOG.

Again this is accessed and used from the Effect menu:

1. In an open project, choose the text tool and select an already created text box with content residing in it.

2. From the main menu, select **Extensions** and then **Text** and **fLIP cASE**.

Random case

This is also a fun text effect; it takes the text contained in a text box and arbitrarily toggles letter case throughout. To use it:

1. In an open project, choose the text tool and select an already created text box with the content residing in it.

2. From the main menu, select **Extensions** and then **Text** and **rANdOm CasE**. The result looks something like this:

tHe qUICk bRoWn FoX JUMps oVEr tHe lAZy DOg.

Now that we have learned the basics of creating text and manipulating it in Inkscape, let's learn some more advanced techniques, so that by the end of the chapter we can create a new title bar and a banner for our example web site project.

Using reflections, shadows, and glows

One of the most common effects seen with text elements on the web—and one of the easiest to do—is creating a reflection or shadow of the letters in the word. These effects give a title, which is often a business or site name, more presence without much additional work (and doesn't over-do the text). We'll learn how to do both with some example text.

Reflections

In this example, we're aiming to create a simple text heading that has a reflection below it and then add a little something special to the text (but very simple) to make it stand apart with very little other effects. Here's what we'll create:

1. Open a new document in Inkscape, create a text box, and enter some text. In our example, we'll use the words: **Simply beautiful**

2. Next, we are going to clone the image. From the main menu select **Edit**, **Clone**, and then **Create Clone**.

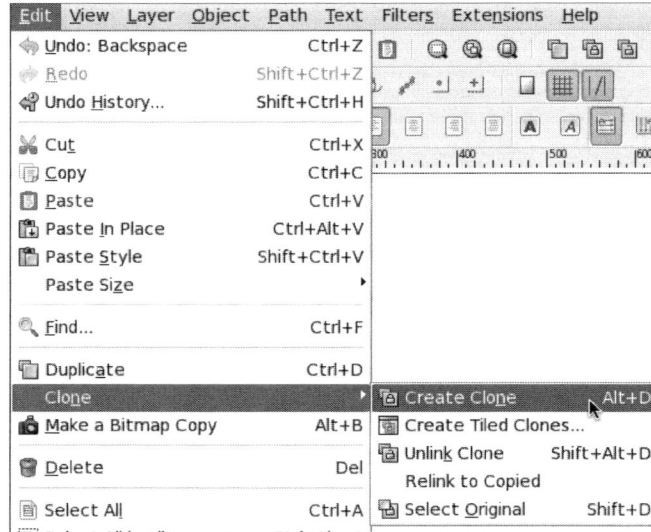

3. Now we need to flip the cloned image vertically to create the basics for our reflection. An easy way to do this is to press the *V* key (or from the main menu select **Object** and then **Flip Vertically**).

4. Move the "flipped" below the original text.

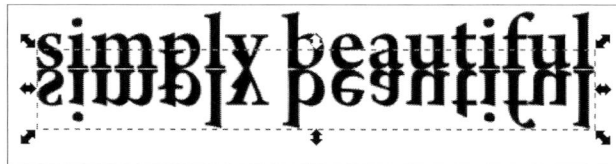

5. From the tool box, select the rectangle tool and create a rectangle that covers the reflected (or cloned) image.

6. Since this image has the letter Y in it, and it dangles/overlaps the main text, we need to clip the text so there is no overlapping. Select this new rectangle and the text underneath it.

Or you can select the text below by using *Alt* and clicking the text's approximate location and then pressing *Shift* and clicking on Rectangle.

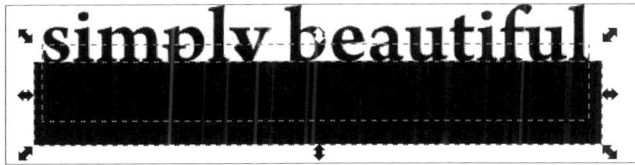

7. From the main menu select **Object** and then **Clip** and **Set**. You'll see that the Y dangler on the reflection now doesn't exist.

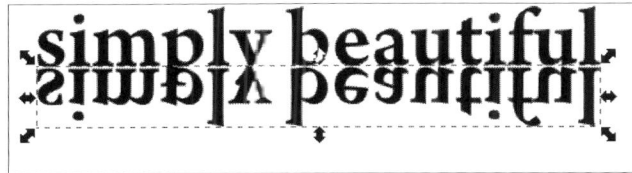

8. Now create another rectangle, and cover the reflection again.

9. With the rectangle still selected, open the Fill and Stroke dialog and choose the gradient tab.

10. Set a black to opaque gradient on rectangle, with the gradient white on top and black at the bottom.

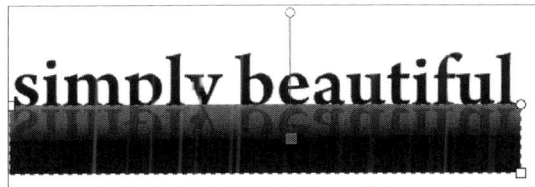

11. Again, select both the rectangle and the reflected text behind. Use the Select Tool, and drag around the rectangle. You should see a dotted line around the rectangle and the text behind it. Or you can select the text below by using *Alt* and clicking the text's approximate location and then pressing *Shift* and clicking on Rectangle.

12. From the main menu select **Object** and then **Mask**, and **Set**.

13. Now you have a reflection!

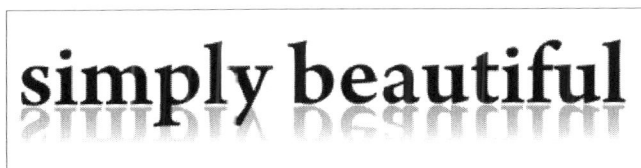

14. If the reflection still seems a bit dark for your taste, change the opacity in the Fill and Stroke dialog box.

15. But let's spice up this text just a bit more. Select the first letter in each word and let's change the color — voila! Since you have cloned the image, any change you make to the original text will also be changed in the reflection automatically.

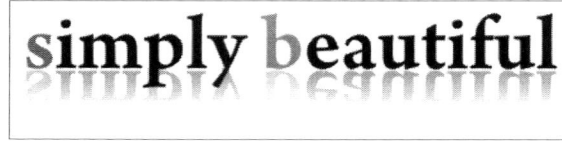

simply beautiful

16. And that even includes if you changed the words entirely like this:

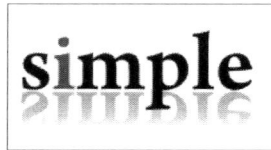

simple

17. Feel free to save this file for future reference or to use in your current projects.

Shadows and glows

We created simple drop shadows around our title area in the design mock up in *Chapter 2*. You use the same principles for creating text shadows as well. Let's work through an example.

1. Open a new document in Inkscape, create a text box, and enter some text. In our example, we'll use the words: **Darkness & Mystery**.

2. With the text selected from the main menu select **Filters**, **Shadows and Glows**, and then choose **Drop Shadow**.

3. In the Drop Shadow window, choose the settings that work for the drop shadow you want to create. We'll use a Blur radius of five pixels, Opacity of 80%, and offsets for horizontal and vertical set at five pixels.

4. Press **Apply** and the drop shadow will be set.

Darkness & Mystery

But there are a lot more filters here that you can use that will give neat effects for your text. These include cutouts, cutout and glow, dark and glow, drop glow, fuzzy glow, glow, in and out, inner glow, inner shadow, and inset. See the following screenshot for what each of these filters looks like when applied to our text examples:

More about text and paths

Using paths with text is a great combination to make unique web elements such as banners, logos, and headings or footers. They work together and allow you complete control over how the text will look. Let's review how we can make them work together.

Using a path for text

In Inkscape, you can put text onto a path and have it follow its shape—and when you do this the text and the path remain editable. This means you can still change the text, the shape of the path, kerning, and spacing elements in the text. Let's look at an example.

1. To start, draw a path with the Bezier path tool.

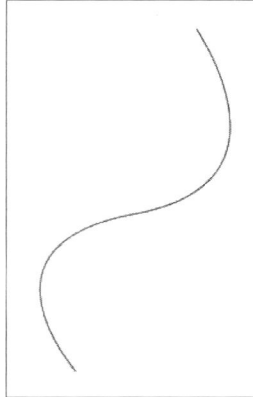

2. Then use the text tool and type text that you would like to place on the path.

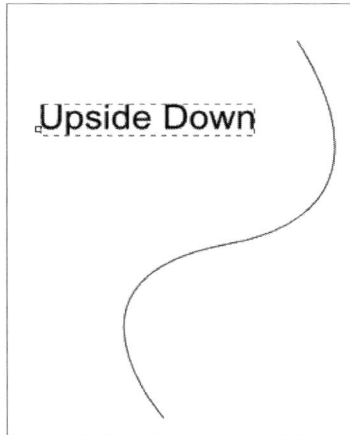

3. Select both the text and path.

4. From the main menu select **Text** and then **Put on Path**. You'll see that the text is then literally placed on the path of the line you had drawn.

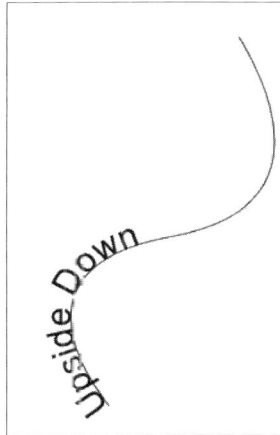

5. You can now move the original path and the text moves along with it. Or you can move the text away from the path, edit the text, or transform the text using kerning, text size, rotating letters, moving them from the baseline—but it still holds the shape of the path.

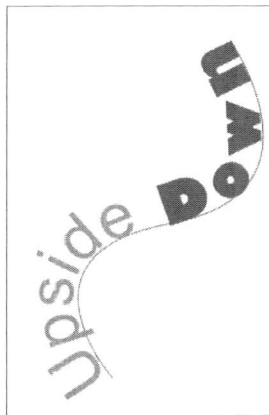

6. If you need to remove the shape from the text, from the main menu, select **Text** and then **Remove from Path**. You'll see that the text will turn back to a regular text object.

7. Again we don't plan to use this image in our current project, but if you want to save it for future reference, you can save it in Inkscape SVG format to open and edit as needed.

Placing text within a closed shape

Another unique text styling can be done, by placing text within a shape. Automatically words will wrap so that the text fits as best as possible within the shape. You can, of course, still edit the text after this, and even change some of its features. Let's walk through an example.

1. First create a shape in a new Inkscape document.

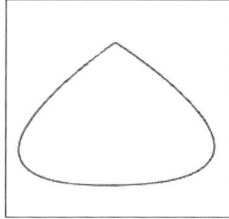

2. Next create some text to place within the shape.

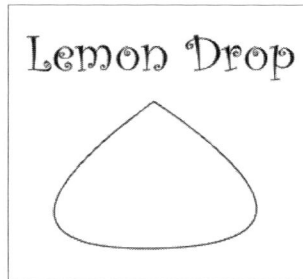

3. Select both the text and the shape and from the main menu choose **Text** and then **Flow into Frame**. Instantly, you'll see that the text is placed, as best as it can be, within the confines of the shape.

4. Feel free to manipulate the text to make it look just right. Even changing color, kerning, and spacing if needed. Same with the shape—feel free to change its border color or stroke and or a bit with it's shape and see how the text reacts or the impact on the overall design.

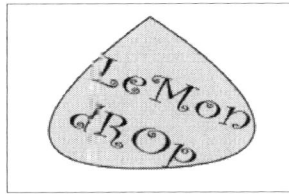

5. If you ever want to remove the text from the shape, from the main menu choose **Text** and then **Unflow**.

6. Save the file in Inkscape SVG format if you plan to use this file in any future projects!

Using perspective

Similar to placing text within a shape, let's learn how to give text some perspective—put it in forms that make it look like it is farther away and zooming forward and more. Here are a few steps to give this a try:

1. First, open an Inkscape document and type some text. Make sure the text is a larger font size to best see the results of this effect.

2. Select the text and then from the main menu choose **Paths** and then **Objects to Paths** to change the text into paths. Once you do this the text cannot be edited, so make sure it says exactly what you want it to say.

3. Next, use the Bezier tool and draw your irregular shape around the words with a smaller height in the back and larger in the front to simulate the words coming toward you on the screen.

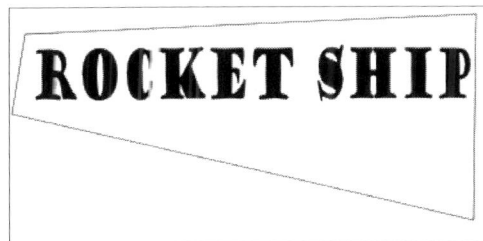

4. Select both the text and this new shape.

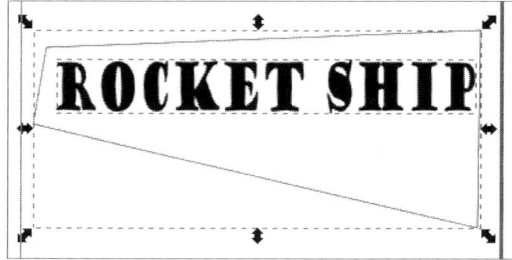

5. Then from the main menu select **Extension** and then **Modify Path** and **Perspective.** The letters will then fill out and stretch to meet the edges of the shape. And as the shape simulated perspective, the words should look smaller (or farther away) in the beginning and come toward you.

6. Delete the shape and, again, fiddle with the text until it is to your liking.

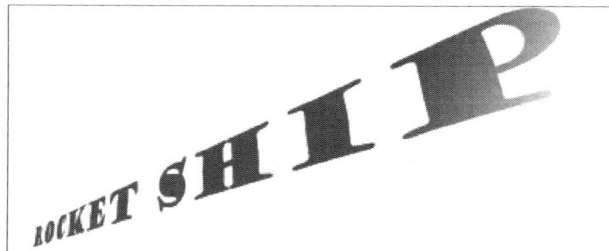

7. Then you are all set! You can save the file as an Inkscape SVG and/or export as a bitmap PNG file for use in a web page.

Pulling it all together

Let's take a sample heading and use a combination of the effects used in this chapter to create a unique heading logo.

1. Open a new Inkscape document.

2. Choose a large font to start for the text. Type the copy you want to use in this header.

**GiGi's
Fun Travel**

3. Now let's adjust the kerning between some select letters using the *Alt + Right Arrow* and *Alt + Left Arrow* keys to add some interest.

4. Along those same lines, since the name of this company implies it is fun (and maybe a little bit funky), let's also take some key characters and rotate them slightly. Use this *Alt + [and Alt +]* keys to do this rotation.

5. For the letters we just rotated, let's also move them from the baseline as well—shifting one letter up and the other down to further give this business name a little bit more fun feeling. We do this by selecting the letter and using the *Alt + Up Arrow* and *Alt − Down Arrow* key combinations.

**GiGi's
Fun Travel**

6. We're almost there! Now let's give it an even more unique feel. We'll use something called a text envelop to bring all of the text together. Select the text, and then from the main menu select **Path** and then **Linked Offset**. This creates a single node that we can drag 'out' to enclose the text in a 'border' or envelope.

7. Grab the node and pull it outward. It should look like your letters 'puff' out. Don't worry. You'll be able to see your lettering again shortly.

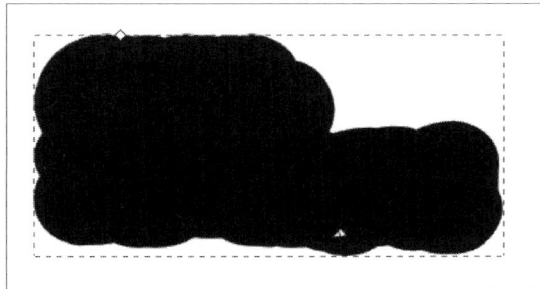

8. Drag and drop a color from the palette to change the color of the envelop to something that complements your companies colors/logo or site design.

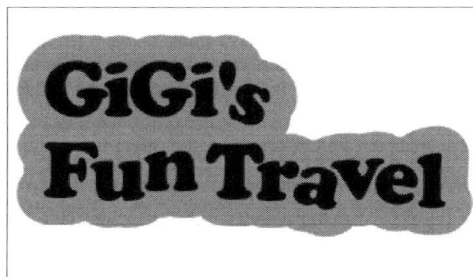

9. Now select the text and change its color to white (drag the white from the color palette).

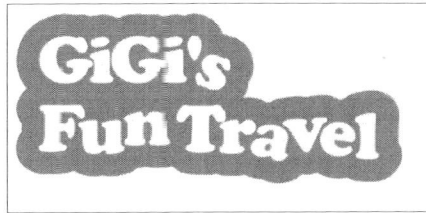

10. Can we add more flair? Of course! Select the envelope portion of our image, and give it a stroke color. Let s choose a color that is darker than or original and complements it.

11. Next, let's make that stroke thicker so we can really see it in the design. In the Fill and Stroke Dialog, change the Stroke Style width to 5 pixels or more.

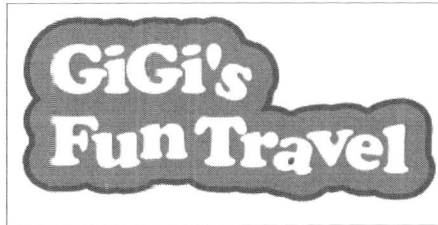

12. Also, let's select the text itself and add a stroke to the text and change its width and color as well.

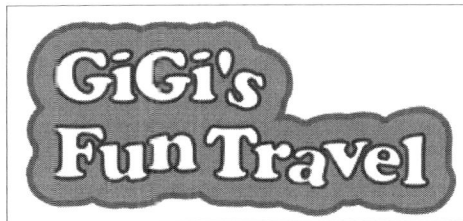

13. Now let's add some simple crop shadows. Select your text first, from the main menu select **Filters** and then **Shadows and Glows** and choose **Drop Shadow**.

14. Choose the Blur radio, opacity and offsets of your choice. In the example, we used a Blur Radius of 2, Opacity 80%, and offsets of 4 pixels for both horizontal and vertical.

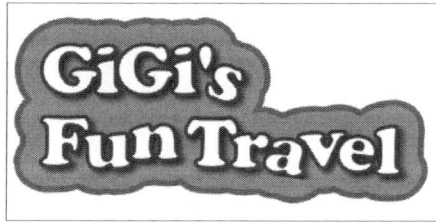

15. And lastly, create a drop shadow for the envelope. Use the same settings as for the text in the previous step.

16. You're all set! A logo that's new, fun, and a little bit funky to use on your website! Make sure you save this as an Inkscape SVG file so you can refer to it later, update colors—and of course use it as our sample web page!

Creating title bars and headings

Throughout this chapter we have learned many ways in which to manipulate text—from changing colors, to working with its shape to customize it and make it as unique as the web page you are designing. Let's use what we've learned so far, to expand the header bar we have on our example design and make it better.

We'll do this by using the new logo we created above and incorporating it into a new heading for our current site.

1. Open a new document in Inkscape. Make this document's size 800 pixels wide by 200 pixels high. This will just be the header portion of our website.

2. Draw a large rectangle that covers most of the canvas. Let's leave a small un-colored portion along the bottom.

3. Now change the color so that it matches but is a bit subdued compared to our newly created logo from the last section. As the original design, we want it to be colorful, but we also want it to align with a new look and design that our logo will define—fun, funky, and fresh.

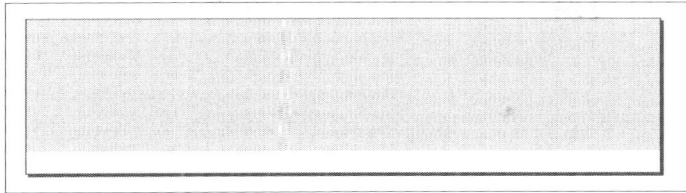

4. Next, we want to pull in our main piece—the new logo. Create a new layer and call it Logo.

5. From the previous section, import the SVG file of the new logo and place it along the left side of the header. We're going to make it a bit larger, rotate it slightly, and have it bleed off the edge of the rectangle we created in Step 2 to add interest.

6. We still want to add in a bit more flair—so from the main menu select **File** and then **Import from the Open Clip Art Library**. Search for some additional flair to add to the header and place it in the design where it works.

7. Feel free to get creative here, and even choose some colors from the palette. Let's change the clip art so it matches our color scheme and makes the logo more unique.

8. Make sure you save your file.

Exporting title bars for use as a design element

So now, as you are refining your design skills, some elements of your original design are being updated, given more flair, and generally helping shape the design of the original site. Let's open the original design and import some of these new design elements.

1. Open the SVG project file in Inkscape.

2. You'll need to go to the Header layer and delete all the current objects (make sure your layer is unlocked so you can edit it).

3. From the main menu, select **File** and then **Import**. Select your new header file and place it along the top.

4. Enhance the design so it now fits this new header. Change footer colors to match, re-align items on your overall page and save the SVG file again to maintain all of your edits.

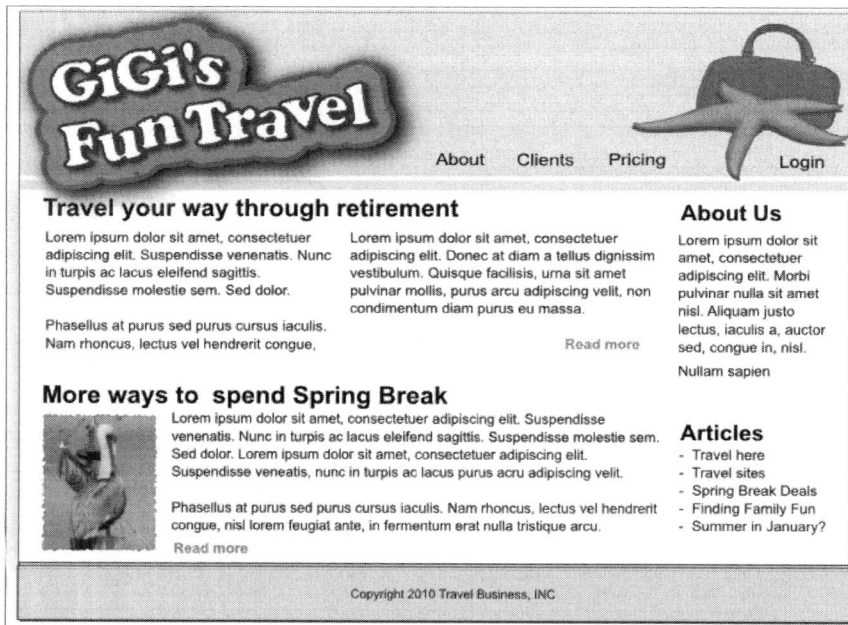

Again, you need to perform the export process as explained in *Chapter 2, Designing Site Layout Mockups*, if you are ready to implement your design. You'd need to provide the following files:

- The PNG image files you exported from your design (likely within a folder called images)

- And the source Inkscape SVG file of your design mock up with all images used in the creation of it (including the five we just made) and any uncommon fonts used in text elements.

Summary

You've learnt a lot about text editing and styling in this chapter. Specifically there were details about kerning, rotating, moving letters from the baseline, reflection, following paths, shadows, the perspective tool and even some cool envelope effects. Then we created a new, fun, and funky header for our project and imported it into the files so it is ready for integration into the overall web page. There are many more options and text manipulation tools within Inkscape—try them out, experiment, and create logos that "WOW" your clients and peers.

Next up are wallpapers and backgrounds that can show off even more of your Inkscape talents.

5
Creating Wallpapers and Pattern Backgrounds

Backgrounds with unique designs and patterns are a fun tool for web designers. It creates visual interest in your design and can give more creativity if used in compelling designs. In this chapter we will:

- Create repeating pattern-based backgrounds such as pin-stripes and tiled backgrounds
- Create swirls and spirals
- Create a unique background with the swirl and the spiral patterns we created
- Export the graphics and backgrounds we created to use them in the example design layout and implementation into HTML

Let's get started!

Using wallpapers and patterned backgrounds

Let's first distinguish between wallpapers and backgrounds. **Wallpapers** are typically used on your computer system itself—as the desktop wallpaper. These are also now commonly used (and downloaded) for cell phones and other electronic devices.

Common computer wallpaper (display) sizes to design for are 800 pixels x 600 pixels and 1024 pixels x 768 pixels, whereas 1024 x 768 is becoming increasingly the norm. For mobile computing (or cell phone), the common sizes are much more dependent on the hardware that is displaying the content—and offer much more diversity in designing for them. But, there are some standard sizes to consider. These are: 240 pixels x 320 pixels, 320 pixels x 480 pixels, 640 pixels x 360 pixels, 800 pixels by 480 pixels.

Backgrounds, on the other hand, refer to the overall background color or pattern 'behind' the overall design of a web page. These need to add a design element to the web page without distracting the content. Meaning, we still want to be able to read or view the web page without the background over-crowding the space.

One way to do this is to use subtle patterns—such as pinstripes or dots. These can be very simple but add interest to the web page instead of using a simple solid color—as seen in our example web page below:

When creating patterns in Inkscape, here are a few things to remember:

- As with any of the shapes you create in Inkscape, they are all vector-based. Which means that they can be resized to any size, initially created as small (or large) as you like, and are scalable (if needed) without losing any of the original designs quality.

- If you want sharp edges, your pattern will need to be drawn to the exact dimensions. Best practice is to use a grid and then use the **Snap to Grid** option.

- To make easy seamless patterns, use square-based designs with a common dimension like 40 x 40 pixels, 100 x 100 pixels, etc.

Using the built-in patterns

Inkscape has a number of simple patterns in the built-in library. Here's how to see what they look like:

1. Open Inkscape and create a new document.

2. Create a rectangle with the shape tool.

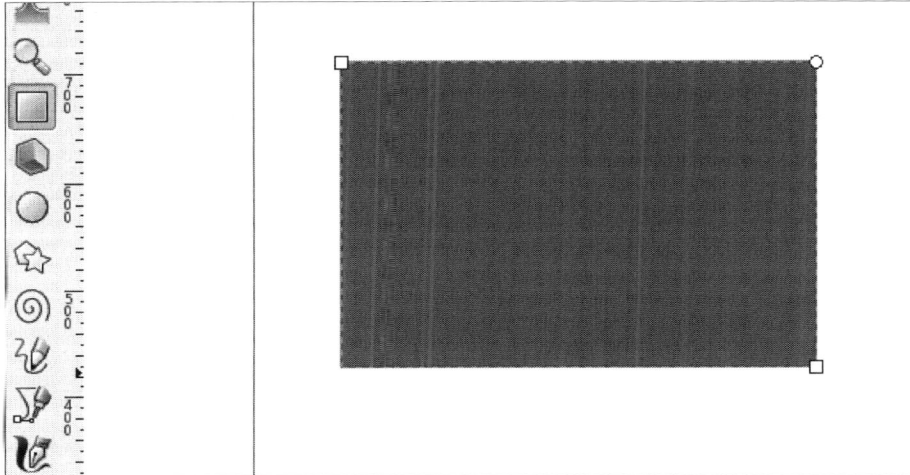

3. Make sure the rectangle is selected.

4. Open the Fill and Stroke dialogue box and select the pattern fill option.

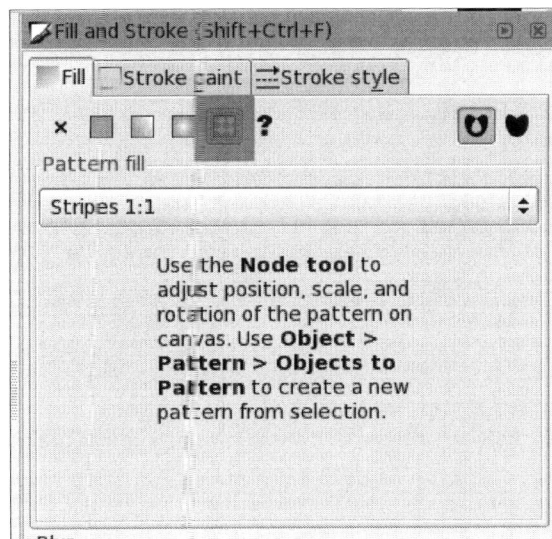

5. Then select one of the pre-installed fills for the shape.

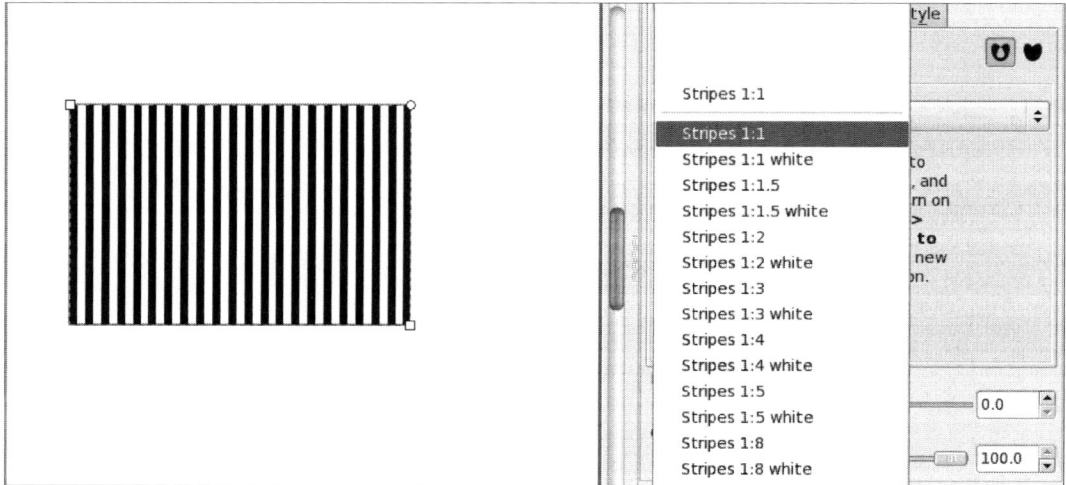

But let's see what else we can do here, like custom patterns!

Creating a simple pattern

Let's start with a simple custom pattern. For this example, let's create a star pattern, like this:

1. Open Inkscape and create a new document.
2. Create a star with the shape tool.
3. Make sure the star is selected.

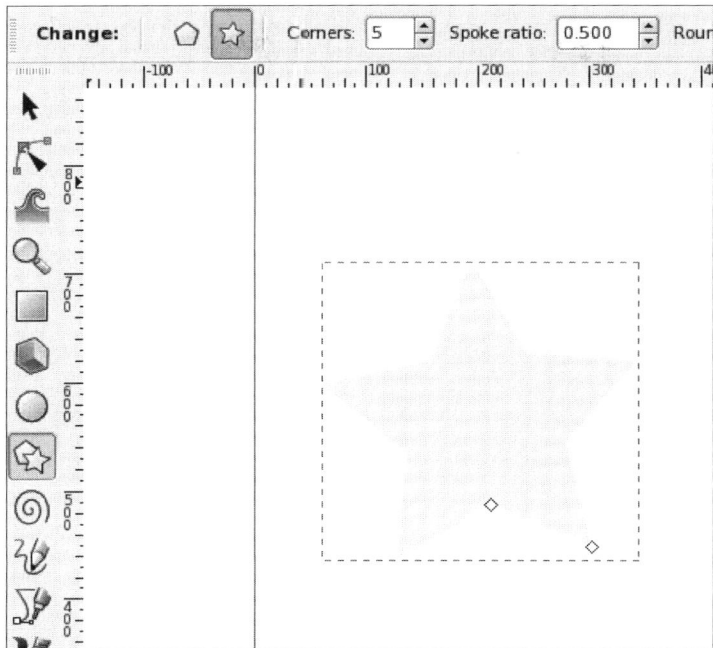

4. Then from the main menu select **Object**, **Pattern**, and then **Object to Pattern**.

5. Next, you need to create a shape in which to place this pattern. In this example, we're going to just create a box.

6. Then open the Fill and Stroke dialogue box and select the pattern fill option and the desired pattern for the fill.

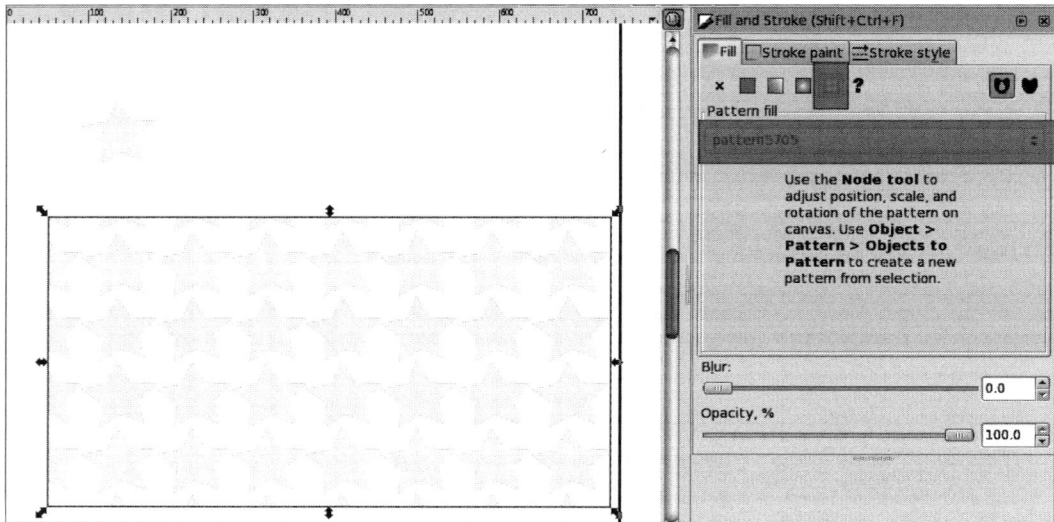

Note that, each time you create a pattern, it is saved to your personal pattern library (as long as you save the pattern SVG file when you're complete). Each pattern is given a unique name as seen in the pattern fill box dialog.

7. Want to give this pattern a little bit more excitement? Say by adding different colors into the mix? Create a new star next to the original — using a different color.

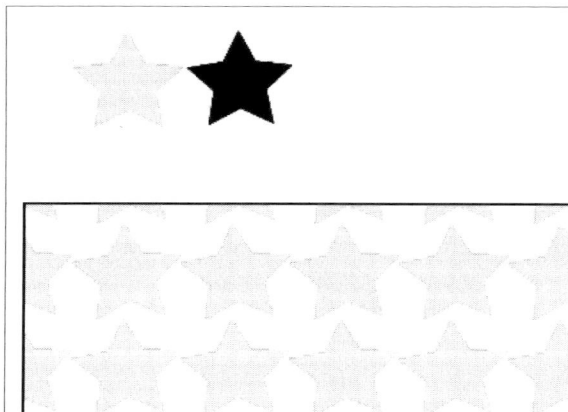

8. Select both the stars and then from the main menu select **Object, Pattern,** and then **Object to Pattern**.

9. Then change the pattern fill of your rectangle to this new pattern.

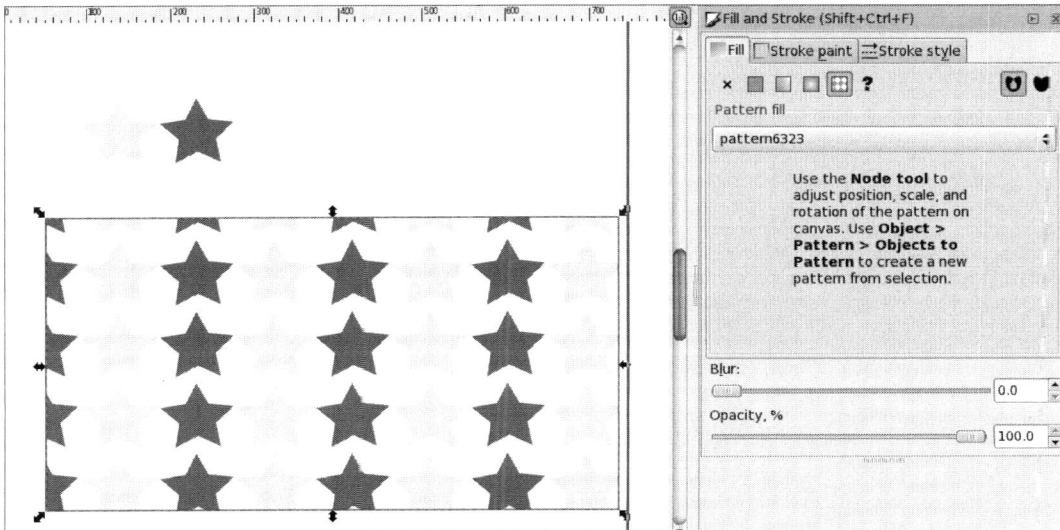

10. You can even try creating stars with unique colors, and using that fill for your rectangle. The possibilities are endless!

11. Or try diamonds!

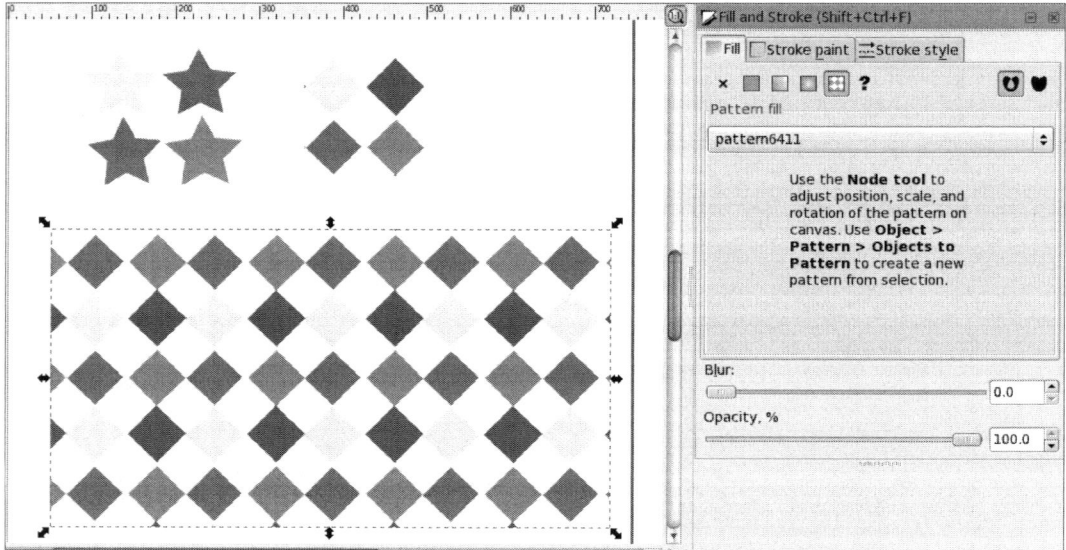

12. Do remember, save this file if you think you might want to use these patterns again. This can be useful if you spend a lot of time creating a custom pattern and you want to use it on a variety of objects as a fill option.

Creating a pin-stripe background

Now, we can create a pattern that is a bit more difficult. Let's try the pin-stripe pattern that can be used as a background for a website or desktop wallpaper. First, we will have to create the pattern tile and then this time clone the tile instead of using it to create a pattern to alleviate some spacing issues.

1. To begin, open Inkscape and create a new document. We'll set the document dimensions to be 10 x 10 pixels. You can do this by going to the main menu and selecting **File** and then **Document Properties** and changing the **Page Dimensions**.

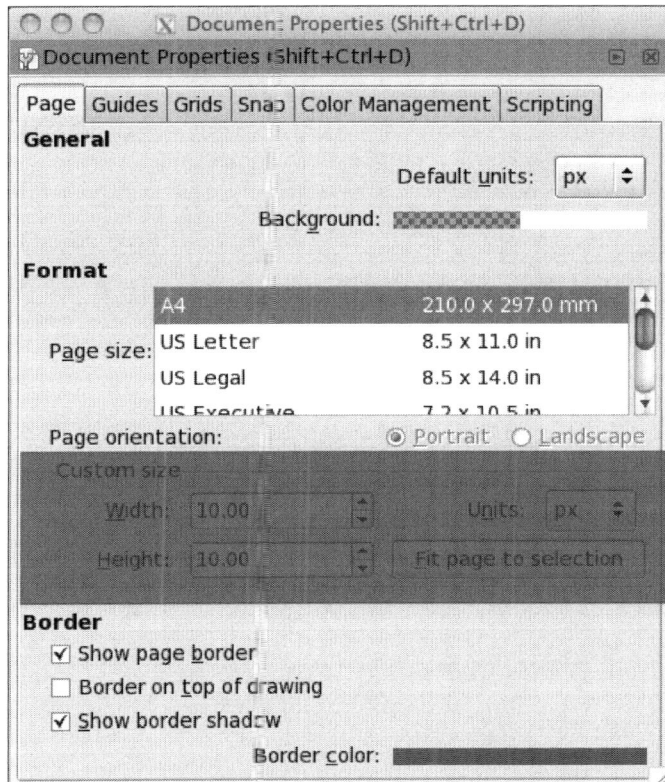

2. Next make sure the **Snap to grid** option is on. From the Document Properties window, select the **Snap** tab and choose **Always snap** from the **Snap to grids** section.

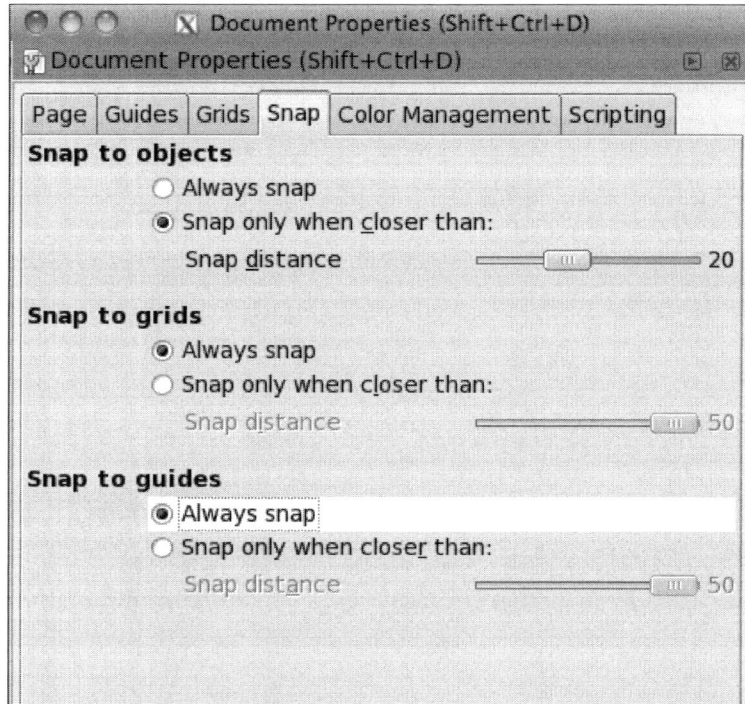

3. Close the Document Properties window and zoom to the page view. Go to the main menu and select **View**, **Zoom**, and then **Page**. This should magnify your canvas, so you can easily see it in your Inkscape window.

4. Now turn on your grid. From the main menu select **View** and then **Grid**.

5. Use the Bezier tool and draw a triangle in the upper left corner. Like this:

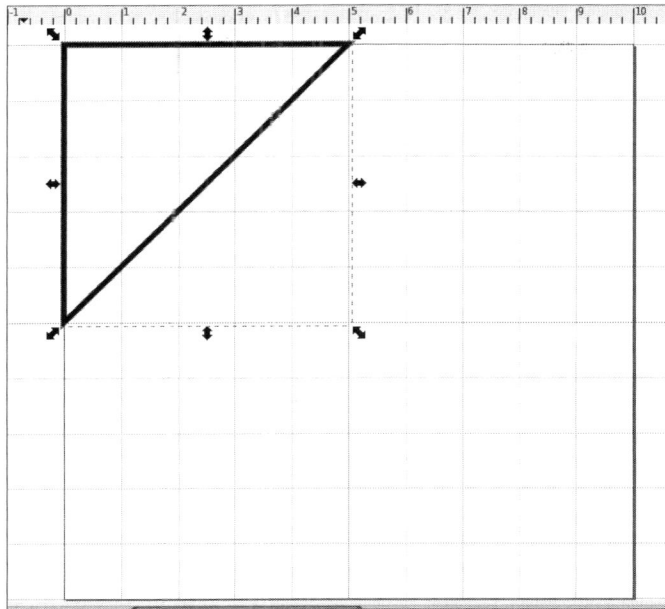

6. I used a 5 x 5 x 5 sided triangle. This is important to note as you make the next shape.

> Also note that, you might need to change the stroke style/thickness of your triangle so it doesn't interfere with your measurements. Open the Fill and Stroke menu, and then choose the **Stroke Style Tab** and lower the number in the **Width** field. In this example it is set to 0.100 px.

7. Next, still using the Bezier tool, draw the stripe using a rectangular shape as seen below—making sure you are aligning the bottom points with those of the bottom of the triangle.

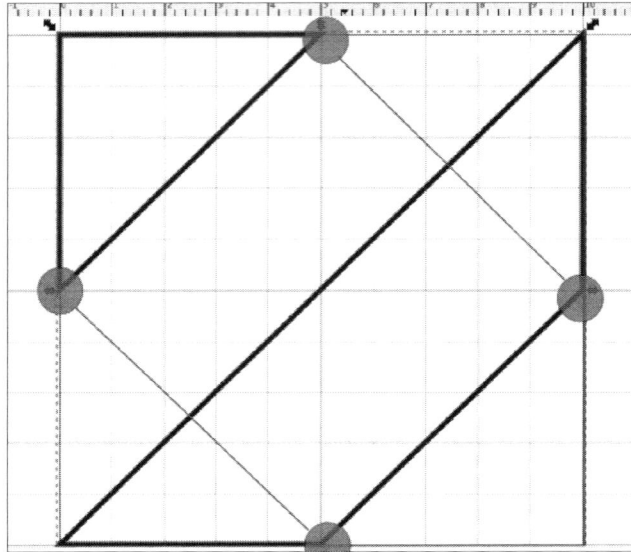

8. Note: The portion left at the bottom right of the rectangular shape is also a 5 x 5 x 5 size triangle.

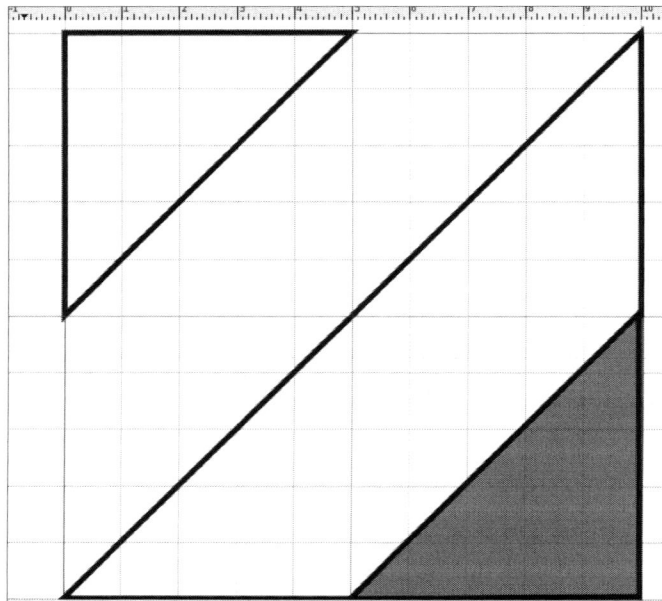

9. Once complete, we'll combine the objects into one—selecting them both, from the main menu choose **Path** and then **Combine**.

10. With this new object selected, again use the Fill and Stroke menu and remove the stroke and give it a black fill (for now).

> **Changing your pinstripe colors**
> Now's the time to get creative with your pinstripes if you want to! Switch the fill of the stripes from black to another color. Even try adding in a border.

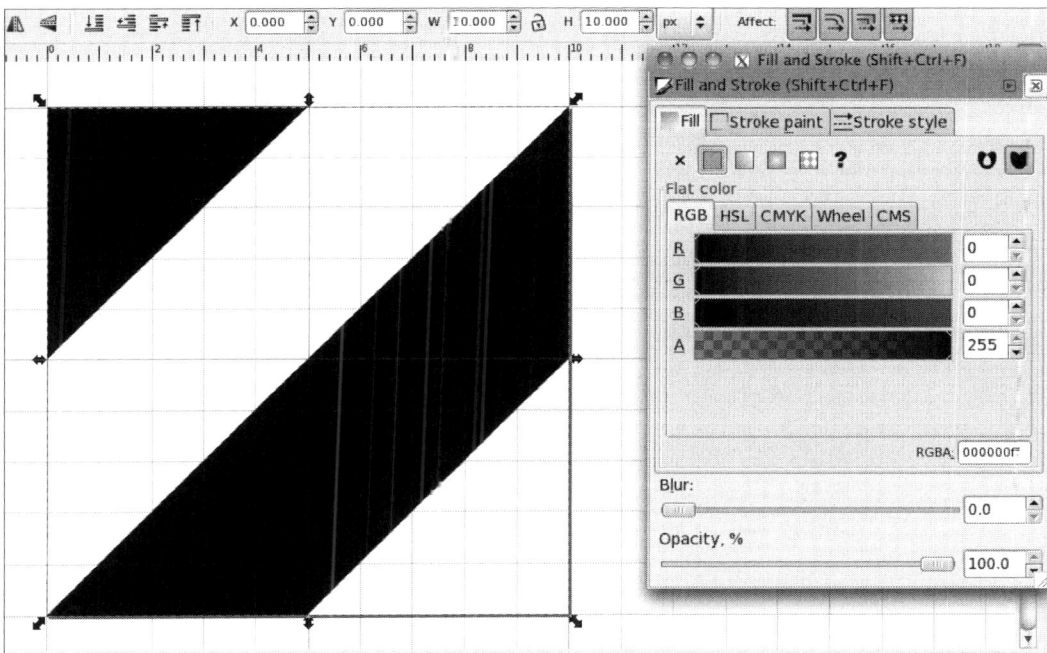

11. With the object still selected from the main menu, choose **Edit**, **Clones**, and then **Create Tiled Clones**.

12. The Clone dialogue box is displayed. Keep **simple translation** selected, enter your desired height and width or number of clones you would like to create. For us, let's create one 20 rows x 80 columns.

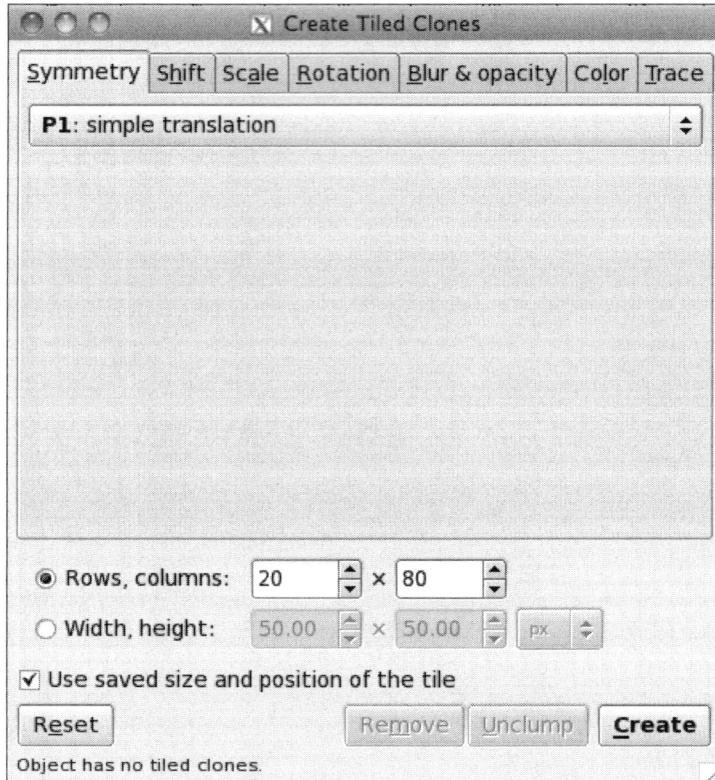

13. Click **Create**. Inkscape will then create a larger space of cloned stripes!

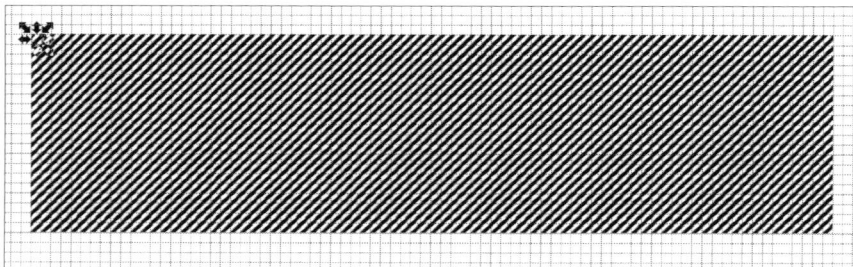

[🔆 Having issues seeing the entire cloned tiles? Then zoom
out your canvas, so you can see them all!]

14. If this is as far as you want to go in creating this pattern you can save the file — both as an Inkscape SVG file and then export it as a PNG (which will have a transparent background with our current settings) and use it as a background image.

However, you can also change colors, stroke colors, and use this pattern to style another shaped object. Let's learn how.

Use the pin-stripe as a fill for another object

You can use the pin-stripe pattern you just created via clones and have it 'fill' another object (much like you did in the Star Pattern example earlier in this chapter).

1. First, select your original tile (it should be the one in the upper left corner), and from the main menu select **Edit, Clone,** and then **Unlink Clone**. This will "detach" your clone from the rest of the other tiles and allow us to combine and manipulate the rows and columns of our tiles.

2. Next, let's make all of these tiles, one large object. From the main menu, select **Path** and then select **Combine**.

3. Now, we need to make this large block of stripes into a pattern which we can apply to an object. Again, select all of the tiles, and then from the main menu choose **Object, Pattern,** and then **Object to Pattern**.

4. Don't worry if this takes a few minutes to convert to a pattern. We are converting essentially hundreds of tiles into a pattern and depending on your computer's processing power, it could take some time.

5. Next, create a new shape using your Inkscape Toolbox bar.

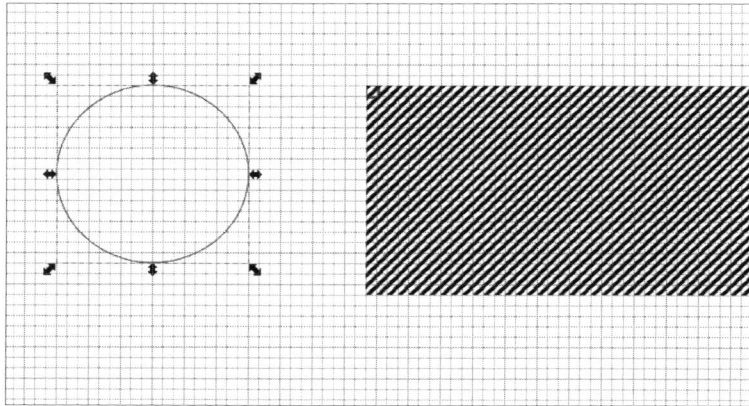

6. Just remember, this object needs to be smaller than your rows and columns of pin-stripes. This pattern will only be as large as the area you created it on (which in our case is about 200 pixels high by 800 pixels wide).

7. Next, select the new object and open the **Fill and Stroke** menu, choose pattern, and choose the new pattern you just created.

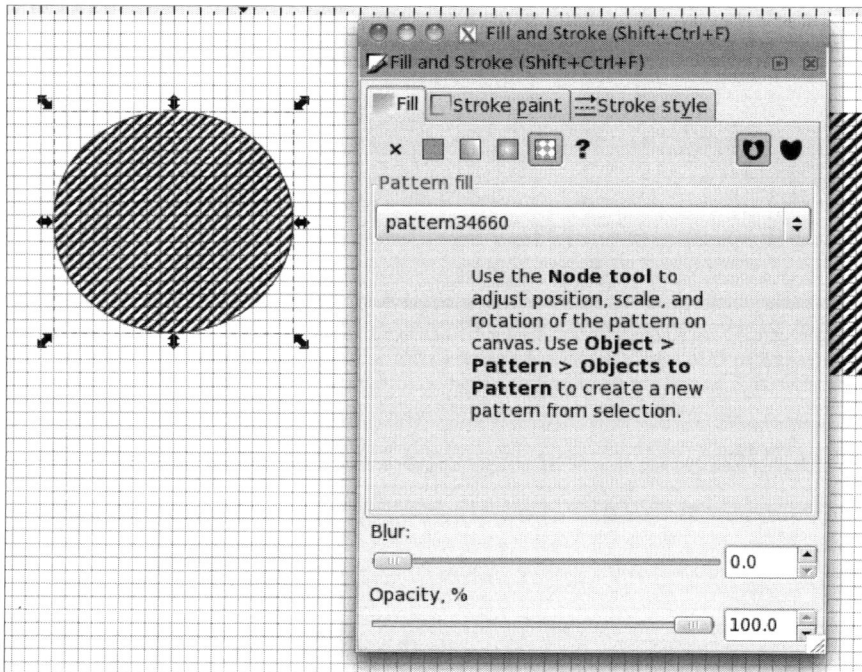

Creating advanced tiled backgrounds

Do you want to create something even more complicated than what we've done so far? Well, you have all the tools to get started. Let's create an advanced tiled background with a completely unique design. Just remember, your measurements must be exact to make this work. So it is important to set up your document properly for the best results. Here are the basic steps we'll be completing: setting up Inkscape for advanced tile design, setting up your document to create the base or original tile, and then creating the pattern.

Changing Inkscape bounding box preferences

Bounding boxes in Inkscape are the black, dashed lines that appear around an object or "frame" when selected. Many times black or white nodes appear with the bounding box as well. These nodes are squares or circles that allow you to manipulate the object.

To create unique tiled backgrounds, we need all objects to be spaced correctly. To do this, we'll need to first change the bounding box preferences in Inkscape.

1. Open Inkscape and then from the main menu select **File** and then **Inkscape Preferences**.

2. Select **Tools** to see the Bounding box settings.

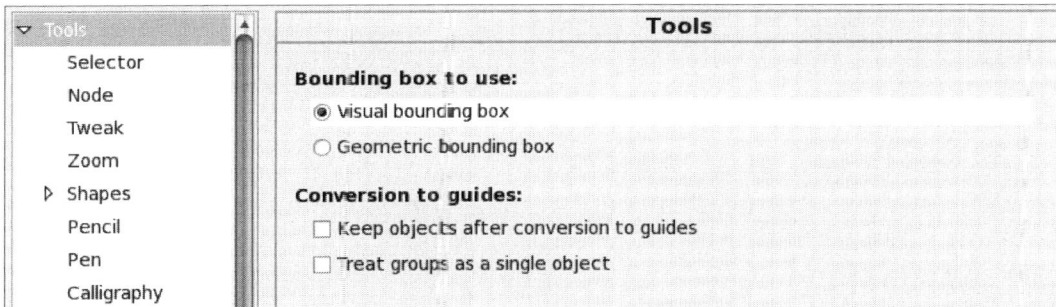

3. When set to **Visual bounding box**, measurements take all parts of the object *including* the stroke thickness into account when calculating sizes. On the other hand, **Geometrical bounding box** uses the nodes of the objects for measurements. That being said, we want to set this to **Geometrical bound box** settings (since our stroke thicknesses could vary).

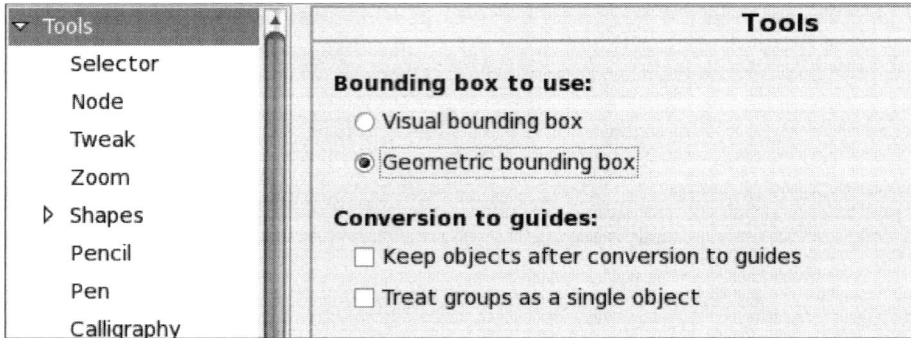

Tools	Tools
Selector	**Bounding box to use:**
Node	○ Visual bounding box
Tweak	⦿ Geometric bounding box
Zoom	
▷ Shapes	**Conversion to guides:**
Pencil	☐ Keep objects after conversion to guides
Pen	☐ Treat groups as a single object
Calligraphy	

Creating your base tile

Now we want to set up a file whose base tile we can design. In the next section, we will create a pattern from this.

With Inkscape open, create a new document with these settings:

- Canvas size of 800 x 600 pixels (just like your web page dimensions)
- Create a grid with spacing of 10 pixels (in **Document Properties, Grid** tab)
- Make sure the Snap to grid option is on
- Turn on the grid (so you can use it for accurate measuring)

When you are ready you can get started in the main document as.

1. Create a square that is 100px × 100px in size. Use the Control tool bar to make this exact size if you need to.

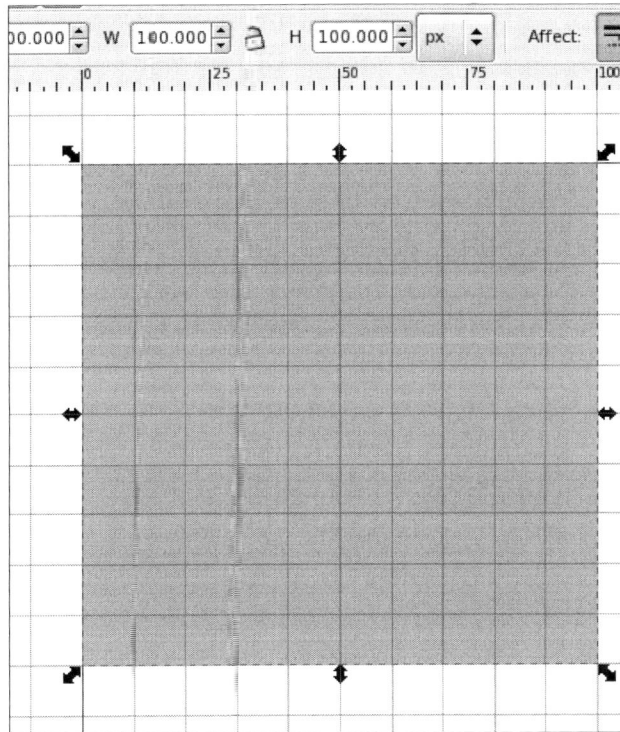

2. Set the fill of the rectangle to a light grey and remove the stroke.
3. From the main menu select **Object** and then **Group**. This will be your base or template tile.

Now, we need to clone the template tile for which we create a full background.

Cloning the template tile

It is important to remember how this tiled background will be used during this step. For us, we are going to create a full background or wallpaper for our website mock up. So we'll need to use the same canvas size for our cloned objects in order to fill that space.

1. Select your template tile.

2. From the main menu select **Edit**, **Clone**, and then **Create Tiled Clones**.

3. In the **Create Tiled Clone** dialogue, **Symmetry** tab, select the following: in the **P1** field: **simple translation** from the drop-down, in **Rows** put **6** and in **Columns** put in **8**. Make sure the **Use saved position of the tile** option is checked. We do this so that you can move the original template tile without moving the layout of the cloned tiles.

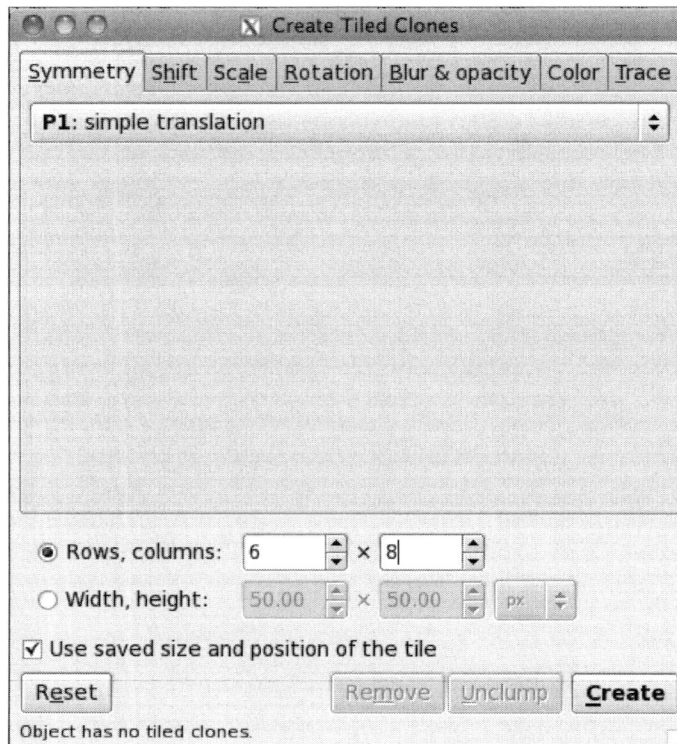

4. Click **Create** and close the **Create Tiled Clones** dialogue window. You should now see an 8 x 6 set of tiles on the canvas with your template tile still selected. This should cover the entire 800 x 600 tile canvas we created.

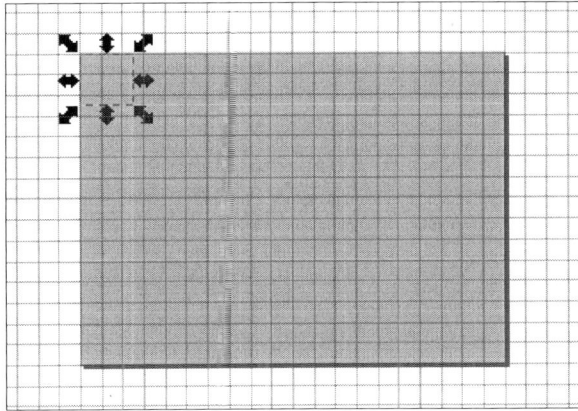

5. We're going to move the original tile of the clones and outside the canvas so we can decorate it separately and use the clones to see how it would look tiled together.

The base tile should still be selected after you have closed the dialog. To verify, look at your status bar—it should read: **Group of 1 object**. If for any reason, it states a clone is selected, select the original tile by pressing *Shift* and the *D* key.

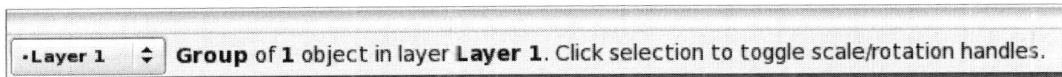

6. Now to make sure we move only the original base time, we'll use the Transform menu. With the tile still selected from the step above, from the main menu select **Object** and then **Transform**.

7. On the **Transform** dialogue **Move** tab, you'll see a **Horizontal** field; change this to -200 and click on **Apply**.

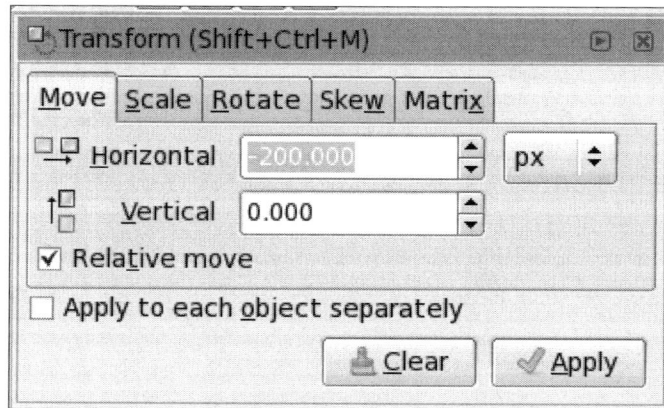

8. You'll see the original base tile move to the left 200 pixels.

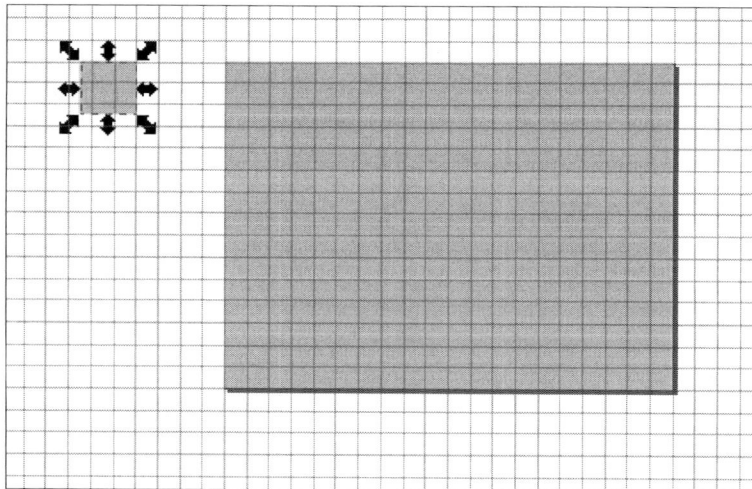

9. From the main menu select **View** and then **Grid** to turn off the grid and concentrate on creating your pattern.

Now we are going to create a design on the tile so that when the squares are tiled together (like your clones) you can see a pattern.

Decorating your tile

As this is just an example, we'll create a very simple design on the tile(s). But you can do whatever design you like on this tile to see how it would create a pattern for a background.

Simple and less complicated works best if you are going to have this lie behind all of the elements on your web page. If you just want this background to be a part of your title or footer bar, and it doesn't have a lot of text, you can use a bit more complicated pattern.

Here's how to get started:

1. On your template tile, you'll need to begin adding a few shapes to create an interesting layout. But in order to do that, you'll first have to make sure you are adding elements to the group you created with the base tile when you initially created it. To do this, right-click (or *Ctrl*-click) the base tile and select **Enter group # gxxxx**, where xxxx is a specific group number for your project from the pop-up menu.

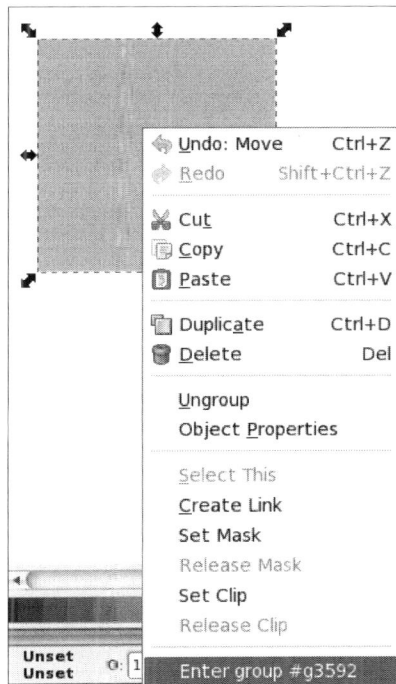

2. You'll notice that your status bar should now have you working within the *group* instead of on a layer.

A group of objects are the ones that are "linked" or "joined" together as one. They can be manipulated as one object—instead of separate items. Layers separate different objects of an image. This is much like a transparency where you are able to place additional images or objects over or under another object/image in the same file.

3. Now start adding objects to your base tile.

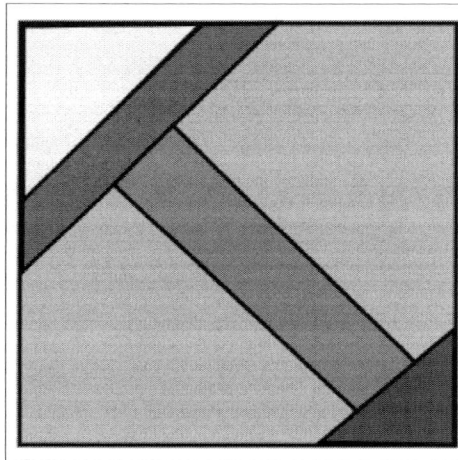

4. You can even try adding some elements that "bleed" over the border of the original tile.

5. Watch the cloned tiles carefully — as you create elements and have
    others bleed over the edge, you will notice that the clones are updated
    automatically. And since they are all grouped together, you see how your
    pattern will look when "tiled" together.

6. We're going to change the gray rectangle to a new color. To finalize the tile and the canvas, select the light gray rectangle from your base tile and let's change it to very pale green. All of your clone tiles also change!

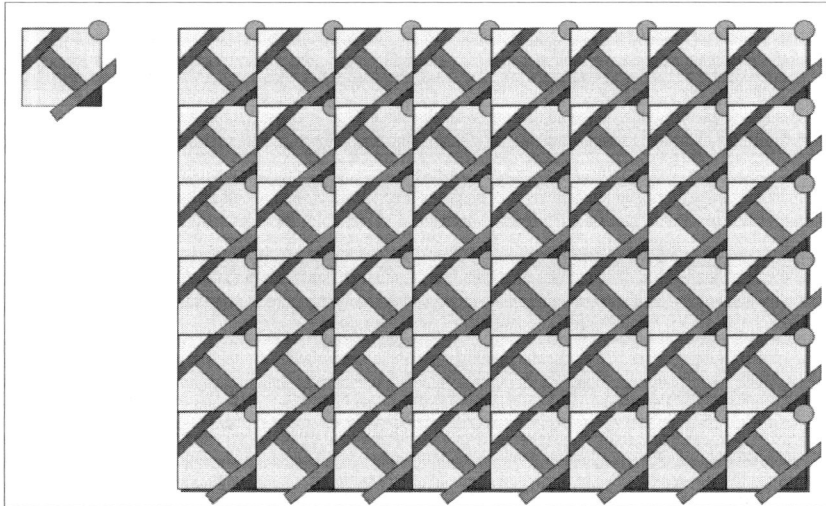

7. If you want to get fancier, use some effects to add in some texture to the background as well. In the example below, we applied the Evanescent blur:

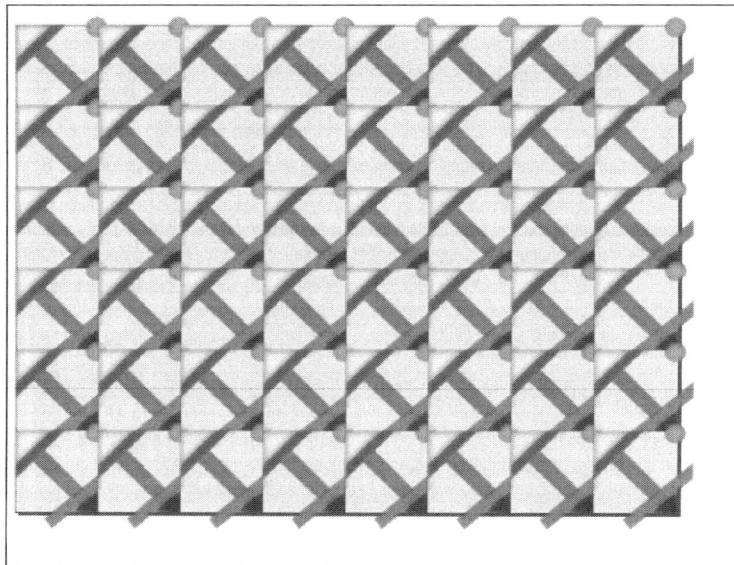

8. You'll notice that some tiles along the top, right, and bottom edges, in our example have bleeds. Let's create a clipping mask to make all of our edges clean. Draw a rectangle that is exactly 600 pixels high and 800 pixels wide that covers the part of the tiled background you want to keep.

Remember you can use the control bar to make your rectangle the exact size you need it to be or use the X and Y fields and set them both to 0. This will place the objects directly on the bottom-left corner of the canvas.

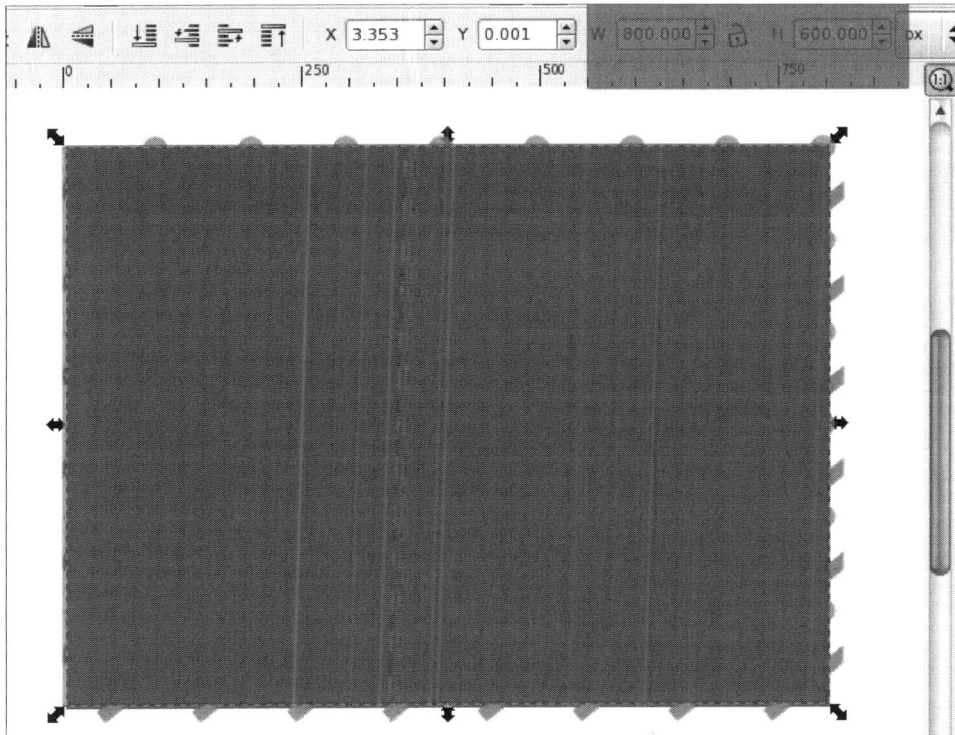

9. Now select all of your cloned tiles and your newly created rectangle.
10. From the main menu select **Object**, **Clip**, and then **Set**.

11. Now it is time to export your tiled background! But before you do that, make sure you save an Inkscape SVG source file for this pattern, in case you need to edit it later.

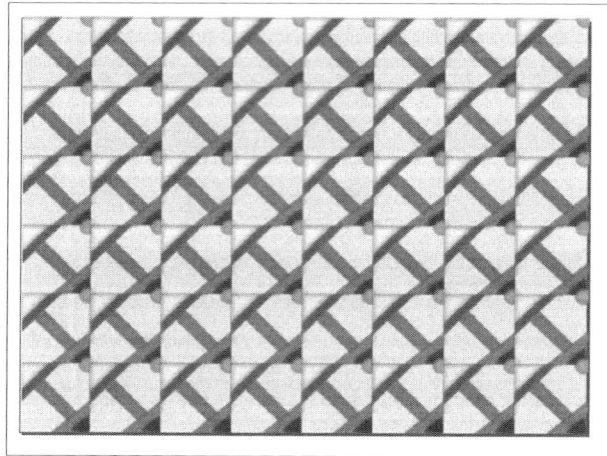

Exporting your tile for a background

These steps should seem very familiar as we have exported many files in the last few chapters. But this time, you want to export your 600 x 800 cloned tiles. Here's how you do that:

1. Select all of the cloned tiles (make sure to "deselect" your template tile, as you don't want this to be a part of the exported image).

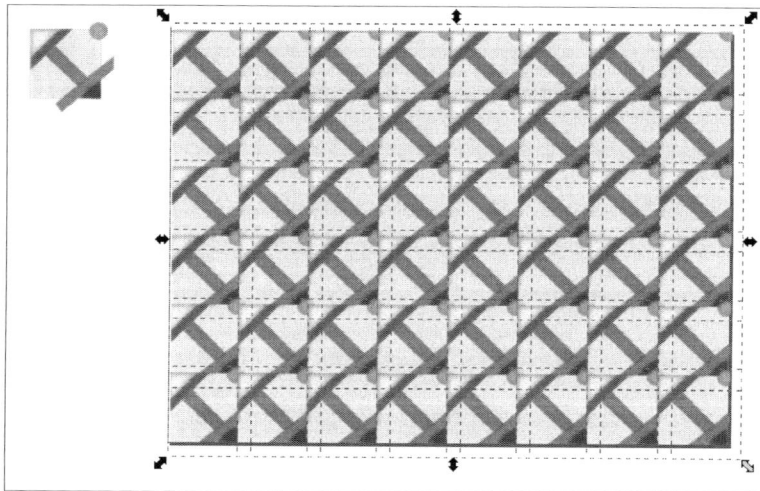

2. From the main menu select **File** and then **Export**.

3. Click on **Selection**.

4. Set an export location and filename in the **Export** text field and click on **Export**.

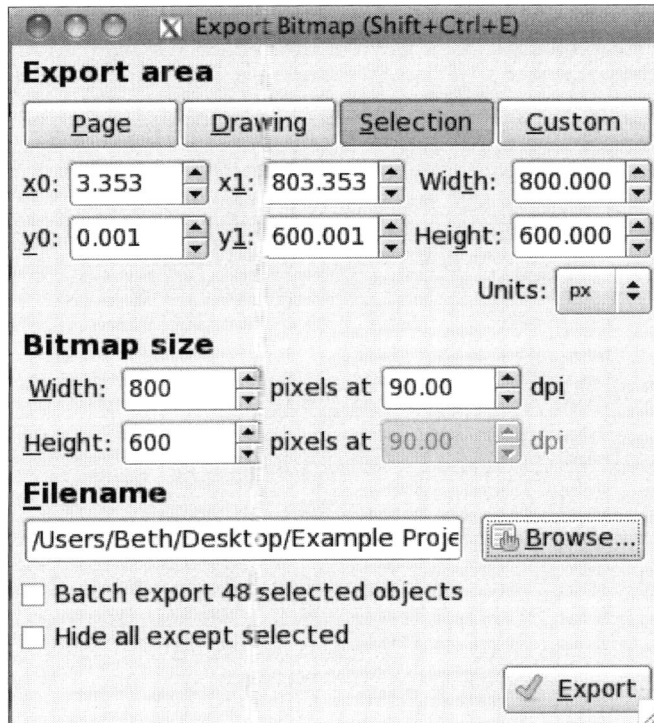

5. A new background image file will be created!

Now you have a complete tiled background to use in a design! In fact, here's how you could incorporate it into our example project:

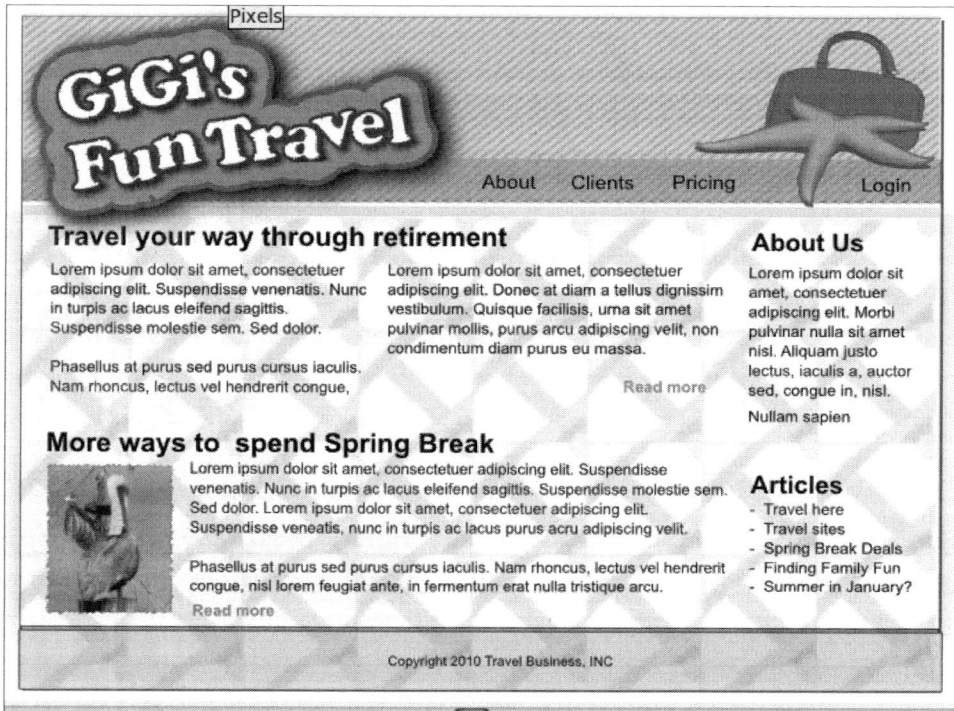

Here are a couple of items you need to remember when working with Inkscape while creating these tiled backgrounds:

- When you render patterns on the screen, Inkscape sometimes shows gaps between the tiles. Don't worry; this is just due to your computer and its screen. When you export, these gaps will not be displayed.

- Make a habit of saving these tiles or patterns. They take a while to create, and once created, you can adjust easily for any future designs. Remember, you can use this file as a template for any other backgrounds you've created with these same sizes if you need to!

Next, let's learn how to create swirls and incorporate them into a background or wallpaper.

Creating swirling design backgrounds

Ever seen a web page design that uses swirls and curve patterns in the background? Maybe it looked something like this:

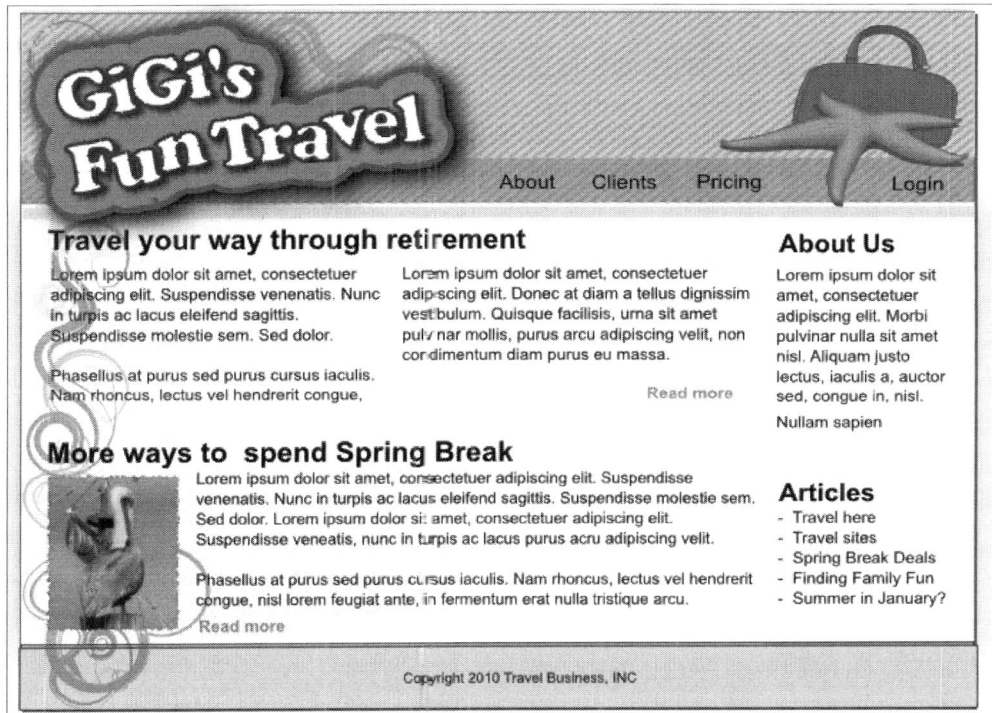

Well now you can make these same sorts of backgrounds for yourself. Let's start with the basics.

Creating a swirl

These are the basics about creating a spiral:

1. Open a new document in Inkscape.
2. Select the Spiral Tool icon from the Toolbox bar.

3. In the Control bar, change the **Turns**, **Divergence**, and **Inner Radius** settings
Change them as shown below to create a smooth curve:

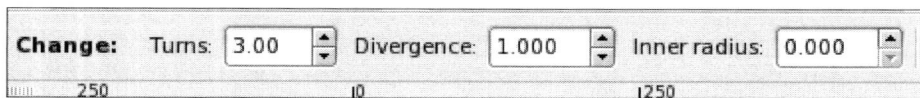

4. Now, draw the spiral.

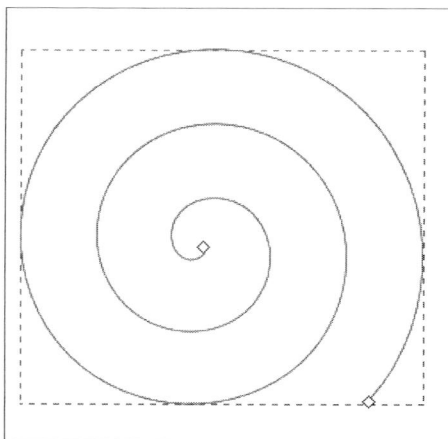

5. If you want to adjust the spiral, select the End Nodes tool and start changing
it to your liking.

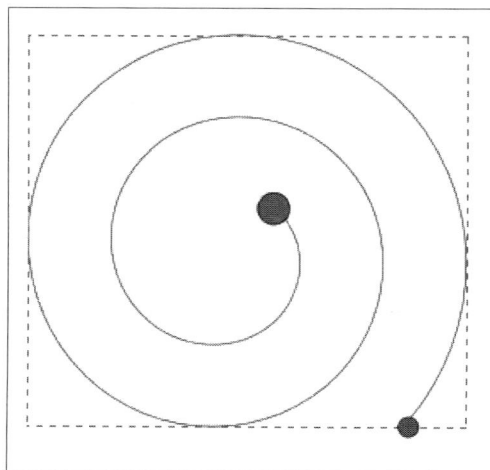

6. Press the *Shift* + *S* keys to see the rotation arrows. Click and drag the center of rotation to the inner end point of the spiral, as shown below.

7. Float your mouse over the tiny cross hair (center of rotation) in the center of the object. Now use *Shift* and drag to place the center of rotation above the location of where the inner path ends.

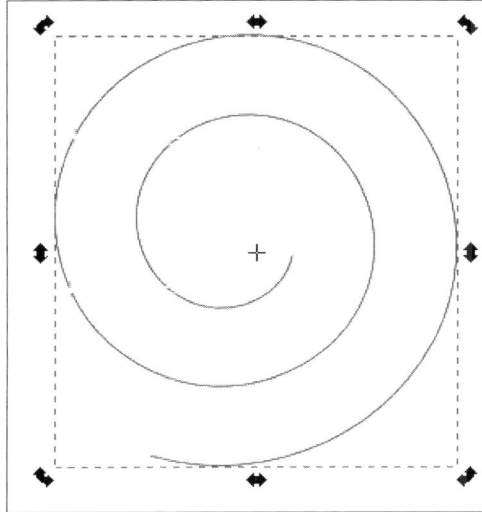

8. Now we need to change the spiral object to a path. From the main menu, select **Path** and then **Object to Path**.

9. Next, from the main menu select **Edit** and then **Duplicate**. We now have two spirals (one on top of another).

10. Choose the Selector tool and then double-click the top duplicated spiral so that the rotation arrow appears and rotate it just a bit.

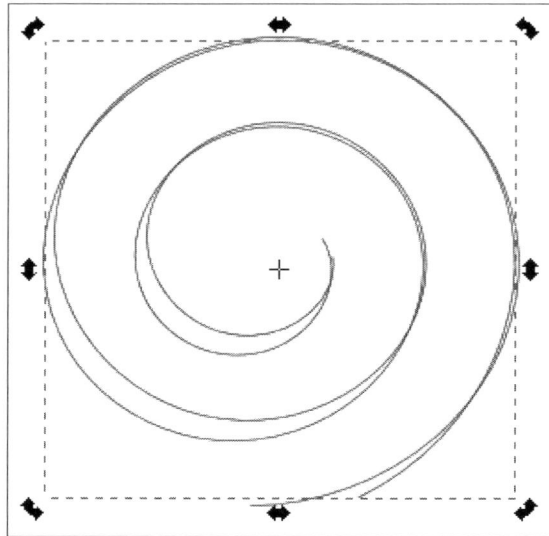

11. Now click the original spiral so that it is selected and you can scale it to a size that makes the swirl interesting. It might look something like the following screenshot:

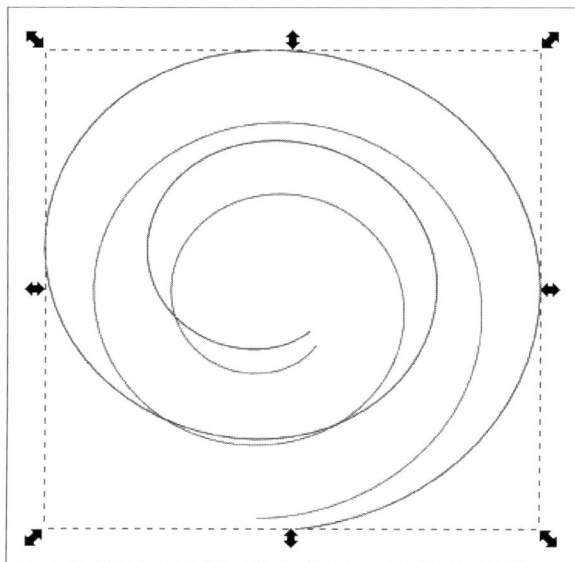

12. While still in the Selector tool, select both spirals by holding the *Shift* key and clicking on the original and duplicate spiral.

13. From the main menu select **Path** and then **Combine**.

14. Press the *F2* key to switch to the Edit Path by Nodes Tool and then select both outer end nodes and click the **Join selected endnodes with new segment** button.

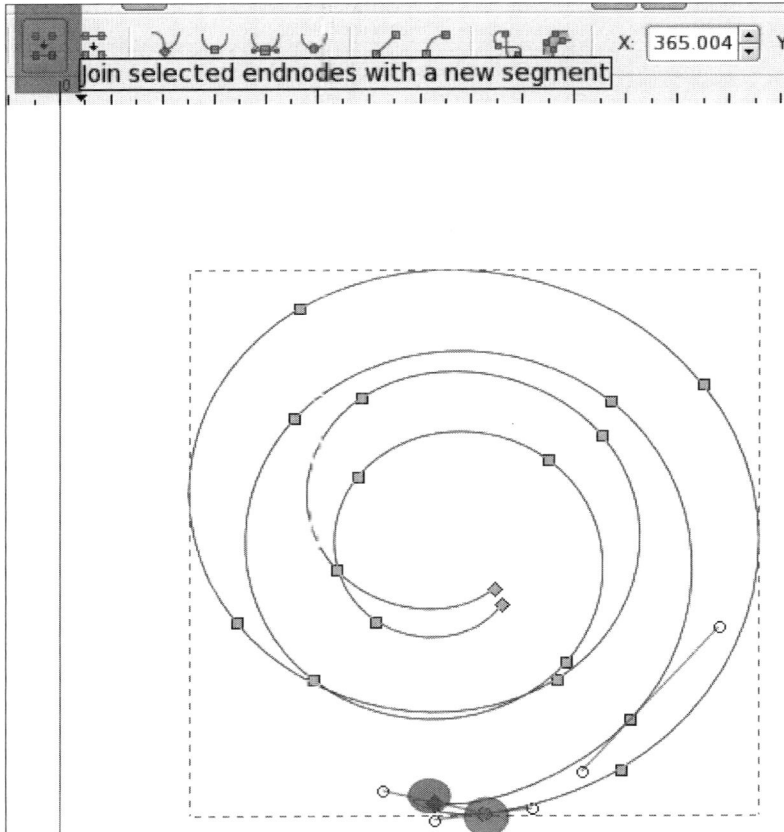

15. This joins the two nodes.

    Do this with any other end nodes that aren't joined and smooth out any areas of the spiral to make it look more appealing.

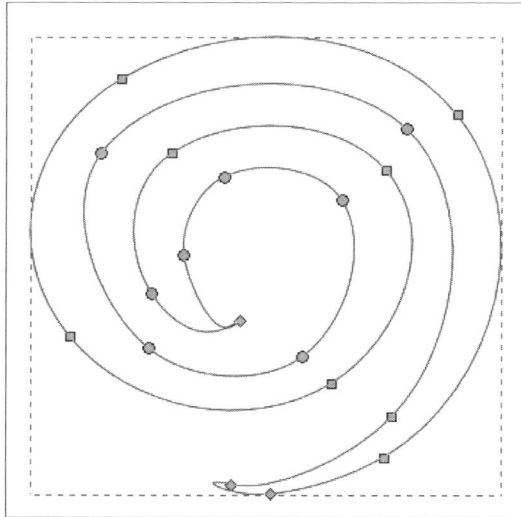

16. Now add a color and fill to this spiral.

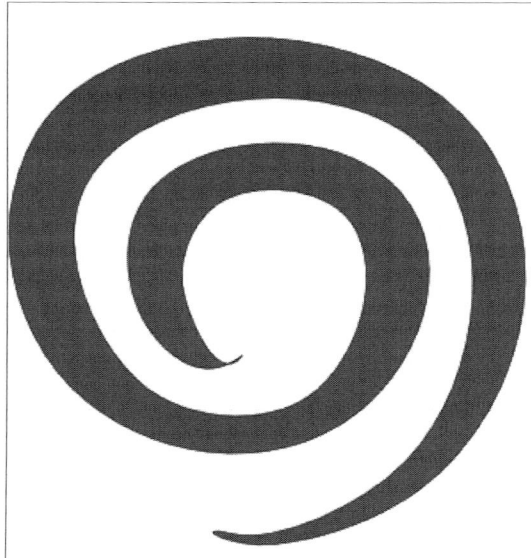

17. Again, feel free to save the file, so you can use this spiral in other projects.

You could continue to create some swirls this way by moving, duplicating, and changing sizes to create the initial background. But let's try something a little easier.

Creating spiro swirls

Here's an easier, more free-form way to create spirals and swirls that work in a background.

1. Again, open a new document in Inkscape. Change the document properties to match that of the area where you want the design, since you will be creating larger and more unique swirls. In our case, let's create a background for the entire canvas with the swirl decoration along the edges. To do this, our canvas size will be 800 x 600.

2. Now select the Bezier Tool from the Toolbox bar.

3. In the Control bar, choose **Create Spiro Path** from the Mode options.

4. Still in the Control bar, from the **Shape** drop down menu, select **Triangle in**.

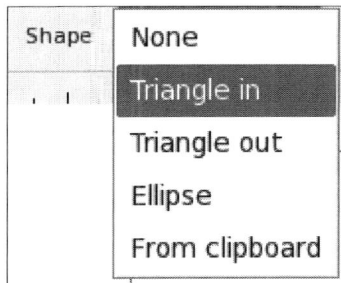

5. Now, draw on the canvas using the Bezier tool and then use click, hold, and drag the technique to create drag curve segments. Don't worry so much about how it looks, but concentrate on the flow or general shape of the line.

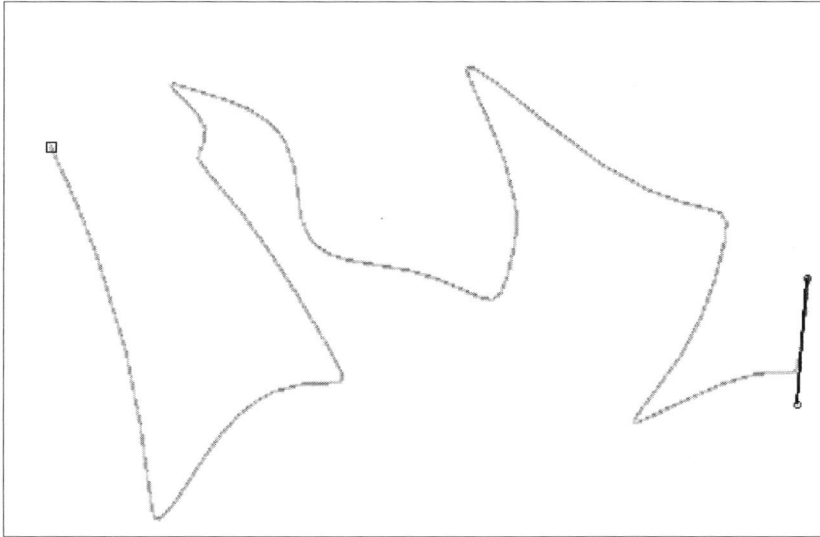

6. Double-click to end the curve. And you should instantly see the Spiro effect take place on your curved shape!

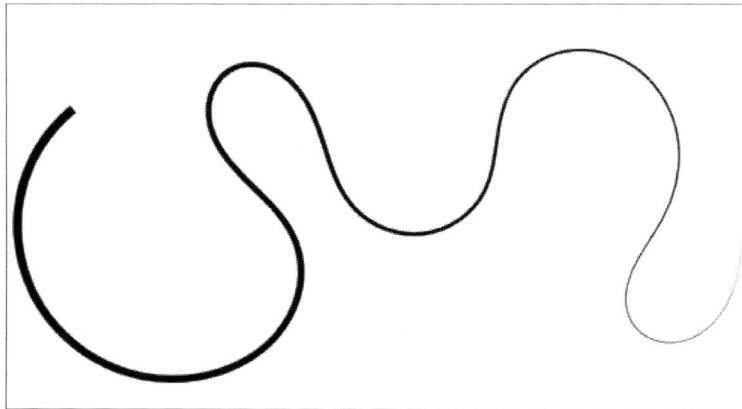

Editing your spiro

Now let's add some more interesting effects to your Spiro! You can edit its path, create your own patterns, and more. Ready to give it a try?

1. From your open project, go to the main menu, and select **Path** and then **Path Effects Editor**. This opens the Path Effects dialogue so that we can adjust, or edit the effects that occurred automatically.

2. The Effects List shows the effects that were applied on our curve. The **Spiral Spline** effect uses all nodes on the path or curve and uses the minimum possible curves. In other words it makes the curve as smooth as possible.

3. Select the spiro and click the Edit Paths by Node (*F2*) icon on the Toolbox bar. Then experiment with this editor by editing the spiral spline.

4. Now select any node and drag it around on the screen, and watch what happens. Move more than one node and see what happens to your spiro shape.

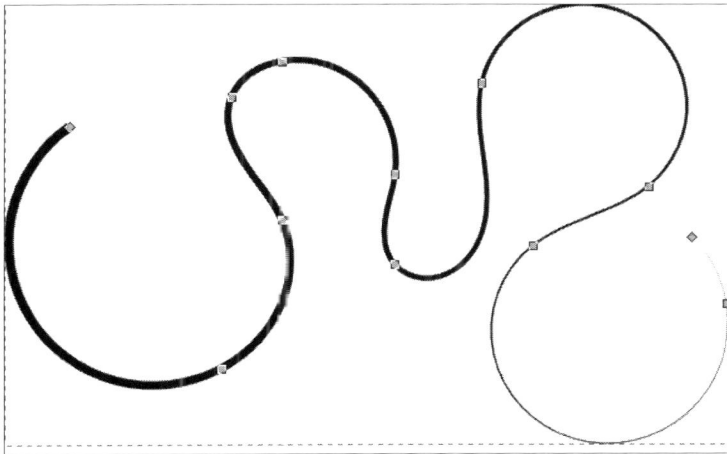

If for any reason you move a node and an undesired effect happens, you can always undo the last node movement by using the keyboard shortcut *Ctrl + Z* or from the main menu select **Edit** and **Undo**.

Now let's edit the other effect that was applied to the Spiro Spline—in the **Path Effect Editor Menu**, click on the **Path along Pattern in the effect list**.

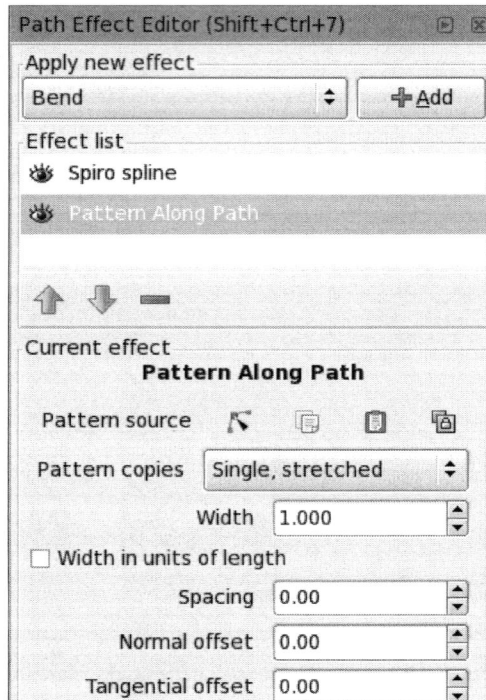

1. The **Path Along Pattern** effect, essentially links the Spiro Spline to a pattern or shape to give it the current shape. But you can edit it for an even more interesting look!

2. When you select the **Path along Pattern** effect, a "pattern source" will be displayed above the upper-left corner of the page layout border.

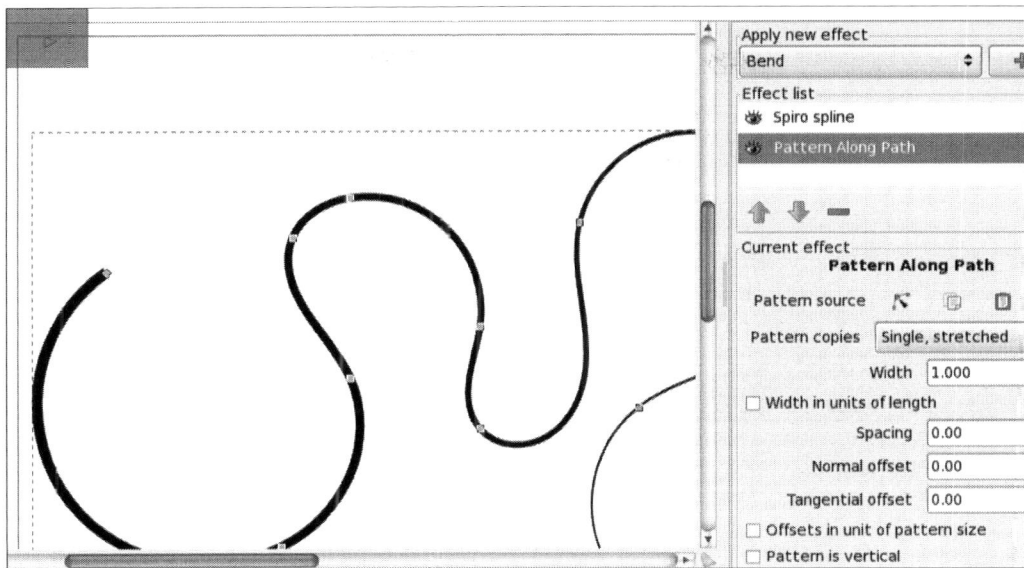

[If you can't see the pattern, zoom out on your canvas until you can see it.]

3. You can "edit" the pattern source directly on your canvas. We're going to give it a try! Back in the Path Effect Editor Menu dialogue, in Path Source, select Edit on screen icon.

4. Then, back on your canvas, select the pattern in the upper-left corner—so that all notes are selected. Also if you need to, move the pattern closer to your Spiro shape so that it's easier to move/edit and see the results.

5. Select and move a node. Move another. See what it can do to your curves.

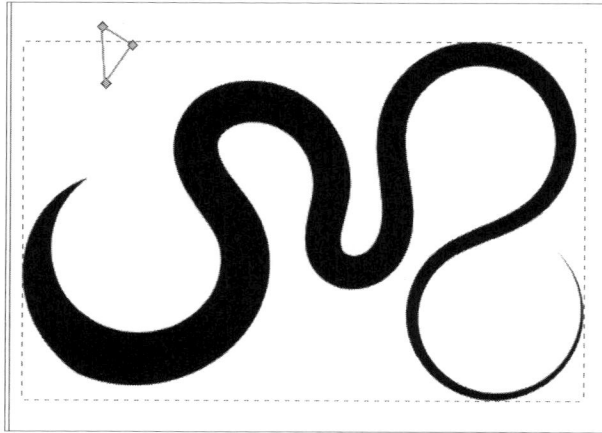

6. Select two nodes that already exist (press and hold the *Shift* key to select more than one item) and then press the **Add Node** button in the Control Bar.

7. This will add a new node between the two selected nodes.

8. Click anywhere else on the canvas to deselect all nodes on the pattern source—and then click the new "middle" node. We're ready to experiment.

9. Drag this new node to the right. Look what happens to your curve!

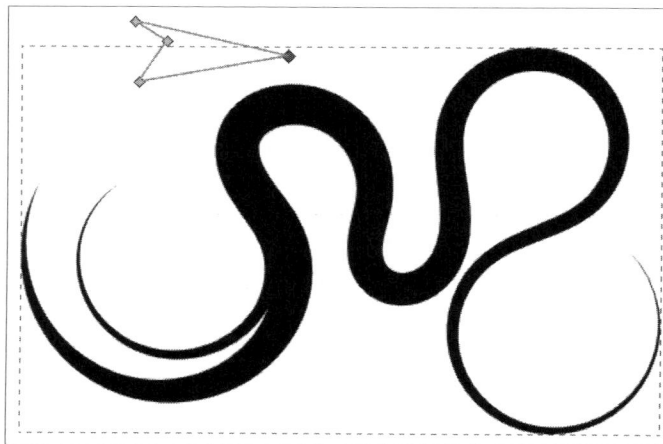

Now let's use all of these new curves, spirals, and Spiro techniques together and create a unique background.

Converting swirls to backgrounds

We've covered all the details for creating individual swirls, but how does that translate into an entire background?

1. Copy and paste different versions of your Spiro swirls created in the previous sections to combine them and create a unique series of swirls that can border a page.

2. Or you can create one large, unique shape that encompasses a large area in the middle of the background.

3. Or you can do any combination of the above to make a background that works for your project.

4. Save any files you create like this in Inkscape SVG format for future editing or even for your own personal example project you are working through with this book.

What's most important now, is exporting backgrounds like those created above in a way that you can use them in your designs.

Exporting for use in a functional web page

Again, you need to perform the export process as explained in previous chapters. But here's a quick recap so that we can import it into our sample design.

1. Open the Inkscape SVG file for any one of the backgrounds you've created in this chapter. As an example we will open the Spiro example we just completed.

2. From the main menu select **File** and then **Export Bitmap**. The Export Area screen is displayed.

3. Select **Page** and then the location of where to save the file (and a filename).

4. Clicking **Export** Inkscape will automatically save to the location as you specified. It will be a PNG image files.

Now you're ready to import this graphic into our design.

Using the design in the layout design

Now, it is time to place these new background images. You can import these so that they cover the entire background of your web page, only on the edges, or even one big design in the middle. It is all dependent on the type of design you created. The idea is, however, that if you have a background created once, you can re-use that image across all pages in your design for consistency. Let's try to place a background in our example design, just to demonstrate how you might use a background like this.

1. Open the SVG project file in Inkscape.

2. Select the Background layer.

3. From the main menu, select **File** and then **Import**. Select your new background image file and place it in the design.

4. Make sure it fits right with your content and enhances (not clutters) your current design.

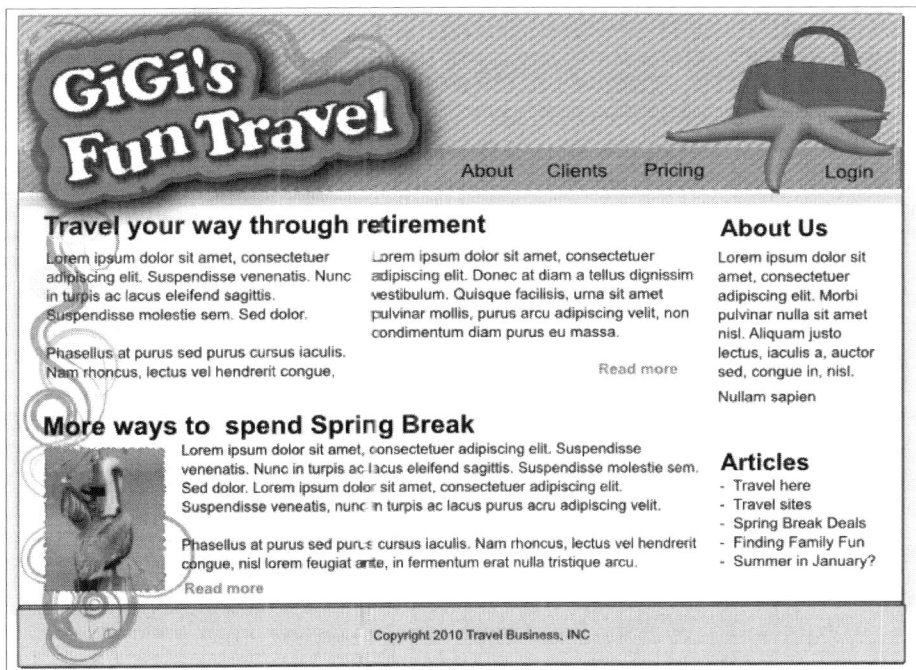

5. When you are ready, save your project SVG file as it stands.

Remember that when you hand off your files, you need all SVGs, all PNG images, and all fonts—even this new background image—and you need to hand it all over in the current directory structure. It will make it easier to program the final web pages.

Summary

Who knew we could have so much fun creating backgrounds? We started at the basics and used the built-in patterns within Inkscape, created our own simple patterns, with stars and stripes. And we even made a pin-stripe pattern and some unique tile designs. Lastly, we learned all about spirals and using the Spiro effect. We learned how to manipulate each to make an even more intricate then incorporated one into our example project.

Next, we'll be moving on to icons, buttons, and logos!

6
Building Icons, Buttons, and Logos

Other elements used in web design are icons, buttons, and the all important logos. In this chapter, we're going to:

- Create example icons, buttons, and logos concentrating on the importance of similar shapes, sizes, and styles to keep the design elements consistent
- Develop both simple and more complex icons and discuss how to export these elements to use them within the programming side of a website
- Use standard file naming standards for a collection of items

We'll also discuss logos and their creation at length. We'll discuss:

- The importance of logos for companies and how this affects web design projects
- Logo design principles
- How to tackle a logo design project
- Redesign our fictional company's logo
- Import our logo into design layout

Using icons, buttons, and logos in web design

Let's discuss how we *could* use each of these items in design and make it look the best it can be.

Icons can be the basis for a consistent, clean design, Especially if used in a minimal fashion and as a visual representation of a concept. Menu items can either be represented by well-thought icons or a combination of icons, text and more. Here's another potential view of using icons to represent menus:

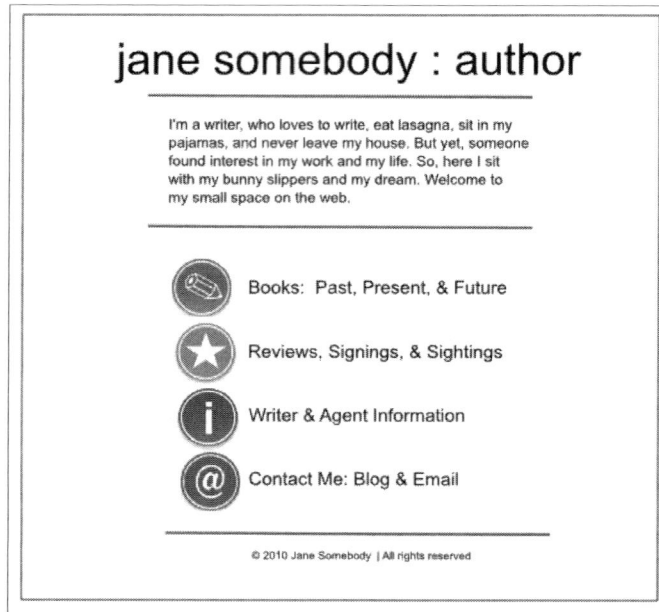

Buttons are most commonly used in forms or web pages where you want to enter information via text fields, etc. Sometimes it is common to use "standard" buttons that look much like the interfaces we use on our computers, but a well-designed custom button can make your design more consistent and professional looking. Here's an example of using a button in a design using an input form:

Lastly, **logos** can be a critical part of a web design. This is particularly true if the business you are promoting has a logo that is the centerpiece of its brand. Can you imagine a Nike website without prominent placement of its logo? There is also an opportunity here if the logo is well designed, to make it the centerpiece of a site design. Here's an example of a web page with a logo as a major design element:

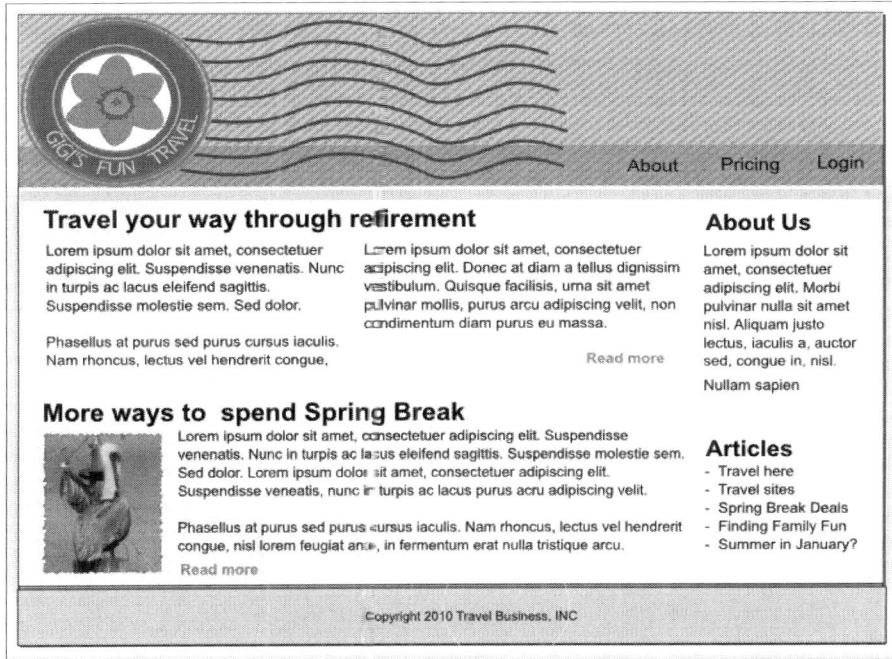

Creating icons

There are no hard and fast rules about creating icons. You make what you want of them. But, my suggestion is that if you make them clean, easy to 'read' or visualize what they are meant to represent, then you've reached your goal. But remember, it is important that each set of icons has similarities. Here are a few guidelines to remember when creating a set of icons (or a collection of icons to be used together on a web page):

- Keep the same height and width.
- Use a color palette that is pleasing and is used across the entire set of icons.
- Use gradients, shading, and reflections consistently across the entire collection.
- Use consistent perspectives, for example, Tango icons (found here: `http://tango.freedesktop.org/Tango_Icon_Theme_Guidelines_` have a guide about how to do this.)

- If you use lettering, use the same fonts for any lettering and shapes using similar angles or curves. However in icon creation, it is best to shy from text, as it can keep icons more universal in nature and avoid translation if used universally.

Let's get to a few examples!

Using grids and snapping

When creating icons it is recommended that you use the grid (by making it viewable) so that you can keep all elements within its boundaries. Here are the initial steps to set this up:

1. From an open Inkscape window select **File** then **New**, and **icon_64x64**.

2. Then select **File** and then **Document Properties**.

3. Select the **Grids** tab and verify that **Spacing X** and **Spacing Y** are both set to **1.0** and that **Major grid line every** is set to every **4** pixels.

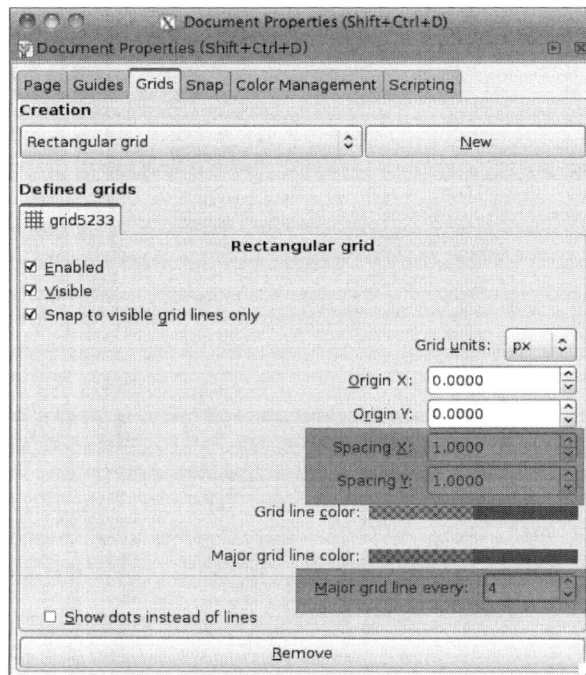

4. We do this so that when you are creating icons, you keep all lines within the gridlines.

5. For example, when you look at the following screenshot with enlarged edges of two different icons, you will notice that the icon "edge" on the left is outside the gridlines (or over the page edge) because of the 1 pixel stroke. The icon on the right, accounts for the stroke thickness and stays within the gridlines.

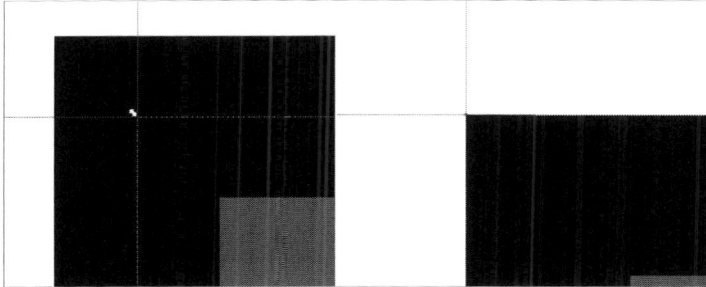

All screenshots in the following sections will not show the gridlines. We do this so that the directions and images are clear.

Also, within any icon file, you should make sure the Snap bounding box corners icon is selected, as seen in the following screenshot:

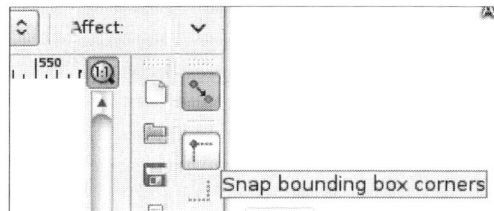

This document setting will make sure that all bounding box corners are always snap points. The bounding box is the smallest rectangular box with sides parallel to the x and y axis that encloses an object.

Simple icons

We'll start with some simple and easy icons. We'll only create one, but here's a whole suite that you could create using the simple steps below:

Here's how to get started:

1. From an open Inkscape window select **File** then **New**, and **icon_64x64**.

2. Then, as described in the previous section, let's set the grid. From the main menu select **File** and then **Document Properties**.

3. Select the **Grids tab** and verify that **Spacing X** and **Spacing Y** are both set to **1.0** and that **Major grid line every** is set to every **4** pixels.

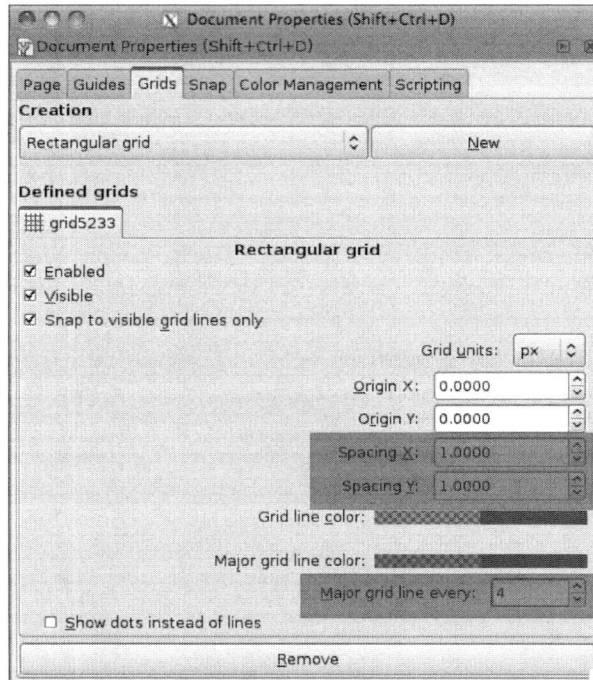

4. Make sure the Snap bounding box corners icon is selected.

5. Draw a circle on the page.

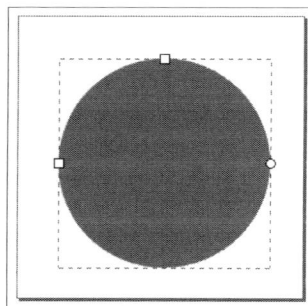

6. Make sure the circle is still selected and then look at the Control Bar. Make the **W:** and **H:** both 64 pixels. You want to make your circle fill the entire canvas.

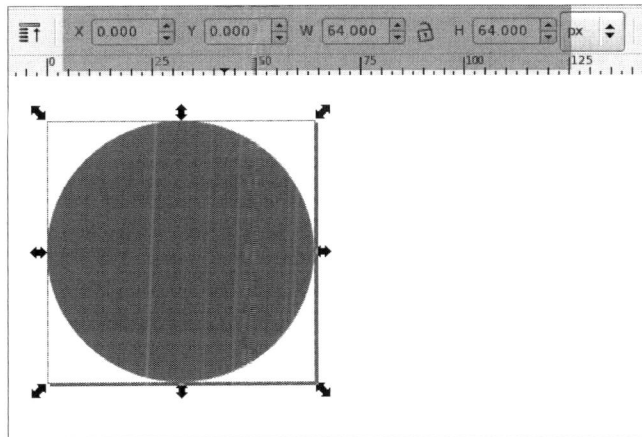

7. Also in the Control Bar, set both the **x** and **y** coordinate fields to **0** so that we are positioning the circle in the exact center of the canvas.

8. Now let's set the color of this icon's background. Open the **Fill and Stroke** dialog box, and set the color to one of your choosing. We'll use a green color.

Using the color pallet menu

You can also enable the Ubuntu color palette by clicking the arrow at the end, right side of the palette bar opens the color palette menu. These pre-defined colors are ideal choices for icon use. Again, in the **Fill and Stroke** dialog, select the stroke tab, and click the **X** box. This sets the stroke to 0, which will give the circle no outline.

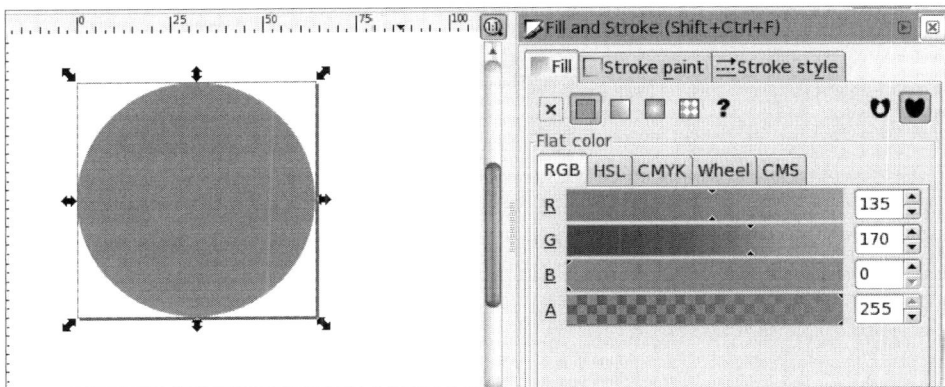

9. Next we are going to draw another circle to be the small white outline within the first. Draw a circle within the first one.

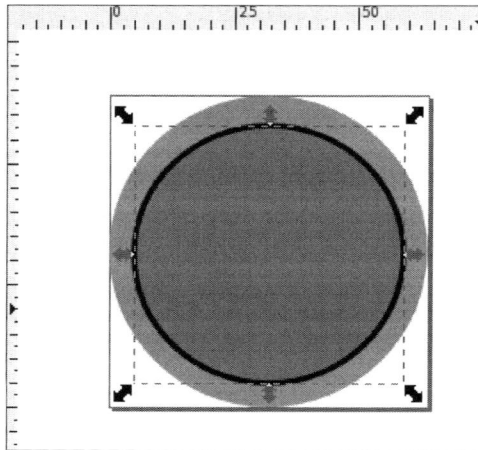

10. Then in the Control bar, set the width and height to 58 pixels.

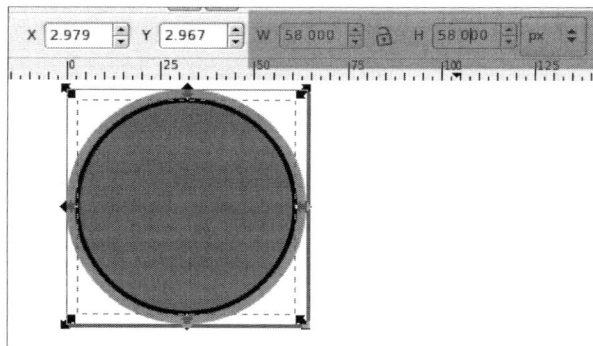

Sometimes, when you use absolute values here, there will be some offset by the computer based on how your circle is drawn (i.e. setting might be 58.001 or 59.994). Exact numbers should be used to avoid anti-aliasing (or blurred edges). Adjust the circle measurements accordingly.

11. Next we need to make sure this circle is aligned correctly within the first circle. Use the keyboard shortcut *Shift + Ctrl + A* to open the alignment menu. Choose **Page** in the **Relative to:** drop down menu and then click the **Center Horizontally** icon and the **Center Vertically** icon.

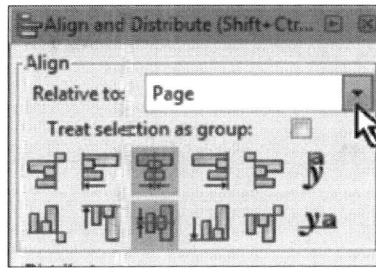

12. Back in the **Fill and Stroke** dialogue, set the fill to none and give this circle a white stroke; set it at 2 pixels.

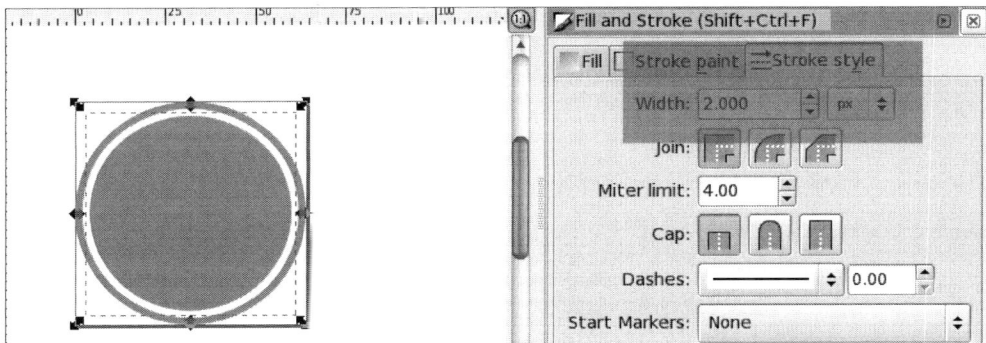

13. Let's add the critical graphical element to this icon. Select the Text tool and type **?**.

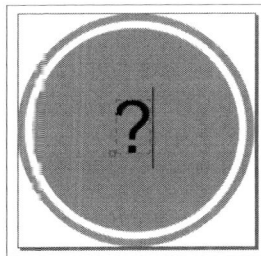

14. Make sure the **?** is selected and then open the Font dialog.

> The keyboard shortcut to open the Font dialog is *Ctrl + Shift + T.*

15. Choose a font that best displays your **?**. In the example, **Charcoal CY** font is used because it is bold and thick enough to be noticeable within a colored background.

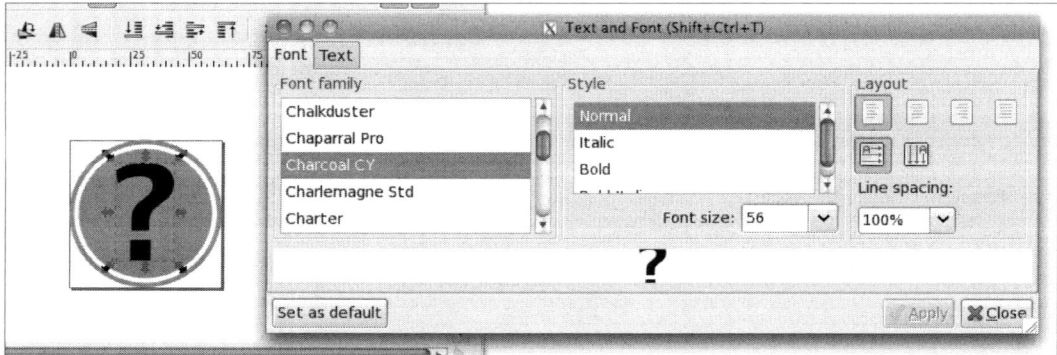

16. With the ? still selected, choose white in the color Palette bar. This changes the font to be white, so it matches the color palette of the rest of the icon so far.

17. Let's add a gradient for the main green circle. Select the main circle, and the **Fill and Stroke** dialog using the keyboard shortcut *Shift + Ctrl + F* and then choose the line gradient option.

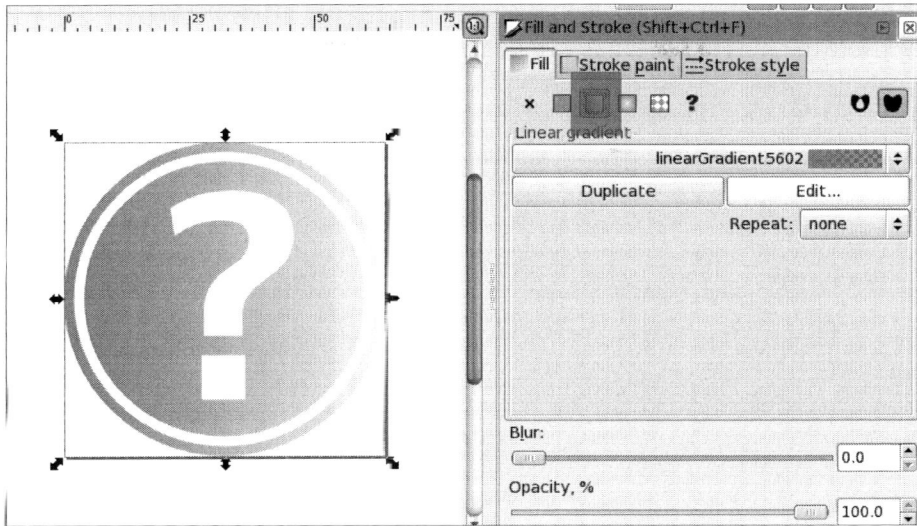

18. Next, go back to your image, select the Bezier tool, a line appears on your drawing. This is where you can set how your gradient appears.

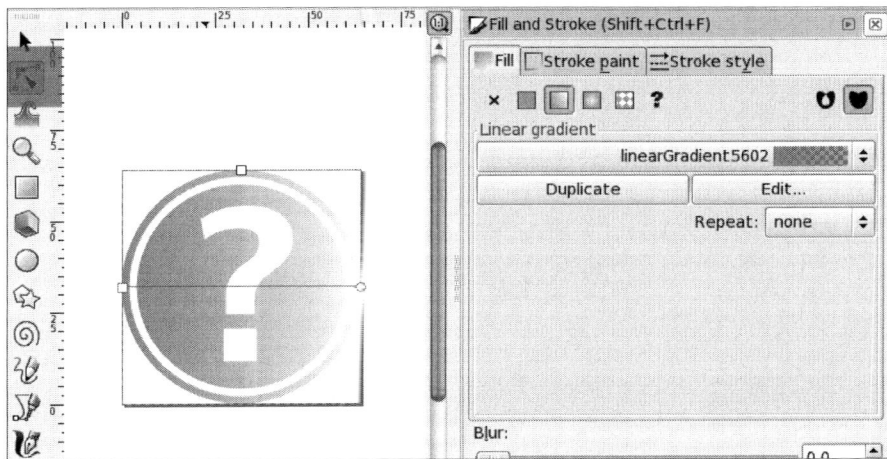

19. Drag it so the gradient goes from dark on top to transparent on the bottom—moving the starting point to the center of the circle, and dragging the gradient end point to well outside the canvas. This is shown in the following screenshot:

20. By default the Inkscape gradient applies an Alpha setting of 0 to the stop gradient, which will be fully transparent. This means, in the above settings, the bottom of the gradient would be transparent.

21. In the **Fill and Stroke** dialog, click **Edit** to change the transparent setting.

22. From the Linear gradient field, choose **Add stop**.

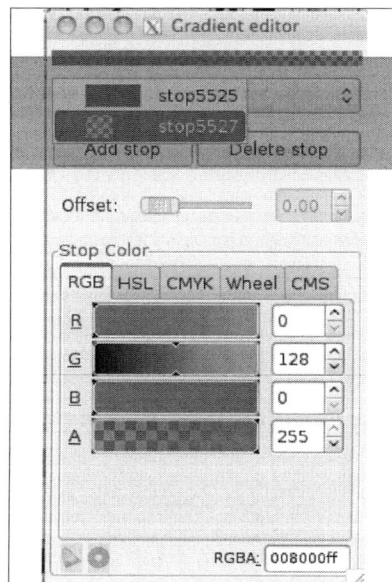

23. Change the Alpha opacity setting (**A**) to a solid color—either move the slider to the left side of the screen or change the value to 255.

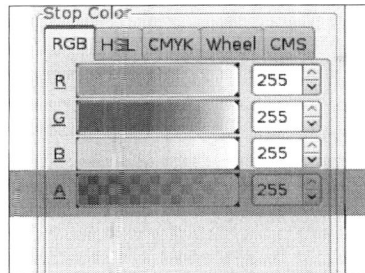

24. Next change the solid color value. In this example, we used white and changed the **R, G, B** values to achieve the results.

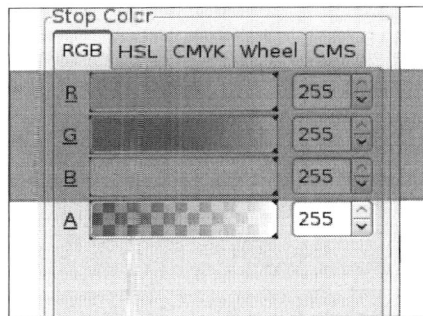

25. Now our gradient will go from dark green on top, to a lighter green on the bottom.

26. Select all of the icon elements using the keyboard shortcut *Ctrl + A*, then in the control bar, set the height (**H:**) and the width (**W:**) to 62.

27. Then use the keyboard shortcut *Shift + Ctrl + A* to open the Alignment menu. Choose **Page** in the **Relative to:** drop down menu and then click the **Center Horizontally** icon and align top edges.

> To see what each of the alignment icons means, you can hover your mouse over the icons to see the text descriptions of each.

28. Let's also add a light drop shadow to the main circle. Make sure the main circle is selected and from the main menu select **Filters, Shadows and Glows,** and then **Drop Shadow**. As an example, set the Blur settings as shown in the following screenshot:

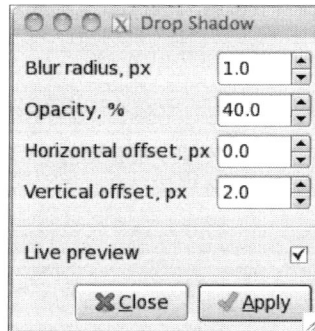

29. And then click **OK**. Your first icon is all set!

30. With this, you can save this file as it is the first of many icons in this set. Save this file with a unique name, like: `help_icon_simple.svg`, where `help` is the name of the icon, and `simple` is the icon set name.

31. Now, to start the next icon in this set, select the background circle (click on it) and then select a new color from the palette. Instantly, you have a new icon color.

32. Now, change the **?** to and **i** (for information) and you've got your second icon in the set.

33. Again save this file with an appropriate name (i.e. `info_icon_simple.svg`) and get ready to make more!

> To actually save these icons in usable formats for the web or programmers, you have to export them as PNG files. We'll discuss this in detail later in this chapter in section *Exporting logos for use on the web*, but you can do this now quickly by choosing **File** and then **Export Bitmap** from the main menu to open the Export dialogue box.

Also note, in the example icons provided at the beginning of this chapter, I used special font (**Webdings** and **Wingdings**) to create some of the special characters like the skull, pencil, and star. You can do the same—just change your font and start placing them into your simple icon template!

More detailed icons

Icons can be much more than basic shapes and font characters as seen in the previous section. You can draw shapes and objects and create your own. As an example, let s create a home or house icon, as shown below in this collection:

Again the same consistency rules apply with more detail as they do with simple icons—use the same dimensions, color palettes, shapes, shading, and more—so collections of icons look like they belong together.

And also note, depending on your skill and level of illustration in Inkscape, you can make these icons as complex as you would like them to be.

1. From the main menu select **File, New,** and then **icon_64x64**.

> Icon sizes can vary depending on your design (or what operating system you might be creating them for). So feel free to change your canvas sizes accordingly.

2. From the main menu select **View** and then **Grid**. Having the grid viewable will help us with spacing of all of the objects.

3. Let's again set the grid properties. From the main menu select **File** and then **Document Properties.**

4. Select the **Grids** tab and verify that **Spacing X** and **Spacing Y** are both set to **1.0** and that **Major grid line every** is set to every **4** pixels.

5. Make sure the Snap bounding box corners icon is selected.

6. Let's start by creating the main part of the house. Draw a square just below the center horizontally, and try to center it in the width of the canvas.

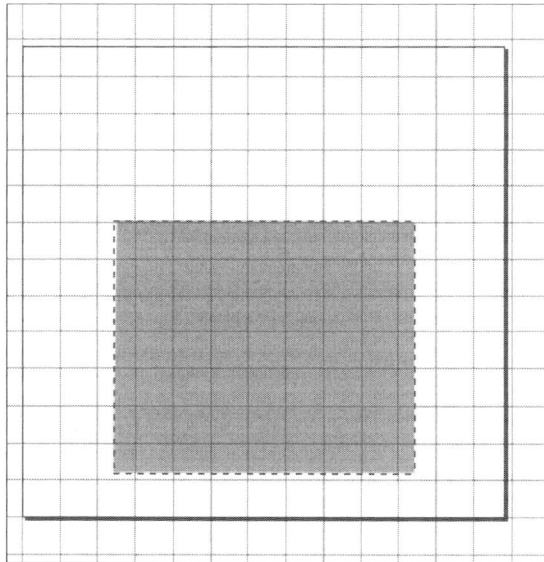

7. Give the square a one pixel border in a color a bit darker than the fill. This will keep the edges of the icon clean and crisp.

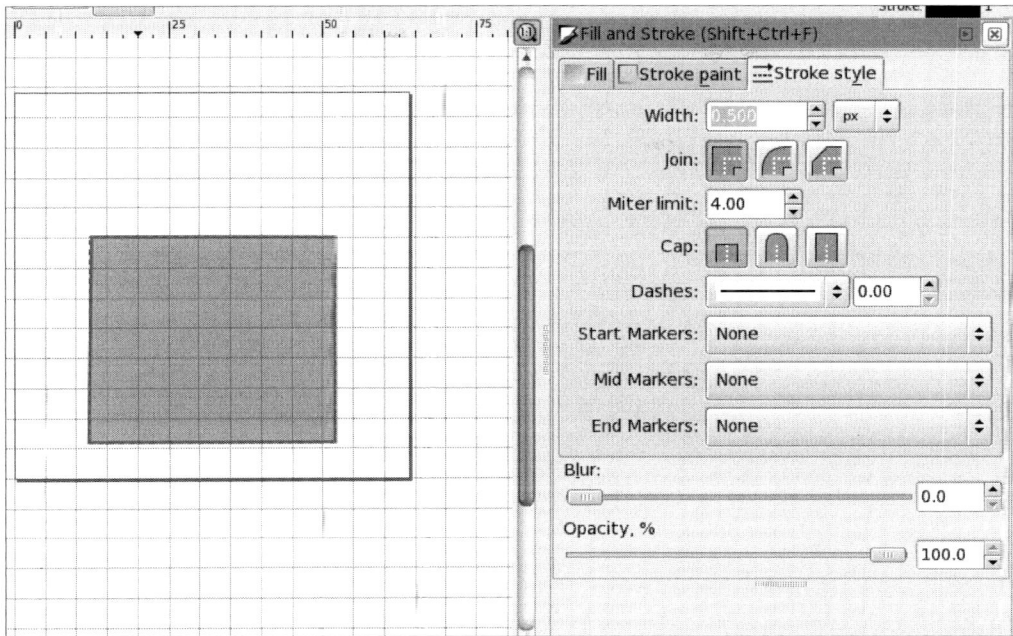

8. Next we'll create the roofline of the house. Select the Bezier tool and create the roofline. Feel free to adjust nodes to get the roof exactly as you would like it.

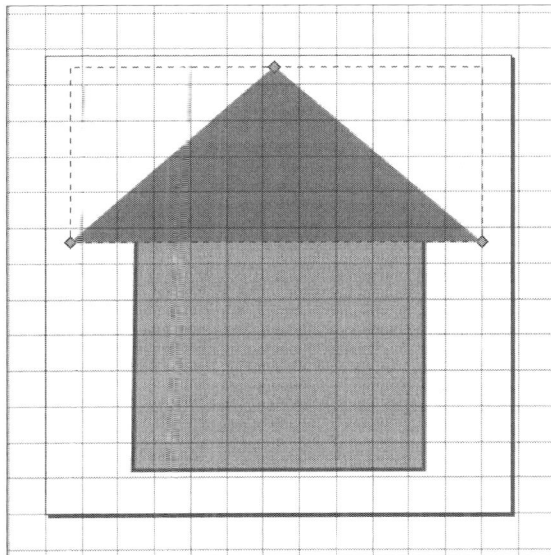

9. Give the roof a one pixel border of colors a shade or two darker than the fill just like you did for the main part of the house.

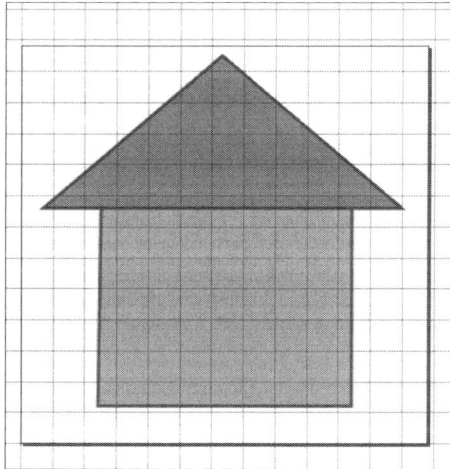

10. Select all of the icon elements using the keyboard shortcut *Ctrl + A*, then use the keyboard shortcut *Shift + Ctrl + A* to open the Alignment menu. Choose **Page** in the **Relative to:** drop down menu and then click on the **Center** on **Vertical Axis** icon.

11. Now let's give the roof and house a drop shadow. Select both objects, and then from the main menu select Filters, Shadows and Glows and then Drop Shadow. Use the settings similar to what is shown in the following screenshot:

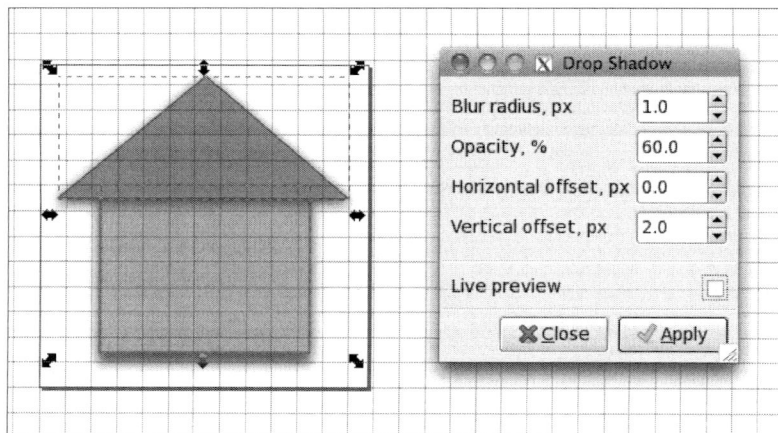

12. Let's give our icon a door. Select the rectangle tool and draw a door near the center of the house frame.

13. Select the door and then the main box of the house.

14. Use the keyboard shortcut *Shift + Ctrl + A* to open the Alignment menu. In the **Relative to:** drop down menu choose **Selected**.

15. Uncheck the **Treat Selection as a group** checkbox.

16. Then click the Center on Horizontal Axis and Align Bottom Edges icons.

17. Give the door a darker gray fill color and a one pixel stroke outline, as done with all other objects.

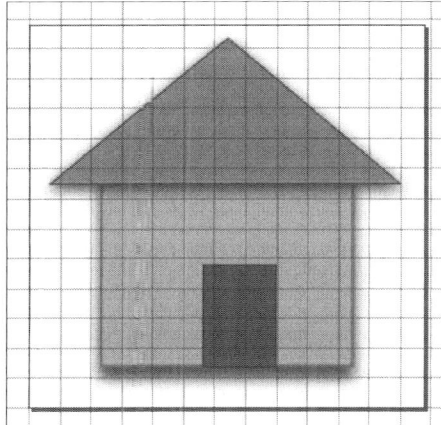

18. Lastly, fill in some other details on the house. Here, I added a door knob and a small window. Again, you can get as detailed or simplistic as you like here.

19. Save your file, again using a nomenclature that represents a collection of icons that you can create with these same document properties, color characteristics, and similar styles for future project use.

Creating collections of more complex icons isn't as easy as it was for the simpler ones. The only 'template' you can create is the one that has the canvas size set and a few other items. The rest require you to remember details such as color palettes, shadow settings, and others so that it can be recreated for all the other icons you create.

Creating buttons

Much like icons, you can create simple or complex buttons on Inkscape. Buttons are used on any forms or fields that require action by the end-user. We'll be creating this simple one to indicate that you want to submit the information in the form.

1. In Inkscape, create a new document.

2. From the main menu, select **File** and then **Document Properties**.

3. Change the canvas width to 140 pixels and the height to 40 pixels.

4. Turn the grid on. From the main menu select **View** and then **Grid**.

5. Then, as described in the previous section, let's set the grid. From the main menu select **File** and then **Document Properties.**

6. Select the **Grids** tab and verify that **Spacing X** and **Spacing Y** are both set to 1.0 and that **Major grid line every** is set to every **4** pixels.

7. Make sure the Snap bounding box corners icon is selected.

8. When ready, draw a rectangle. Make sure the rectangle fills the entire width of your canvas.

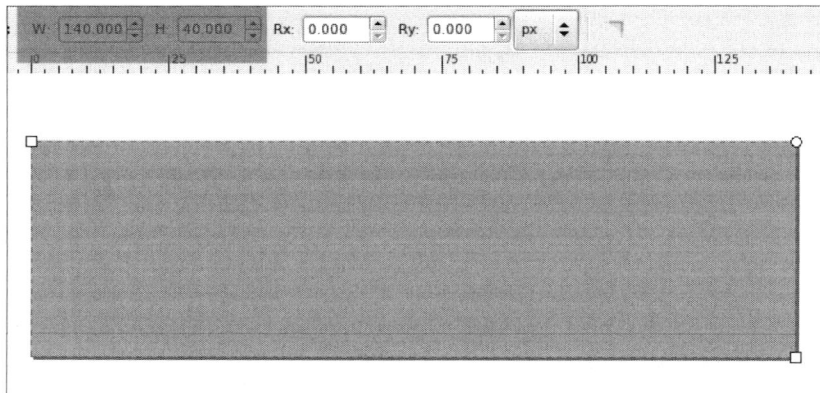

9. Set the Rounding radius **Rx** and **Ry** as 10 pixels in the Tools Control bar. This will give the rectangle rounded corners.

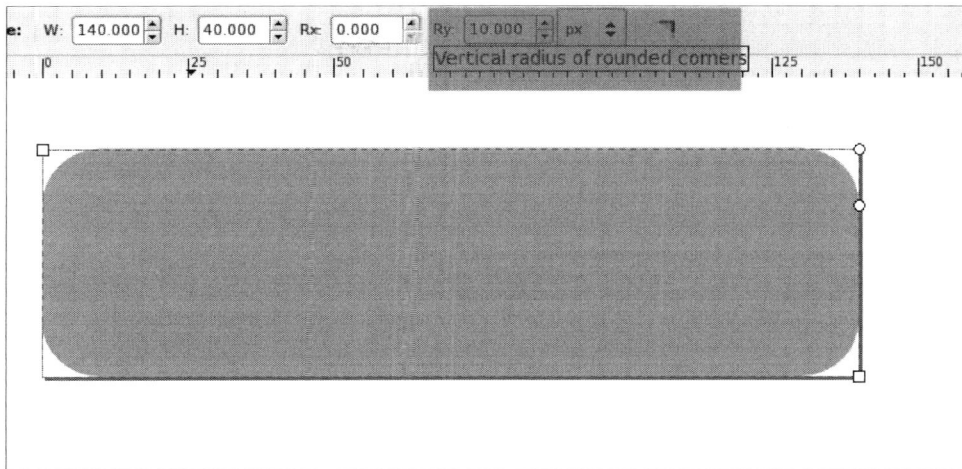

> You can also adjust the radius by pulling the corner nodes inward on the rectangle to find a suitable curve for your button corners.

10. Next select the rectangle and duplicate it. From the main menu select **Edit** and then **Duplicate**. This is the beginning of creating a mask, for a gloss-type effect on the button

11. Next, with the duplicate object selected, give it a linear gradient fill. You do this in the Fill and Stroke dialog.

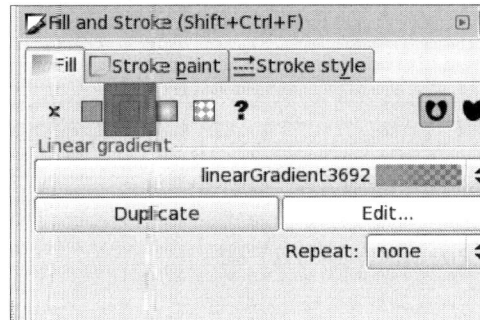

12. We'll need to add a stop, white colored, into this gradient. Again, in the Fill and Stroke dialog, click **Edit**.

13. In the Gradient Editor, click **Add Stop**.

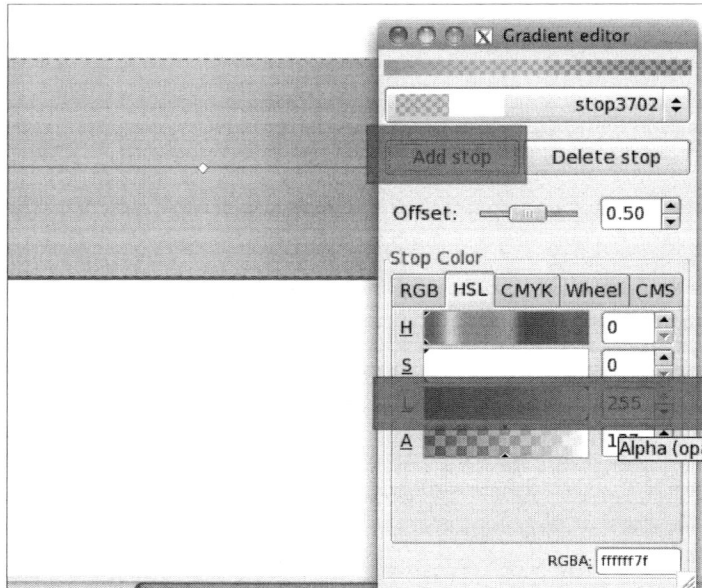

14. You may not be able to see this new gradient in your button graphic yet. To do this, choose the Edit Paths by Node tool in the tool bar and nodes will appear.

15. Drag the square node from the left of the rectangle to the top of the button. And then, with the *Ctrl* key pressed take the circle node and drag it down and off the shape as shown in the following screenshot. The *Ctrl* key will allow it to snap the angle of the gradient.

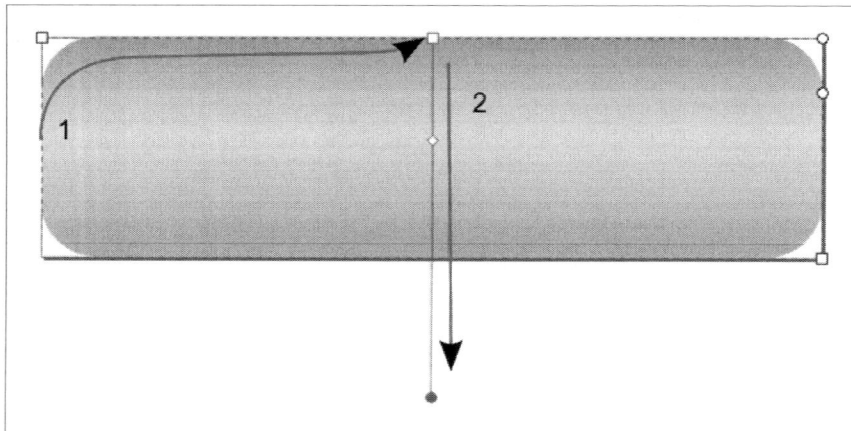

16. You should see the gradient now — with a white portion near the middle of the rectangle.

All we want to be viewable now is the top portion of the duplicate graphic. To make this happen, we will create a mask.

1. Draw another rectangle on top of the area we want to *remain showing* in the final button.

2. Select the duplicate and this new object, right click, and select **Set Mask**.

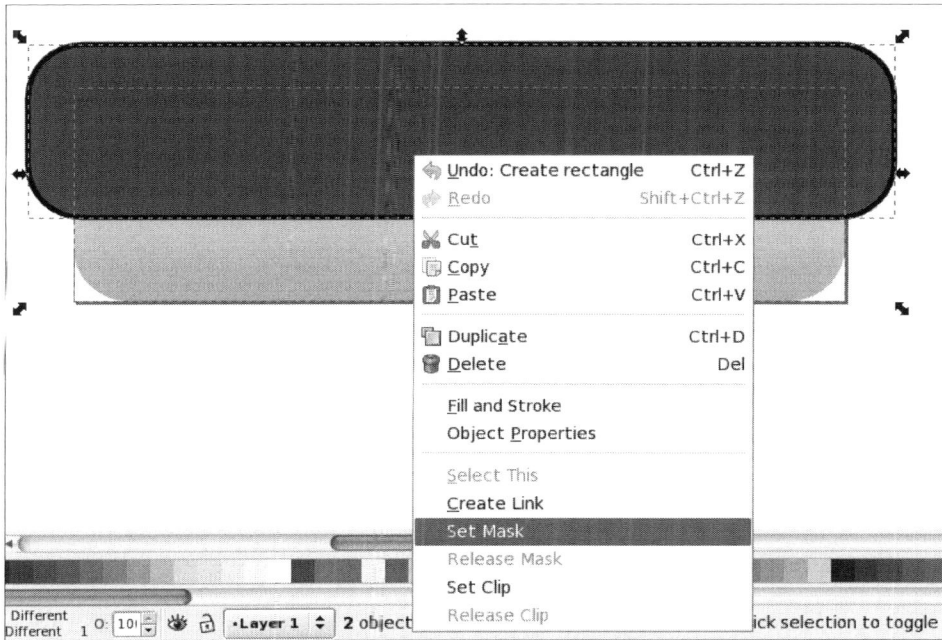

3. What remains should be the base of our button. Or a template to create future buttons, that has a glossy-type effect near the middle.

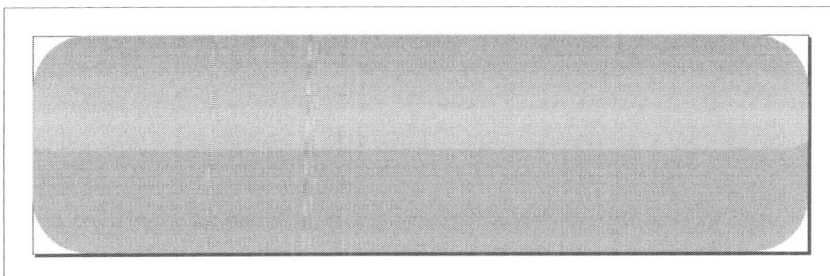

4. Now we'll add some text. For this example, we are going to add the word Submit — so that this button would be used to submit any form of information on our web page. Select the Text tool, type the word, and place it where you would like it.

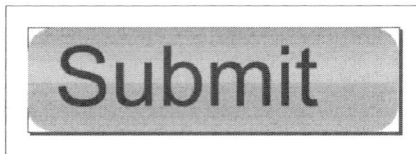

5. You can also add a graphical icon to this button to represent its function and a drop shadow for some finer tuning.

Just remember when adding any more text or graphics, it might look better to select those objects and drop them below the gloss mask. Just select those items and then from the main menu select **Object** and then **Lower**.

6. When you are ready, save the file in SVG format so you can use it again for any other buttons you might want to create for this set of web pages.

7. It's easy to change the text and/or the graphics used on this button by just selecting the text and graphic used on the buttons. Here are a few quick examples of other buttons you can create using this same template as a base:

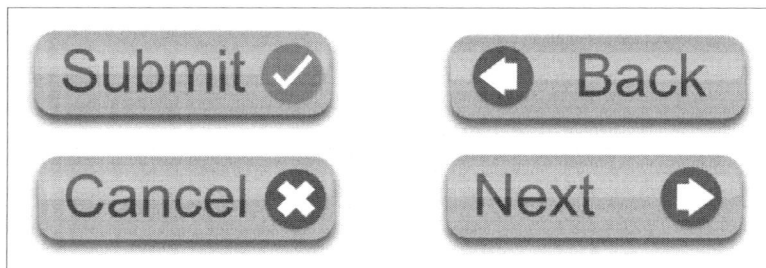

And remember, there are no rules for button sizes and shapes. If your design calls for something original — feel free to experiment and make your use of buttons unique and fun.

Logos as the cornerstone of the design

Logos are the graphical representation or emblem for a company or organization—sometimes even individuals use them to promote instant recognition. They can be a graphic (a combination of symbols or icons), a combination of graphics and text, or graphical forms of text.

Why are they important in web design? Since most companies want to be recognized by their logo alone—the logo is the critical piece of the design. It needs prominent placement to work flawlessly with the design.

Best practices for creating logos

Designing logos could be a book topic itself—there are a lot of guidelines and principles to the best logo designs. And they start with some simple ideas that have been reworked and discussed intensely since the start of the Internet. But it never hurts to review the best practices. You want your company logos to be:

- **Simple**: That's right, you want to keep them clean, simple, neat, and intensely easy to recreate. If you nail this attribute, the others listed below will be easy to achieve.

- **Memorable**: Think of all the great company logos. You remember them in your mind's eye very easily right? That's because they are unique and in essence simple. These two attributes together make some of the best company logos today.

- **Timeless**: These logos will last many years. This not only saves the company or individual money, but it also increases the memorability of the logo and brand of the company.

- **Versatile**: Any logo that can be used in print (color and black and white), digital media, television, any size, letterhead, billboards, and small iconic statements along the bottom of web pages or promotional materials—is a successful logo. You never know where a logo might be placed, especially on the web. You want something that can be used in a prominent location on the company web site itself, but also something that works in a small thumbnail space for social media or cell phone applications.

- **Appropriate**: We want the logo to be appropriate for the company it is representing. The right colors, images, and more will go along way in giving the company credibility immediately upon first glance by any consumer or potential client. It can also prove to be a great indication of the services one can expect from the company itself.

Seems easy enough right? It is, after some practice and some processes are in place. It never hurts to have a loose process to work with clients to determine their needs and wants in a logo. Some may already have a logo and want to keep parts of the design and revamp others while other clients might be so new they haven't ever had a logo before. As a start, here's a brief process for working with clients and discussing logos.

Information gathering

There's no better place to start than to open the floor for discussion. Here's just the start of what you can ask or gather from your client in an initial information gathering meeting:

- Does the client already have a logo?

- If yes, do they intend to keep that logo to use in the web design? Again if yes, get the source files. Hopefully they are in vector graphic format so they are scalable and usable right away in the web design. If not, return to *Chapter 3, Working with Images* as it explains how to trace elements in Inkscape to create vector graphics.

- Are they interested in a logo redesign? This can be beneficial if they are rebranding themselves as a business or having a 'grand re-opening' of some sort. It can breathe life into a stale business and sometimes garner some new interest.

- If yes, is it a complete (open to anything) redesign? Or are there certain elements that need to stay? Sometimes color is important, or a certain font or even a certain graphical element needs to stay within the logo. Listen and take notes; it is important to work with the client to try to fulfill their needs as much as possible.

- If the client is open to a complete redesign, brainstorm a bit with them about their needs and wants. Colors, fonts, graphical ideas. Don't be afraid to bring out some paper and pencils and start sketching some ideas. Sometimes it can be most productive to work through some rough ideas this way to get a feel for what the client likes most and not. Consider it a working session.

- Try to understand where the client wants to use this logo most prominently. Keeping that in mind you will design something that is versatile and could be used in most mediums; you still want to know where they plan to use it the most. That way, you can tailor the logo as much as possible for that space—especially if you can use more color.

- What are the primary goals of the company? What is their mission statement?

- Does the client already have brand guidelines to consider?

Creating initial designs

After the initial informational session it is your turn to start designing. Take the paper and pencil sketches (if you had any) from the initial meeting and expand on them. In fact, spend a bit more time with your team and flesh out a few more of those ideas in a true brainstorming session. It can be beneficial to start this way first before jumping on to the computer and getting caught in details like typeface and effects.

Once you have some solid ideas, bring it over to the computer and start designing. Focus on only three of your best ideas. That way you bring only your best to the client to review and discuss.

Much like with the web design process, the logo design process takes a very similar route. You bring design mock ups to your client to review, give feedback, redesign, and then you go back and design some more—all until you get approvals. And then you—being an Inkscape expert—can build and then export the logo in any number of vector formats for use in almost any medium.

Importing existing logos

If you are fortunate enough to work with a client that has an established logo that they would like to continue to use in their web space, then you need to be able to pull the logo into your initial mock up designs—and then into your final design and use it as any other object. To do this:

1. While in an Inkscape document (with our without your design already in place), from the main menu select **File** and then **Import**.
2. Find the logo file in the menus and click **Open**.

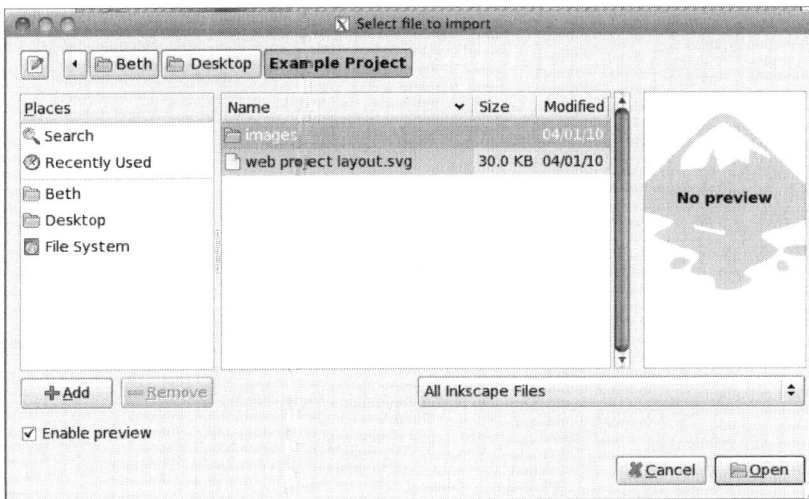

3. Then place your logo where it best fits in your design.

What if the logo is not in the right size and not in a scalable vector-graphic format? Then you need to re-create the logo in Inkscape in a form that *is* scalable. We discussed the details of tracing and recreating items in *Chapter 3, Working with Images*. It's definitely possible and not difficult to do. It just takes time and a bit of Inkscape expertise.

Re-creating existing logos

Sometimes a client provides you with a logo but it isn't of a good quality and it requires you to 'trace' it to essentially re-create the logo as a vector graphic. There are a few tricks to do this that can save you some time.

If you have an electronic version of the graphic — meaning any PNG, JPG, BMP, or graphical format of the image, you can import it into Inkscape as described above. Once placed, create a new layer on top of the original graphic and start "tracing". Use shapes, tools, images, and more to draw over the initial drawing until you have essentially re-created the logo.

Group all of your objects together to essentially make the logo one object again and hide or delete the original layer. Once saved as an SVG file, you can now make this new logo larger or smaller and not have it degrade in quality. You've recreated your first logo!

What if you don't get an electronic version? What if you are not confident of your re-creation skills? You can use the Inkscape tracing feature. We discussed this in great detail in *Chapter 3, Working with Images*, section *Tracing images*.
It uses Protrace, an extension of Inkscape that scans and finds the "edges" of objects in pictures and allows you to manipulate them.

Logo re-designs

If your client decides that they want to redo their logos, as stated above, your challenge is two-fold: creating a logo that represents their company and then designing a web site that complements it.

Logo design is very personal to the company that it is being designed for. That being said, there are no step-by-step instructions on how to create a logo. But let's run through an example of what one could do to redesign the logo (again) of our fictional company we've been working with from the start of this book. We'll redesign Gigi's Fun Travel logo to go from what we did in *Chapter 4, Styling Text* to something like this:

Let's say we've already brainstormed with our client to determine that the color palette needs to stay the same—but we can work with using different shades and fonts. The logo still needs to be fun, and the client is open to either using the name in the logo or not.

1. Following the logo design principles listed above—we'll go simple, but with an eye towards fun. Let's start with two ideas: a tropical flower and mail stamp as the base of the logo. This affords us the orange and green color palette and allows us to continue the fun theme.

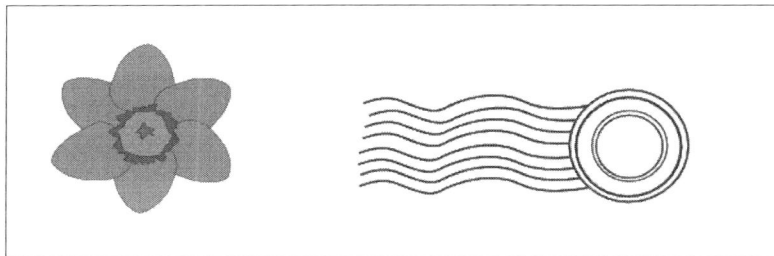

2. Let's first concentrate on getting the flower and the colors within the mail stamp.

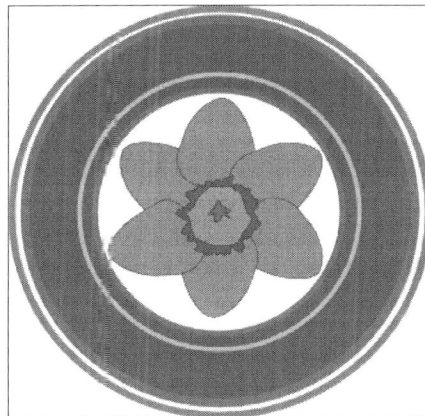

3. Then, we can add in the company name and the stamp 'flyers'.

4. Do we need the flyer lines of the stamp? In some promotional items we could use it, but the logo could stand on its own without it. Here's the finished product:

Again, this is a quick example of what can be done with logo design. There are a ton of materials that can explore this design theory even more and give you even more pointers for the best logos created today.

Exporting logos for use on the web and more

As stated earlier in the chapter, typically you would export your icons, buttons, and logos in a rasterized form—line a PNG format for use in web development. As always you keep the SVG forms so you can scale larger images of the graphics when and if needed.

To export any of the icons, buttons, or logos you created in this chapter:

1. Open the SVG file.
2. Select all the objects in the drawing.
3. Then from the main menu select **File** and then **Export Bitmap**.

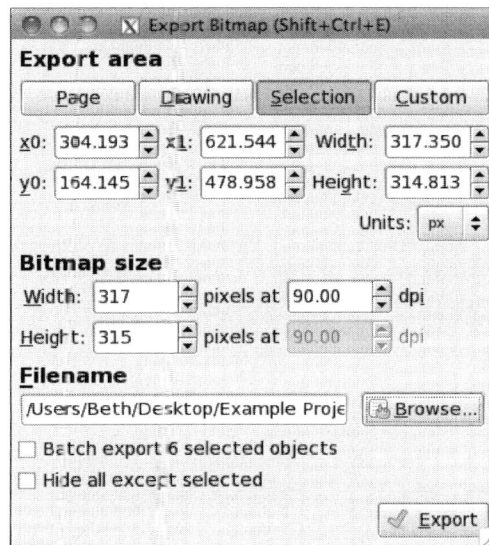

4. On the Export dialog, click **Browse** to find a save location, and then click **Export** to save your files in PNG format.

As always, when providing files to programmers it is a good idea to provide them with:

- The PNG image files you just exported from your design.
- And the source Inkscape SVG file of your logo, buttons, or logo and the design mock up with all images used in the creation of it. That way, they see how they all work together and build it as designed.

Summary

We learned everything from icon and button design principles to creating simple and complex icons for a web site (and how best we might create collections of both), how to export them and save them for continued use. And we even learned a few new techniques like the glow effect and masking while creating buttons.

Then we took a step back and talked about logo design principles, how to best tackle that logo design project, best practices for working with a client and of course—an example of how to redesign a logo we've been working with the entire book so far. As always, we also reviewed again how to hand off files to the web programmers to implement our design wishes.

In the next chapter, we'll learn how to create other elements in Inkscape--diagrams, flow charts, site maps and more.

7
Making Diagrams, Site Maps, and More

Aside from the basic look and feel of a web site, you can also use Inkscape for more technical design—creating diagrams, charts, and site maps. We'll discuss the purpose of each kind of diagram and chart, then how best to create each in Inkscape. We'll focus on the visual aspects and then demonstrate how to create them in a way that can best be exported and used within web pages. This chapter covers:

- Defining diagrams, site maps, and charts
- Creating a basic diagram
- Developing an organizational chart
- Building a flow chart
- Creating a site map
- Exporting diagrams, site maps, and flow charts for web site integration

Diagrams and maps

In web design, you often have a need to show some more technical information and/or organizational charts, site maps, and sometimes diagrams. Inkscape gives you the ability to create these easily and then export for use on the web. Here are some simple examples of what we are going to create in this chapter:

- **Diagram**: It is a graphical representation of information. There are a number of diagram types such as Venn, Activity, Tree, Network, and more. Inkscape can help create all kinds of diagrams.

- **Site tree/Site map**: A site map (or sitemap) is a list of all the individual pages of a web site. Typically the site map outlines how each page is linked to the others. Sometimes it is used primarily for planning, but sometimes it is also used to help web site users find where they need to be on the site.

- **Organizational chart**: An organizational chart (that is, org chart) primarily shows the structure of an organization. It also details roles, job titles, and sometimes the relationships between the jobs.

- **Flow chart**: One of the most common types of diagrams, a flow chart shows the general process for completing a task or decision. It shows each step, decision, and option as a particular box/option/connector. And in general it represents a step-by-step solution to a given problem.

Each of these types of diagrams and charts can land themselves in your web site design depending on your client's needs. Let's look at how you might create these diagrams in Inkscape.

Diagrams

Diagrams come in all shapes and sizes. Some are very graphical versions of step-by-step instructions, others a literal drawing of network configurations, or general diagrams of complex topics. We'll create a simple diagram for a promotional piece for our fictional company Gigi's fun travel—**4 Simple Steps to Prefect Travel**.

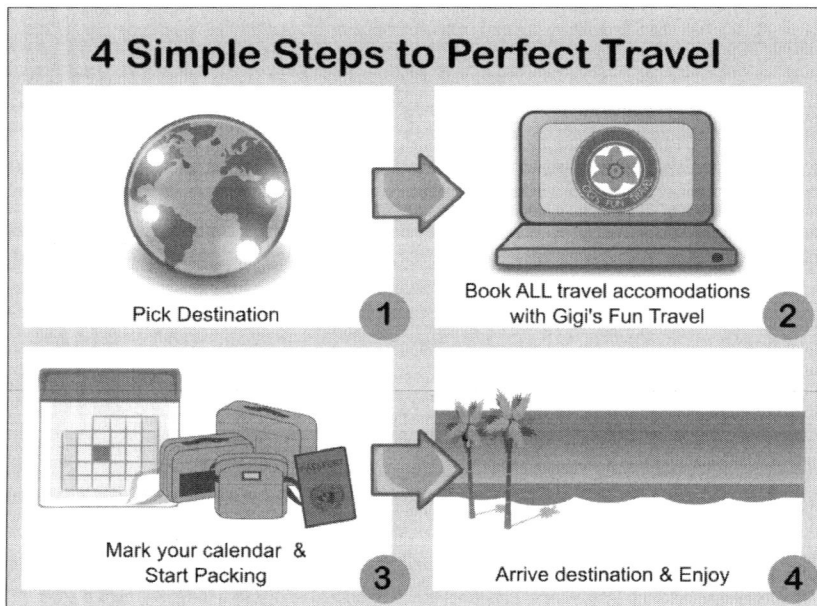

I used simple Open Clip Art library graphics (http://www.openclipart.org) when creating this diagram and then customized their colors and shapes so it fits our design. You can do the same for simple graphics or create a completely custom look for your clients.

To create this diagram:

1. Open a new document in Inkscape. From the main menu select **File** and select **New** and **desktop_800x600**.

2. Using the *Shift* + *Ctrl* + *N* keyboard shortcut, create a new layer called Background.

3. Select the new layer, then click the Rectangle tool in the Toolbar box and create a rectangle on your canvas. The rectangle should cover most of the canvas.

4. Use the Tools Control bar to set the exact size of the box to be that of the canvas. Set the width (**W**) to 800 and the height (**H**) to 600.

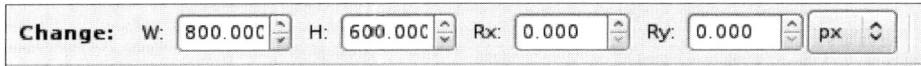

Change:	W: 800.000	H: 600.000	Rx: 0.000	Ry: 0.000	px

5. Use the Color Palette to choose a fill color. For our example, we're using pale green.

6. In the Status bar, right click the Stroke setting and select **Remove Stroke**.

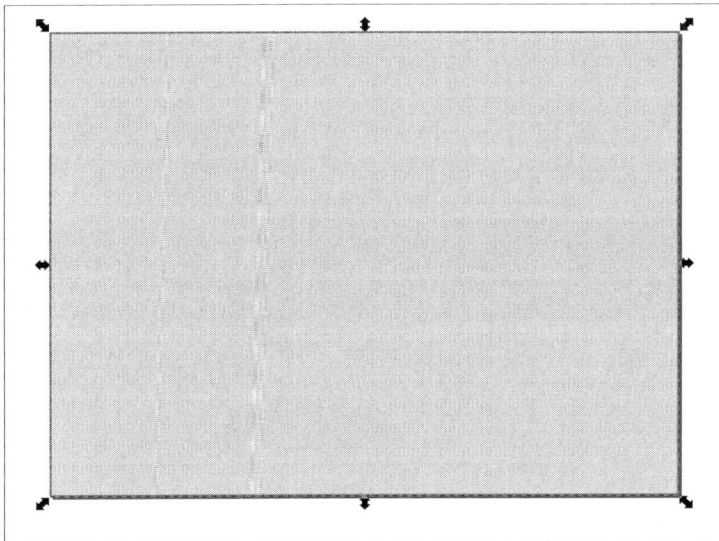

7. Let's begin creating the four rectangles within the diagram. Create a new layer (*Shift + Ctrl + N* keyboard shortcut) with the name: **Main steps**.

8. Select the Main steps layer, click the Rectangle tool in the Toolbar box, and create a rectangle on your canvas.

9. In the Tools Control bar set the width (**W**) to 360 and the height (**H**) to 240.

10. Use the Color Palette to choose a white fill color.

11. In the Status bar, right click the Stroke setting and select **Remove Stroke**.

12. Place this rectangle in the first position.

13. Let's create tiled clones of this first rectangle. From the main menu, select **Edit**, **Clone**, and **Create Tiled Clones**.

14. In the **Shift** tab, make sure the **Rows, Columns** is set to 2 x 2, the **Shift X, Per Column** to 10%, and the **Shift Y Per Row** to 10%.

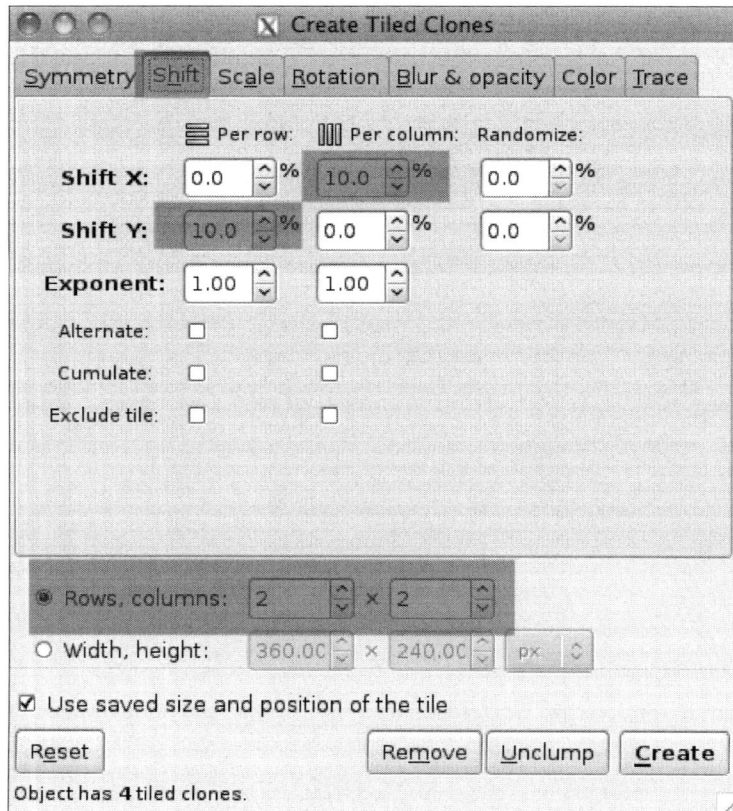

8. Click **Create**.

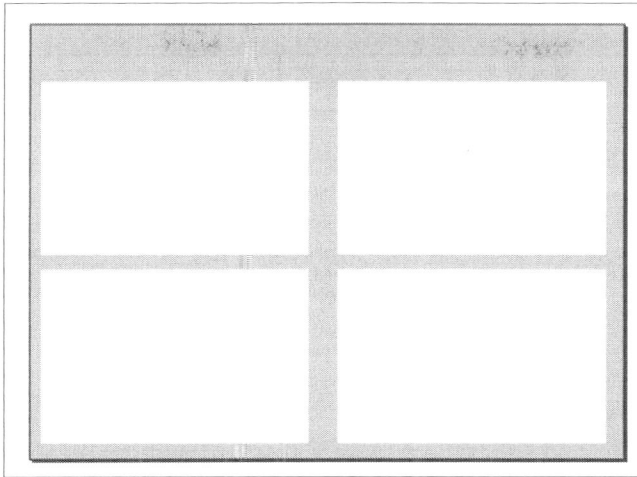

Clones of the original rectangle are created that are spaced evenly on the background.

> Note that not only are the newly cloned rectangles the same size as the original, they also have the exact same stroke and fill information. And, if you were to change any of the features (like fill) or the original rectangle—it will also automatically change for the clones.

9. Create a new layer for the step numbers. Use the *Shift + Ctrl + N* keyboard shortcut, and name the new layer, **Steps**.

10. In the Toolbar Box, select the Circle tool and create a circle in the lower-right corner or the first rectangle.

12. Use the Color Palette to change the fill color to orange and right-click the Stroke Status Indicator and choose **Remove Stroke**.

13. Just as with the rectangles, we'll create tiled clones of this circle. Make sure the circle is selected, and then from the main menu, select **Edit**, **Clone** and **Create Tiled Clones**.

14. In the **Shift** tab, make sure the **Rows, Columns** is set to 2 X 2, the **Shift X, Per Column** to 705% (to make sure the circles move far enough to align with the right side of the rectangles) and the **Shift Y Per Row** to 435% (to verify the bottom row circles move to the lower corners or the rectangles).

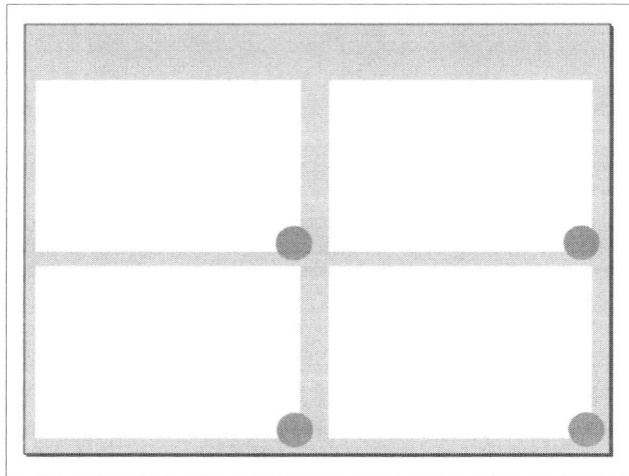

15. Now, it is time to start adding content. Create a new layer (*Shift + Ctrl + N*) and name it as Titles.

16. In the Toolbar box, select the Create Text Tool (or select the *F8* shortcut key), and click on the canvas, within the top area of the background and type the title of the diagram.

17. In the control bar, select the font and size.

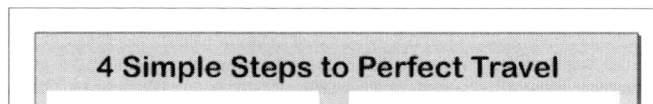

4 Simple Steps to Perfect Travel

18. To make sure this title is centered, select the title, and the background rectangle. Open the Align and Distribute dialog (*Shift + Ctrl + A*) and click the **Center on Vertical Axis** button.

19. Again, use the Create Text Tool (or select the *F8* shortcut key), and create the text for each of the steps. Remember, just like with the title text, you can use the control bar to adjust the font and the size of the text.

20. Make sure the text is placed on the lower portion of the white main step rectangles. Then center the text for each step, select the text and the white rectangle, open the Align and Distribute dialog (*Shift + Ctrl + A*) and click the **Center on Vertical Axis** button.

21. Much like the titles, I created the step numbers the same way. Select the Steps Layer.

22. Use Create Text Tool (or select the *F8* shortcut key), click on the canvas, within a step circle, and type the number 1. Remember, just like with the title text, you can use the control bar to adjust the font and the size of the text.

23. Do the same for making the numbers for steps 2, 3, and 4.

24. Then select each number, and each circle, open the Align and Distribute dialog (*Shift + Ctrl + A*), and click the Center on Vertical Axis button and then Center on Horizontal Axis to center each number within the circles.

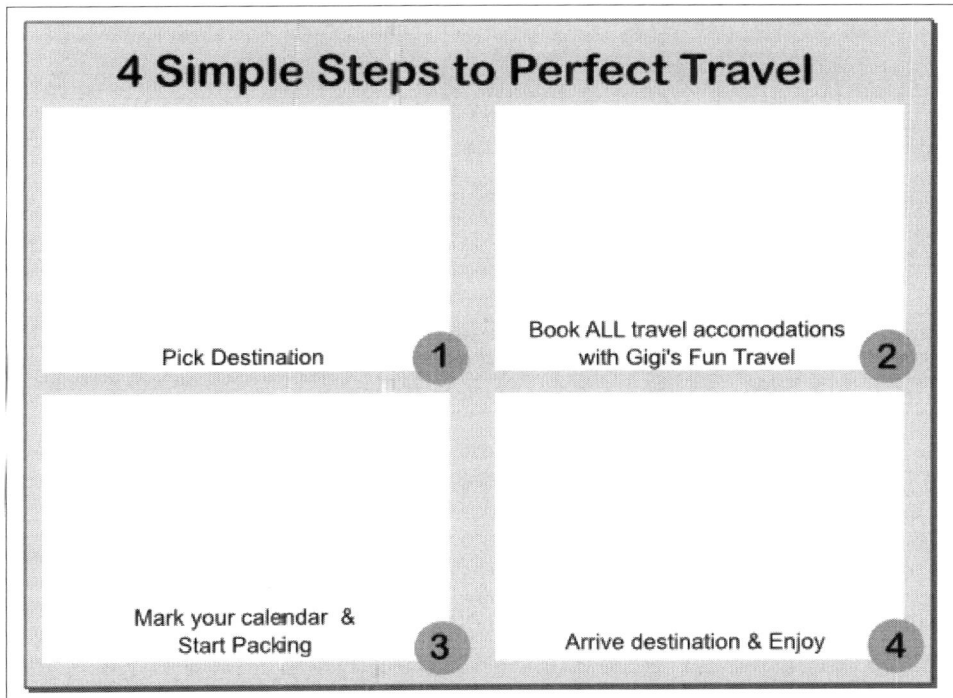

4 Simple Steps to Perfect Travel

Pick Destination   **1**

Book ALL travel accomodations with Gigi's Fun Travel   **2**

Mark your calendar & Start Packing   **3**

Arrive destination & Enjoy   **4**

25. Next I imported the Open Clip Art Library objects. From the main menu select **File** and **Import from Open Clip Art Library** and change their sizes and colors to match my color theme.

Unfortunately, in this release of Inkscape, Open Clip Library via the **File** menu only works for a Macintosh computer user. Windows and Linux users can go to http://www.openclipart.org and download clip art for free.

Then go to the main menu and select **File**, **Import**, and select your downloaded SVG file. This will import the clip art and place it onto your open Inkscape canvas.

26. You can change the object sizes, orientations, and colors as needed to match the colors of the diagram.

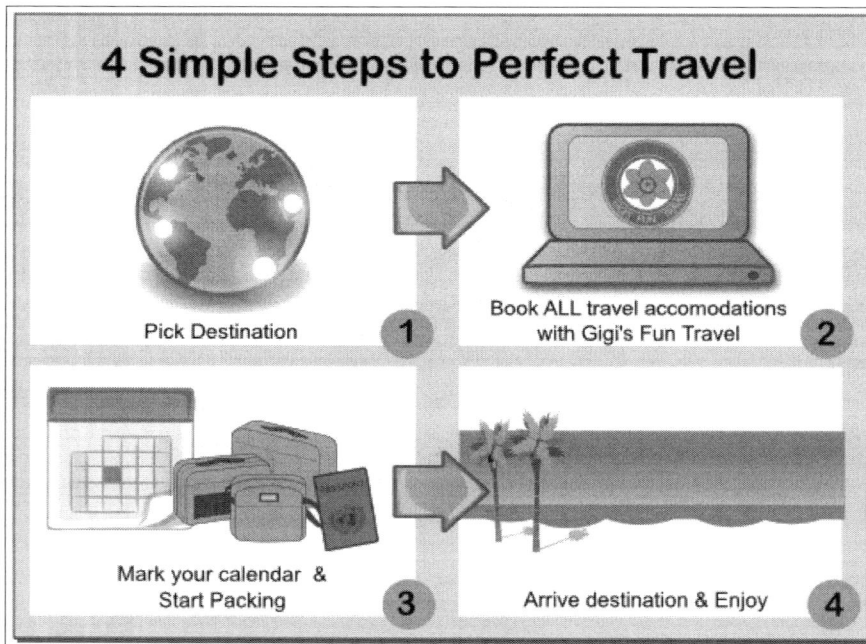

27. With just these few simple steps, our diagram is complete! Make sure to save the file as an Inkscape SVG file in case you want to change any of the content at a later time. From the main menu, select **File** and then **Save As**.

28. You can also export this diagram as a PDF or PNG file to use for integration into a web page or other print or electronic deliverables. From the main menu select **File** and then **Export Bitmap**.

This example was a very non-technical sort of diagram to just illustrate the basics of what you can do with Inkscape. Feel free to use it to do more detailed diagrams of all kinds—including computer networking diagrams, pie charts, Venn diagrams, and more.

Organizational charts

Organizational charts will most likely be used only in corporate environments—and in today's landscape—are often updated when people move around in the company, get promotions, leave the company, or new positions are created. Either way these visual ways at "seeing" an organizational structure can be very helpful and most often used on internal company websites like Intranets. But creating the organizational chart is simply creating a graphic much like you have always done in Inkscape. Just remember to save the Inkscape SVG file so you can always update it!

Before you start, it is wise to:

- Create a color code chart outlining the color theme
- Define what colors are associated with what roles within the company
- Figure out how you are going to show reporting structure (dashed or full lines)
- Get a staff list with names and titles of all the people in the organization and who they report to

All of this, specifically a nice color theme will make the chart look more clean and professional and make this an easy task to accomplish.

Here s how to get started creating an organizational chart (or org chart):

1. Open a new document in Inkscape. From the main menu select **File** and select **New** and **desktop_800x600**. We are creating this graphic the exact same size as our web page template, but you can create it slightly smaller if you want it to fit underneath a title bar on your web site.
2. Using the *Shift + Ctrl + N* keyboard shortcut, create a new layer called Background.
3. Select the new layer, then click the Rectangle tool in the Toolbar box and create a rectangle on your canvas. The rectangle should cover most of the canvas.
4. Use the Tools Control bar to set the exact size of the box to be that of the canvas. Set the width (**W**) to 800 and the height (**H**) to 600.
5. Use the Color Palette to choose a white fill color.

6. In the Status bar, right click the Stroke setting and select **Remove Stroke**.

7. Select the white rectangle and from the main menu select **Filters, Shadows and Glows** and then **Drop Shadow**. For this example, we set the **Blur Radius** to 2.0, **Opacity** to 80%, and **Vertical offset** to 2.0. Click **Apply**.

8. Create a new layer (*Shift + Ctrl + N*) called **Boxes**.

9. Select the new layer, then click the Rectangle tool in the Toolbar box and create a rectangle on your canvas near the top of the page. This will be the "top" of the organizational chart.

10. Use the Tools Control bar to set the exact size of the box to be that of the canvas. Set the width (**W**) to 260 and the height (**H**) to 70.

11. Use the Color Palette to choose a green fill color. Use your prepared color scheme to help know what color to use here.

12. In the Status bar, right click the Stroke setting and select **Remove Stroke**.

13. Give the rectangle a simple drop shadow. From the main menu select **Filters, Shadows and Glows** and then **Drop Shadow**. Like the background, we set the **Blur Radius** to 2.0, **Opacity** to 80%, and **Vertical offset** to 2.0. Click **Apply**.

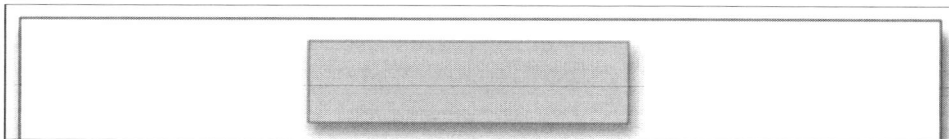

14. Next, we'll create all of the underlying roles/titles in the organization. To do this, you will create a series or rectangles, in additional fill colors with the rectangle tool in the Toolbar Controls. When this step is completed, your canvas will look something like the following screenshot:

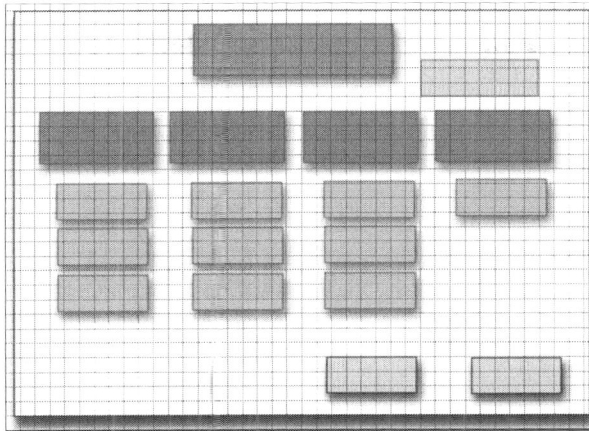

15. Using the Duplicate (*Ctrl + D*) feature helps you create the same size and color rectangles throughout the chart. Select all the rectangles on the canvas, and give them a drop shadow. From the main menu select **Filters, Shadows and Glows**, and then **Drop Shadow**. Like the background, we set the **Blur Radius** to 2.0, **Opacity** to 80%, and **Vertical offset** to 2.0. Click **Apply**.

16. Now we'll create the paths to show reporting structure between roles in the organization. Create a new layer (*Shift + Ctrl + N*) called **Paths**.

17. In the Toolbar box, use the Bezier Pen tool to draw paths between rectangles to show reporting structure.

18. Click the paraxial line mode in the Control bar in the Bezier tool to make 90 degree cornered paths. Using the Paraxial Line Mode will eliminate blurring or right angled lines.

19. To create Straight Paths use the *Ctrl + Left Click mouse* combination.

[Pressing the *Enter* key will end a path where the mouse cursor is located.]

20. Your canvas will look similar to the following screenshot:

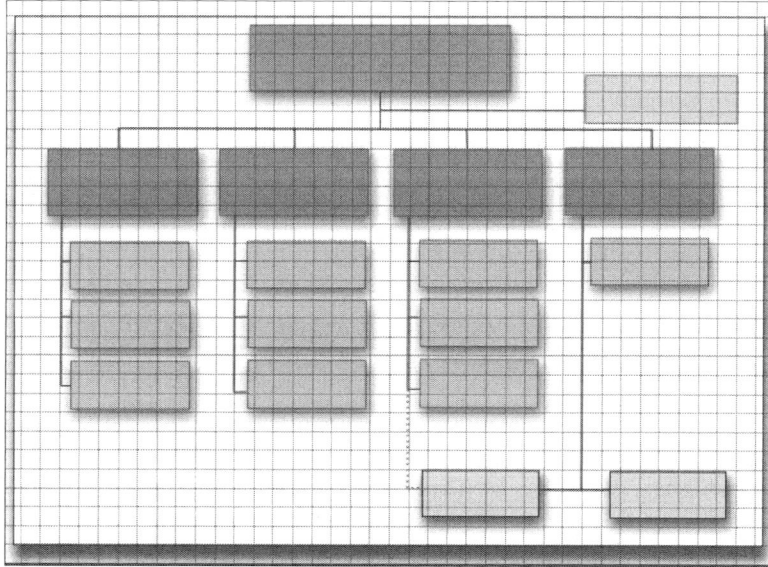

21. Create one more layer (*Shift* + *Ctrl* + *N*), called Employees. We will use this layer to type employee names and job titles into the chart.

22. From the Toolbar Box, select the Create and Edit text tool, place it within the top box, and type the name and title of the person leading the organization.

23. In the control bar, select the font and size.

24. To make sure this text is centered, select the title, and the background rectangle. Open the Align and Distribute dialog (*Shift* + *Ctrl* + *A*) and click the **Center on Vertical Axis** button.

25. Again, use the Create Text Tool (or select the *F8* shortcut key), and create the text for each of the employees in this organizational chart. Remember, just like with the title text, you can use the control bar to adjust the font and the size of the text, as well as center the text on each box. When complete, your canvas will look similar to the following screenshot:

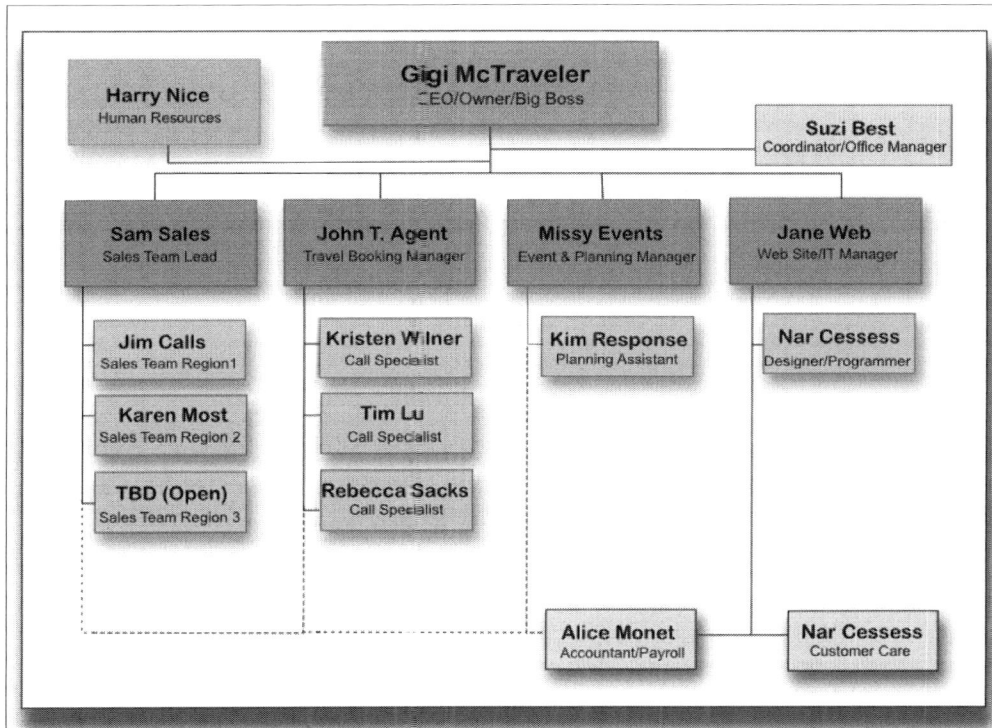

26. Make sure you save the file in the Inkscape SVG format—as organizational charts tend to change over time and ideally you could go back to this file and change it as necessary. If you need to save this file in another file format (.pdf, .eps, etc), use the **File** and **Save Copy** as option.

Flow charts

Just like organizational charts, flow charts are often used as internal corporate documents that document a process. They can also be used to illustrate technical processes. We'll create a very simple flow chart as follows for your reference when creating your own.

To be technically correct, there are standard shapes in flow charting. These are not always followed in all flow charts, but it is a great rule of thumb to try. Color coding is optional, but can make for great definition of ownership if needed. Here are some of the basics to get you started:

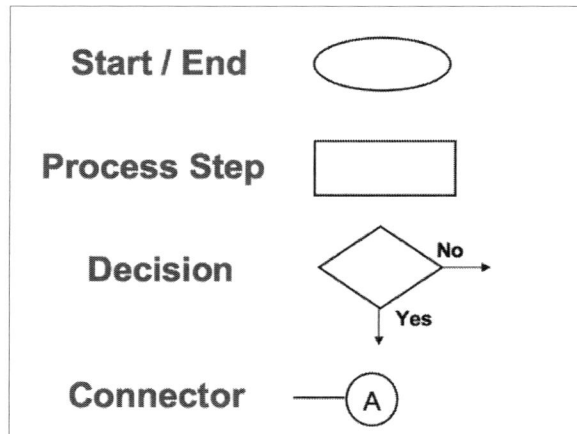

Also, before you start, it might be a good idea, to work with a subject matter expert (your client) to understand the process and sketch it out on paper before creating a flow chart in Inkscape. Then you can work through details on the process itself before creating color schemes and starting the flow chart design.

Here's a simple example of a flow chart for web development and deployment:

1. Open a new document in Inkscape.

2. By default your graphic will have a transparent background. If you don't want this—or prefer a specified background color like white, create a rectangle that covers most of the canvas.

3. Use the color palette to give the rectangle a white fill, and right click the Stroke Status Indicator and choose **Remove stroke**.

4. Create a new layer (*Shift + Ctrl + N*) called **Flow**. Use the standard flow chart shapes, and start creating your process flow. Use the circle and rectangle tool to create and position each step in the process (with the appropriate symbols) on the canvas.

5.   Use the Color Palette to add fill color to each object type.

6.   Select all of the flow objects. From the main menu select **Filters, Shadows and Glows,** and then **Drop Shadow.** Set **Blur Radius** to 2.0, **Opacity** to 80%, and **Vertical offset** to 2.0. Click **Apply.** A simple drop shadow will highlight each process object.

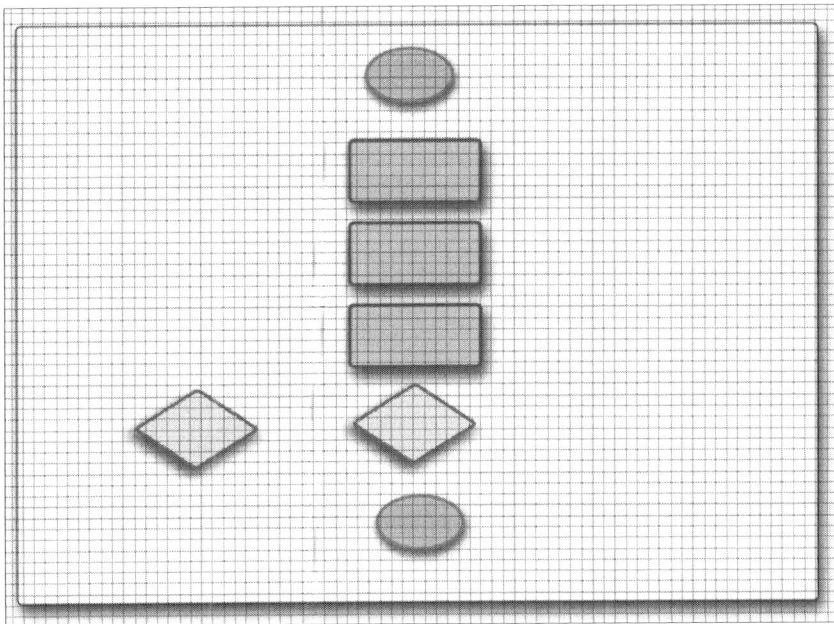

7. Then you'll need to create the connector lines. The easiest way to do this is using the Bezier tool. Select the Bezier tool in the Toolbar box.

8. Click the paraxial line mode in the Control bar in the Bezier tool to make 90 degree cornered paths. Using the Paraxial Line Mode will eliminate blurring or right angled lines.

9. To create Straight Paths use the *Ctrl + Left Click mouse* combination.

[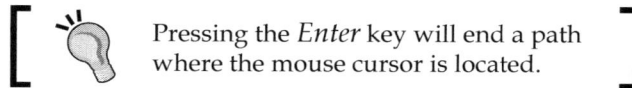 Pressing the *Enter* key will end a path where the mouse cursor is located.]

10. Continue creating paths to connect all parts of the process or flow chart.

11. If you want to add arrows or end markers, open the Fill and Stroke Dialog (*Shift + Ctrl + F*) and select the **Stroke Style** Tab. In the **End Marker** drop down box, choose an option.

12. When complete, your flow chart will look similar to the following screenshot:

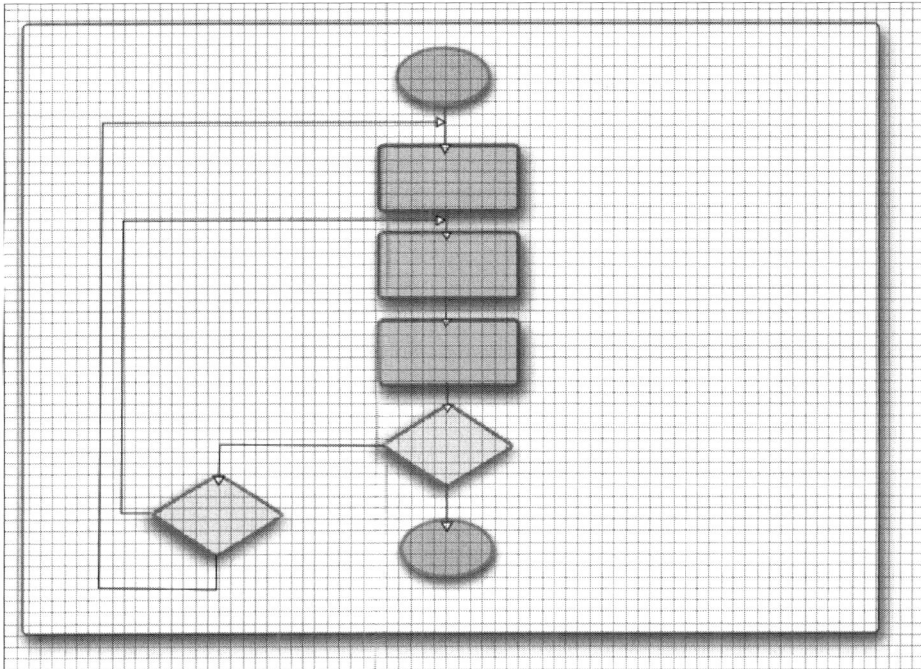

13. Let's add another layer (*Shift + Ctrl + N*) called Text.

14. From the Toolbar box, select the Create and Edit text tool. Place it within the first flow chart object and type its name.

15. In the control bar, select the font and size.

16. To make sure this text is centered, select the title, and the background object. Open the Align and Distribute dialog (*Shift + Ctrl + A*) and click the Center on Vertical Axis and then the Center on Horizontal Axis buttons.

17. For each flow object, you will want to create a name for it. Keep using the Create Text Tool (*F8*), clicking on the canvas where you want it to be placed, and type the flow step title.

18. As needed use the control bar to adjust the font and the size of the text and center the text on each object. When complete, your canvas will look similar to the following screenshot:

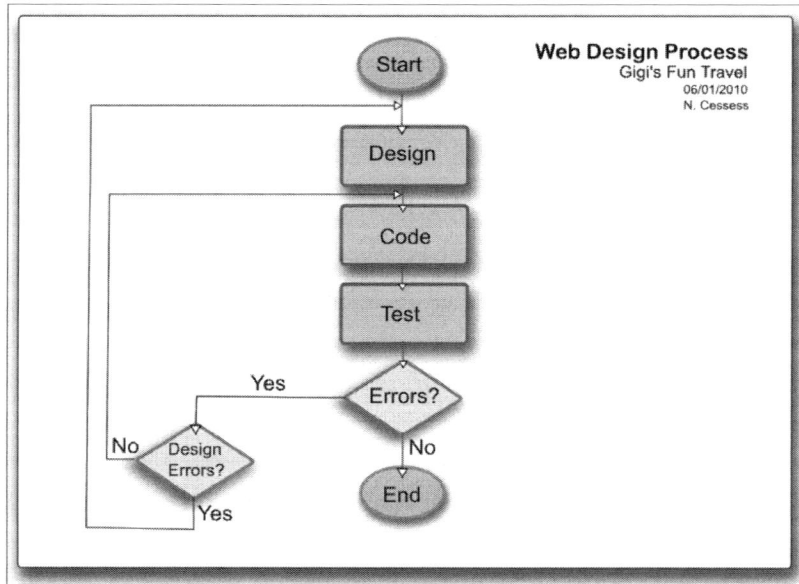

19. Save the file in case you need to do further editing. If you need to save this file in another file format (.pdf, .eps, etc), use the **File** and **Save Copy** as option.

Site maps

Lastly we are going to discuss site maps. As stated earlier in the chapter these are typically used on web site design projects in the planning stages. In fact, you will notice as we work through our example, that site maps are created (and often look a lot like) similarly to organization charts. As they should—there are hierarchical elements. Only in site maps, the lines or relationships are in the form of links to sub-pages in a web site.

Before starting, as with most of these diagrams and charts, map out with paper the site map. Mark the main site, links, or sub page menus seen there. Then map another layer of content pages below those, etc.

Again, we'll take a look at a simple example of how this would look once you move from a pencil sketch to Inkscape to create this type of diagram:

1. Open a new document in Inkscape (**File** and then **New** or *Ctrl + N*).

2. Using the *Shift + Ctrl + N* keyboard shortcut, create a new layer called Background.

3. Click the Rectangle tool in the Toolbar box and create a rectangle on your canvas. The rectangle should cover most of the canvas.

4. Use the Color palette to change the fill to white.

5. Within the Style Indicator, right click and select **Remove Stroke**.

6. Add a drop shadow to the rectangle. From the main menu, select **Filters**, **Shadows and Glows** and then **Drop Shadow**. Choose the desired settings and click **Apply**.

7. Create a new layer (*Shift + Ctrl + N*) called **Boxes**.

8. Next, use the rectangle tool and create a rectangular shape and center it along the top of the canvas. This will represent the main web page—or landing page—of your website.

9. Use the Tools Control bar to set the exact size of the box to be that of the canvas. Set the width (**W**) to 260 and the height (**H**) to 70.

10. Use the Color palette to choose a green fill color. Use your prepared color scheme to help know what color to use here.

11. In the Status bar, right click the Stroke setting and select **Remove Stroke**.

12. Give the rectangle a simple drop shadow. From the main menu select **Filters**, **Shadows and Glows**, and then **Drop Shadow**. Like the background, we set the **Blur Radius** to 2.0, **Opacity** to 80%, and **Vertical offset** to 2.0. Click **Apply**.

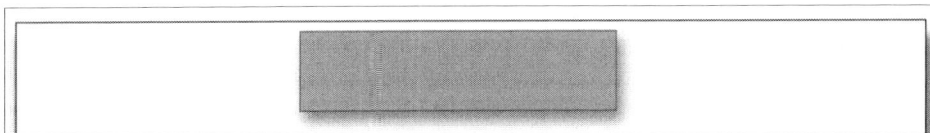

13. Create all of the underlying pages of the web site. Use a series of rectangles, and in additional fill colors with the rectangle tool in the Toolbar Controls. When this step is completed, your canvas will look something like the following screenshot:

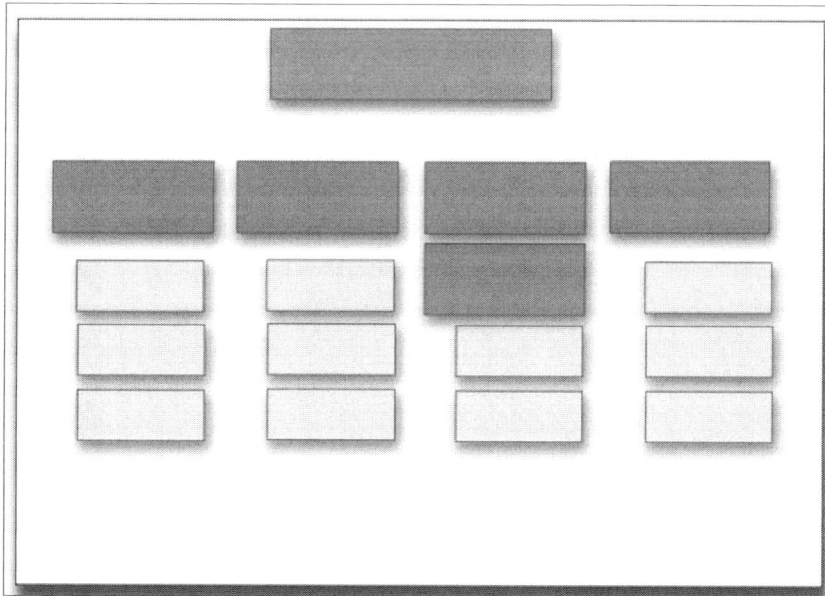

14. Using the Duplicate (*Ctrl + D*) feature can help you create the same size and color rectangles throughout the chart.

15. Select all the rectangles on the canvas, and give them a drop shadow. From the main menu select **Filters, Shadows and Glows** and then **Drop Shadow**. Like the background, we set the **Blur Radius** to 2.0, **Opacity** to 80%, and **Vertical offset** to 2.0. Click **Apply**.

16. Now we'll create the paths to show the links between the web pages. Create a new layer (*Shift + Ctrl + N*) called **Paths**.

17. In the Toolbar box, use the Bezier Pen tool to draw paths between rectangles to show web links. Click the paraxial line mode in the Control bar in the Bezier tool to make 90 degree cornered paths. Using the Paraxial Line Mode will eliminate blurring or right-angled lines.

18. To create Straight Paths use the *Ctrl + Left* click mouse combination.

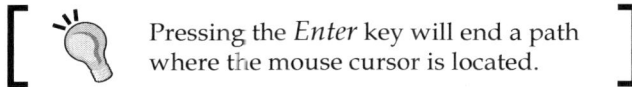

[🔦 Pressing the *Enter* key will end a path where the mouse cursor is located.]

19. Your canvas will lock similar to the following screenshot:

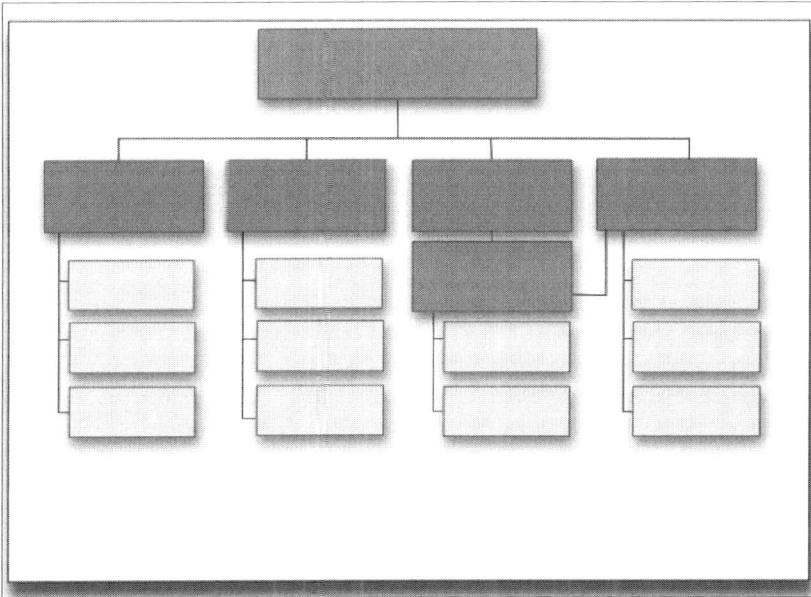

20. Lastly, it is time to start page titles into the chart. From the Toolbar box, select the Create and Edit text tool. Place it within the main web site rectangle and type its name.

21. In the control bar, select the font and size.

22. To make sure this text is centered, select the title, and the rectangle object. Open the Align and Distribute dialog (*Shift + Ctrl + A*) and click the Center on Vertical Axis and then the Center on Horizontal Axis buttons.

23. For each web page object, you will want to create a name for it. Keep using the Create Text Tool (*F8*), clicking on the canvas where you want it to be placed, and type the flow step title.

24. As needed use the control bar to adjust the font and the size of the text and center the text on each object. When complete, your canvas will look similar to the following screenshot:

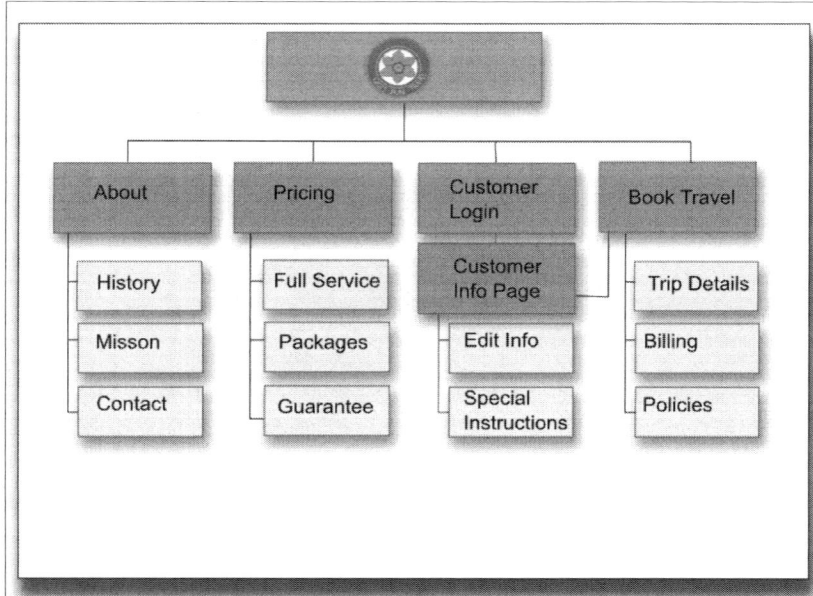

25. Again, always make sure you save your work in the Inkscape SVG format so that you can edit any of these files at a later date. Then you can choose the **File** and **Save Copy as** option to save the file in another format like PDF or a PNG image to share with others.

Exporting for use within a web page

For these sorts of graphics in particular it is very important to provide SVG forms to the web programmers. Particularly for site maps, you might want to link content from that image directly to that we page for easier navigation. You can do this using the SVG XML editor (we'll learn details of this in Chapter 10).

To save in SVG, it is a simple Save As function from the main menu — as you have done throughout this chapter saving your graphics for possible future use. But remember you need to hand off the SVG file and any other graphic file you used in the creation of the SVG to help aid in this process.

To export in PNG—as you have many times—follow the instructions we've always reviewed:

1. Open the SVG file.
2. From the main menu select **File** and then **Export Bitmap**.
3. On the Export dialog, click **Page**, and then click **Browse** to find a save location, and then click **Export** to save your files in PNG format.

As always, when providing files to programmers include:

- The PNG image files you just exported from your design.
- And the source Inkscape SVG file of your logo, buttons, or logo and the design mock up with all images used in the creation of it. That way, they see how they all work together and build it as designed.

Summary

In this chapter we learned about diagrams, charts, and site maps—including the basics for what each type of diagram is, what it would be used for, and then how best to create each of them in Inkscape. Some small types to help create more professional and unique looking designs were also offered as well as the basics, exporting rules, and more.

Up next we will discuss blogs and storefronts and how best to design for them using your web design skills learned so far with Inkscape.

8
Designing for Blogs and Storefronts

On the Internet today one can find varying websites—some are personal sites, others are corporate, informational, instructional, and more. More commonly you can find personal blogs and small business storefronts. These two types of websites offer unique capabilities of creating the entire site with templates—or basic designs that are common throughout them.

Blogs contain entries or posts that can be anything from commentary of life events, videos and pictures to anything else that can be 'posted' online. Blog posts are in reverse-chronological order and allow readers to provide comments and sometime ratings. Sometimes a blog is the entire website, or a blog can be a subset of the entire site. Another critical element of a blog is comments. Readers expect to be able to leave comments about the posts and sometimes rate the content. Thus, the posts themselves and the way they are displayed on a site are important, as it is the main content portion of the site. Clever designs allow for the common elements around the posts to stay the same and consistent, while allowing posts to be updated (and aggregated) frequently.

Small business **storefronts,** or any site that sells a commodity, often has an area that allows you to search through its products and then purchase them through a "shopping cart". These storefronts then need a well designed area to be able to view products, get the specifications, and then add the products to a cart to checkout. It is a process that would be repeated often and used whenever a product is purchased.

In this chapter we hope to provide:

- Web design principles for blogs and storefronts.

- Overview of RSS and ATOM feeds examples of designs for these two types of websites.

- How you can use Inkscape to create basic design templates that can be used with **Cascading Style Sheets** (**CSS**), HTML, and HTML5 in the final implementation. CSS are used with the HTML/XML coding to define the look and formatting of an entire website. One style sheet can be created that determines fonts, colors, spacing, placement, and more—reducing complexity and repetition in the coding of the pages themselves.

Web design principles for blogs and storefronts

As with general web design there are some guidelines that can help you create effective, clean, and inspired blog and storefront designs. The web design basics (as described in *Chapter 2, Designing Site Layout Mockups*) should also be taken into account: proximity, alignment, repetition, and contrast—but also here are a few other pointers.

Keeping it simple

For blogs, there are more widgets and plugins you can add into your blog than you have space for—and more than is ever really needed. Be particular and choosy. Use only those that make sense for the type of reader you want to attract. Otherwise it becomes visual clutter. Choose sidebar features wisely and keep it to a bare minimum. Some basics are: a picture or more information about yourself, how to contact you (if you like), links to other similar blogs links to some of your past posts (favorites, archives, most mentioned), and links to any other websites you contribute to and/or own.

When designing storefronts or any websites where your end goal is to have someone purchase an item—don't distract a user from their main goal of purchasing an item. If you add in sidebars with too much distraction, you'll lose the ever-dwindling window of opportunity for a purchase. Keep the important items front and center: a shopping cart, account information, check out.

Identifiable

You have about a five second window to attract *and keep* a reader on your website. So, use those seconds wisely and give your viewers everything they need to know about you and your blog or store within that first five seconds.

How can you do this? Use your header wisely. A graphical title, tagline that is prominent and expressive can do it all, and quickly. This should be placed in the "header" location of your web design.

When blogging this is critical, since most blogs are text-based, most viewers won't take the time to read but a few sentences unless you entice them to stay on your site and read along for a while.

For any storefront, if you keep your company name, and a graphical representation of what they might find in your online store, then you too will encourage a casual browser to "click around" and see what else you have for them to browse. This also increases your chances at making a purchase.

Making your site navigationally easy

Everyone hates a website where they can't figure out "where to go next". So make your links and navigation very easy to find. Top or sidebar locations are the most obvious and natural locations for these, and probably the best locations for any of the key places you want any visitor to your site to see.

You can also incorporate other forms of navigation like breadcrumb trails, tree menus, and submenus. **Breadcrumbs** are visual navigational elements. They show the 'trail' of where you are in the site, and how you arrived at your current location. Most often breadcrumb trails are near the top of the web page. An example of breadcrumb trails is seen in the following screenshot from the online Inkscape Manual `http://tavmjong.free.fr/INKSCAPE/MANUAL/html/index.php`:

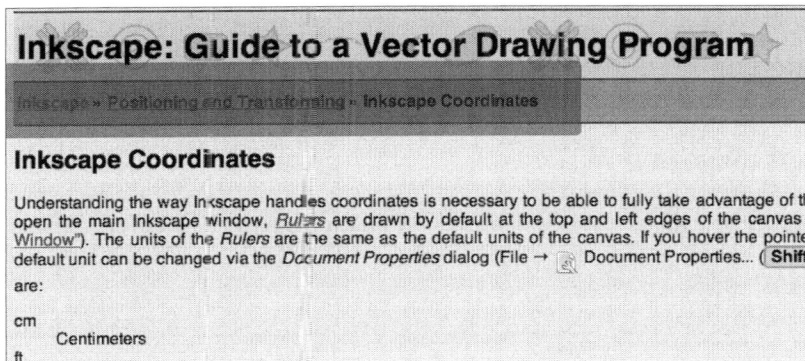

An example of a tree menu is as follows:

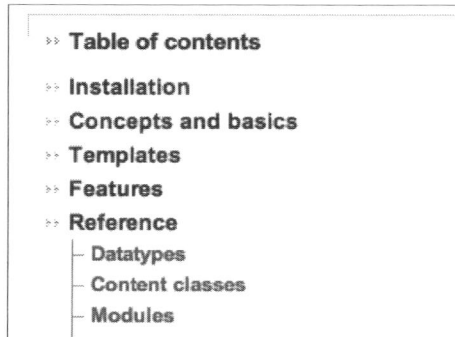

Tree menus are a bit more complicated. They show the main level web pages and then, when clicked, expand to show the next "tier" of pages. Each level can continue to expand if needed.

As seen in the tree menu, main level pages can expand to submenus. This could also be done in a drop down in any horizontal-based navigation as well, like the example shown below:

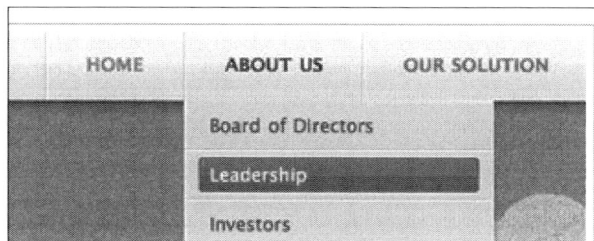

No matter what navigational elements used, the key is to keep them simple and identifiable throughout your web page design and obvious that a user can use these links to get where they need to be on your website.

Feeds and social networking links

More and more people today are taking advantage of RSS feeds. What are RSS feeds? **RSS (Really Simple Syndication)** feeds are a way to continually broadcast (or publish) your blog entries. These feeds are in a standardized XML format and pull the metadata tags you assigned when publishing your blog post and display them in "readers" for others to automatically receive.

Feed readers allow subscribers (those who want to favor your site), to receive updates as soon as you post any new information, in this case, every time you would release a new blog post. When using an RSS reader, the user needs to enter you blog's feed URL to complete a subscription. Then, the RSS reader checks these subscribed feeds' URLs regularly for new updates and then alerts them when new podcasts are available.

So, how do you create an RSS feed for your blog?

- For a website with hosting where you have your blog as part of an entire site, you can create RSS feeds by using a simple RSS feed provider, such as FeedBurner (www.feedburner.com). These services are free, and once you provide a link to your blog, they do the rest automatically for you.

  You'll have to set up an account, and then make a note of the blog RSS feed URL (it typically ends in XML). Then on your website, you can offer a link to subscribe to your blog feed.

- When using a blogging service, there are usually ways to automatically set up RSS feeds to your blog entries. In fact, most blog software has two types of RSS feeds links built in. These can be found in the <head> element of the HTML. There are also many orange 'RSS' buttons that can be easily set up and used within the design itself. Explore your blogging service provider site and set up to determine how best to set up RSS feeds.

Either way you set up a feed, make sure you display the RSS feed link prominently. Put it in the sidebar, under each blog post, up near the titles. And give it a distinct link title like: Subscribe to my blog or RSS feed or something similar.

RSS feeds are most commonly used for blogs, but as a storefront or online merchandiser, you might set up you own blog announcement area where you would want to announce new products or features of your online store. This would be an easy way for your shoppers to stay tuned to your latest offerings.

An alternative to RSS feeds are Atom feeds. Atom stands for Atom Syndication Format which is an XML language used for web feeds. This differs from RSS feeds that focus on post updates; web feeds focus on allowing software programs to check for updates on an entire website. The site owner can use a content management system or other special software that publishes a feed of all the new content that then can be used by a feed reader, another program, or fed into other content management systems.

Making checkout easy

Design the checkout process of your online store to be as easy as entering brief information and clicking a few buttons. Ideally you need to have the shopping cart, checkout, continue shopping, and my account access available from any page within the site. Then, any potential purchase could also be made from any page on the site as well.

Work with the programmers of the shopping cart to create the most efficient checkout process possible. Give them design options that can allow for the fewest number of screens, but that captures the critical information from the purchaser.

Creating Web templates in Inkscape

Blogs and storefronts have some different elements when designing, however they also have "pages" within them that use standard items, those that repeat over time.

Blogs have posts that all have (at least):

- headings/titles
- content in the body
- options to comment

Storefronts have some of the following:

- lists of items to purchase
- prices
- descriptions
- ratings/comments
- checkouts or shopping baskets

And since these items are common on a number of the website pages, it can use templates for the design. Much like how you designed your first site in Chapter 1 of this book—you can create a site based on a template. Here are two quick examples based on each type of site in this chapter.

Designing for blogs

Some common parts of many blog site are: the blog header or banner, a sidebar with recent posts (or archives), about section, recent posts, blog roll and/or links section, a main content section that will contain all of the blog posts, then links to their relevant comments, and a footer of the site. Of course you can get as fancy as you would like here, or as simple, but let's design a site based on these simple sections. Here's how it's done:

1. Open Inkscape, and create a new document. From the file menu, select **File**, **New**, and **Desktop_800x600**.

2. When open, create a new layer (*Shift + Ctrl + N*) and call it **Basic Layout**.

3. Use the **Rectangle Tool** to draw rectangles for each of your layout areas in your blog design.

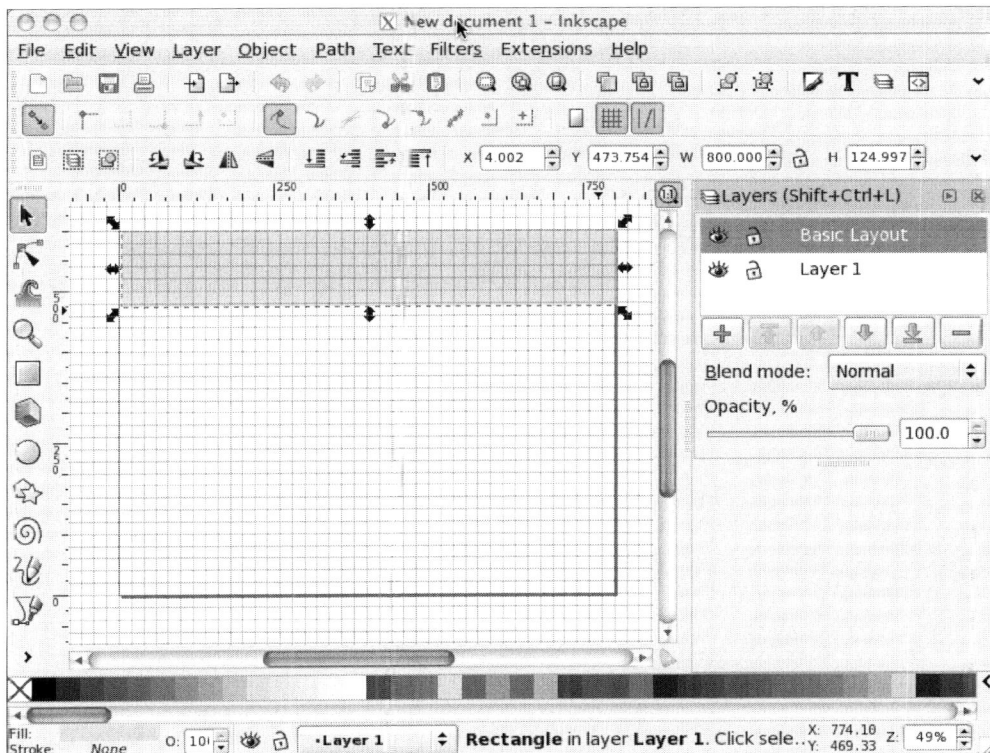

4. For now, use different shades of gray for each area so you can easily distinguish between them at a glance. To change the fill color of a particular rectangle, left click the rectangle and choose a gray shade for the rectangle. Or drag the gray shade from the color palette onto the rectangle.

5. Use sharp edged (not rounded) rectangles. If you need to change to sharp, click the **Make Corners Sharp** button in the Tool Controls Bar.

6. Make sure your rectangle shapes do not have an outline or stroke. Use the *Shift* + Left click keypad shortcut to open the Stroke dialog and choose **No Color** (the icon with an X) to delete the stroke.

7. Position the rectangles so there are no white spaces in-between them.

8. From the main menu choose **Object** and then **Align and Distribute**. In the **Remove Overlaps** section, click the icon. This makes sure that the bounding boxes around each object don't over lap each other and place the objects tangent to each other.

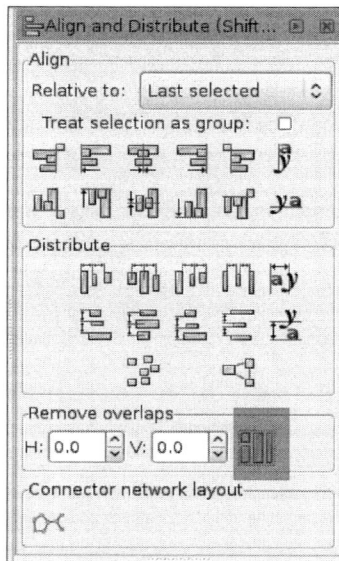

9. Use the Tool Controls Bar **W** (width): number field to apply a setting of 800.0 px so the Header fills the entire width of the web page.

10. Continue using the steps described to add rectangles for all areas shown below in the rough layout of the blog page we'll be creating.

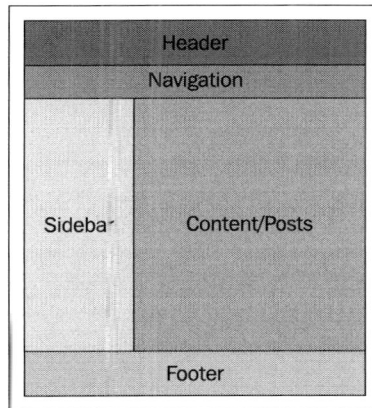

11. Once all of your areas are blocked out on the canvas, we'll need to convert the current rectangles into guides so we can use the guides when creating our web page layout graphics in the next chapter. We can easily keep the Basic Layout Export layer intact; we need to copy all of the rectangles in this layer. On the main menu, select **Edit** and then **Select All** (or use the keyboard shortcut keys *Ctrl + A*).

12. Then select **Edit** and **Duplicate** (or use the keyboard shortcut *Ctrl + D*) to duplicate all of the elements in this layer.

13. Now you are ready to convert these current shapes into guides. First, select all the rectangles in the top (duplicate) layout. Do this by clicking a rectangle and then holding the *Shift* key on your keypad. Then click/select the next rectangle.

14. When you have all rectangles selected, from the main menu select **Object** and then **Object to Guide**. Your duplicate rectangles will be removed from the canvas and replaced with blue guides. To better see the guides, turn off the grid (from the main menu choose **View** and **Grid**) and hide the basic layout layer (click the eye icon).

15. Create a new layer (*Shift + Ctrl + N*) called Background.

16. Use the rectangle tool to draw a background that fills the entire canvas. Use the control bar, to set the width to 800 and the height to 600.

17. Use the Color Palette to choose a fill color of white.

18. In the Status bar, right-click the Stroke setting and select **Remove Stroke**.

19. Create a new layer (*Shift + Ctrl + N*) called Header.

20. Click the Create and Edit tool and enter the header title as shown in the following screenshot. Remember to use the control bar to adjust the font type and size.

21. Then, still using the Create and Edit tool, type the sub-title as shown below and, again use the control bar to adjust the font type and size.

22. Create a new layer (*Shift + Ctrl + N*) called Navigation.

23. Now we need to import the icons that we have created in *Chapter 6, Building Icons, Buttons, and Logos*. From the main menu, select **File** and then **Import.** Select the SVG file for the icon and then place it on the canvas. Repeat this until you have all five icons on the canvas.

24. Use the rectangle tool to draw the horizontal bars below the title and then below the navigation icons. Use the Color Palette to choose a fill color for the rectangles. For our example, we're using a turquoise color.

25. Select both rectangles, and then in the Status bar, right-click the Stroke setting and select **Remove Stroke**.

26. With the rectangles still selected open the Align and Distribute dialog (*Shift + Ctrl + A*) and click the Center on Vertical Axis button.

27. Select all of the icons and then open the Align and Distribute dialog (*Shift + Ctrl + A*) and click the Distribute Centers Equidistantly Horizontally button.

28. Next we will create the sidebar content. Most of this will be the links to help with navigating to previous posts or static content—content that doesn't change. Create a new layer (*Shift + Ctrl + N*) called Sidebar.

29. Import a photograph (**File** and then **Import**).

30. Place it on the upper left side of the page. Use your guides to place it appropriately on the page.

31. Select the Create and Edit tool, and drag it across your canvas in the area you want to add a block of text to create a textbox. Then start typing placeholder text for an author bio.

32. Use the control bar to adjust font styles and sizes.

33. Again use the guides for left alignment placement.

34. Continue to use the Create and Edit to create any Headings and other text content on the left sidebar. Note that Inkscape does not support bullets or numbers. So any "bullets" will need to be created manually with dashes (-) or importing graphics.

35. Your blog web page should look similar to the following screenshot:

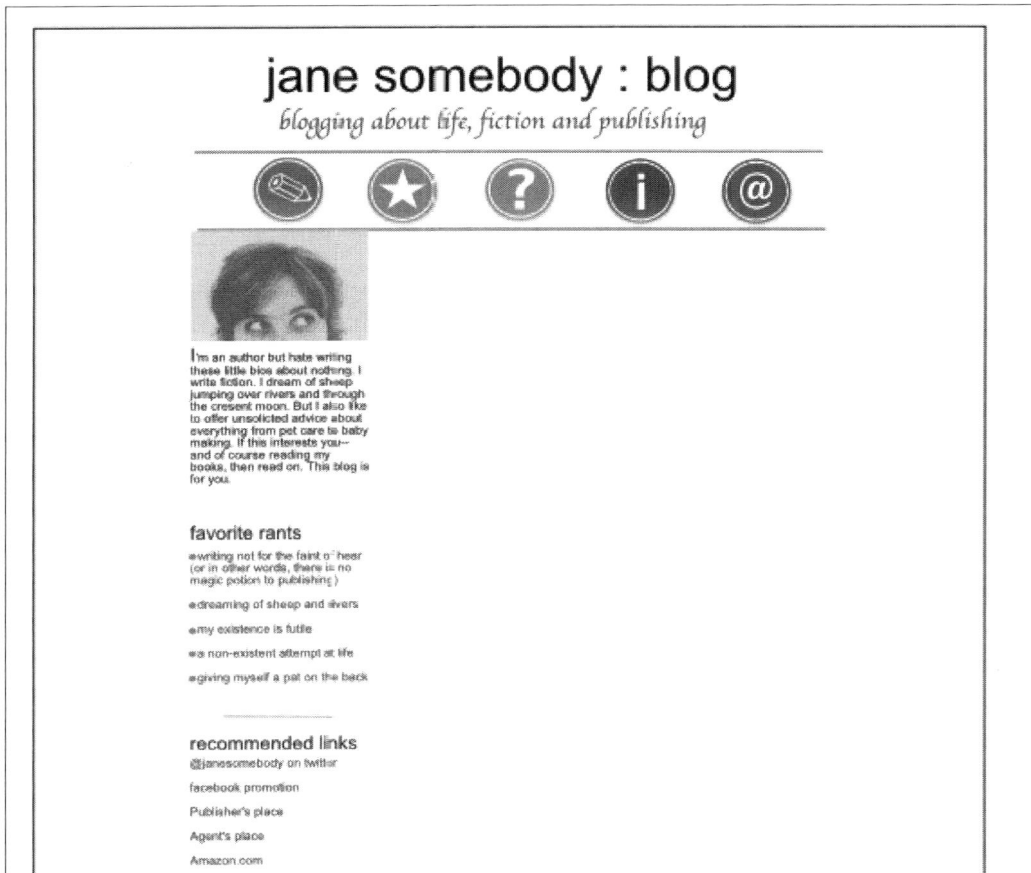

36. Now it is time to create the look of the content portion of the site — where the blog posts will appear. Create a new layer (*Shift + Ctrl + N*) called Blog Post.

37. Just like with the sidebar text, use the Create and Edit text tool to create text and use the control bar to adjust fonts and sizes. Start with a heading.

38. Then with the Create and Edit text tool selected, drag it across the screen to create a textbox. Add in dummy text or write some placeholder blog post. Again, use the control bar to adjust font and size of the text.

39. Select the heading and the blog post text and align it within your guides. Or use the Align and Distribute dialog (*Shift + Ctrl + A*) to align items on the page correctly.

40. Now it is time to create the comment, permalink and share this link text. Create a new layer (*Shift + Ctrl + N*) called Blog Post Footer.

41. Again select the Create and Edit text tool, and type: **comment | 0 comments | permalink | share this post**.

42. Use the control bar to adjust font and size as needed.

43. Then use the color palette to change the text to red.

44. If desired, use the rectangle tool to draw the horizontal bars to show a break between blog posts. Use the color palette to choose a fill color for the rectangles. For our example, we're using turquoise color.

45. You can save the file, or add additional post examples. Use Steps 37 – 44 to do a second blog post. Your page should now look something like the following example:

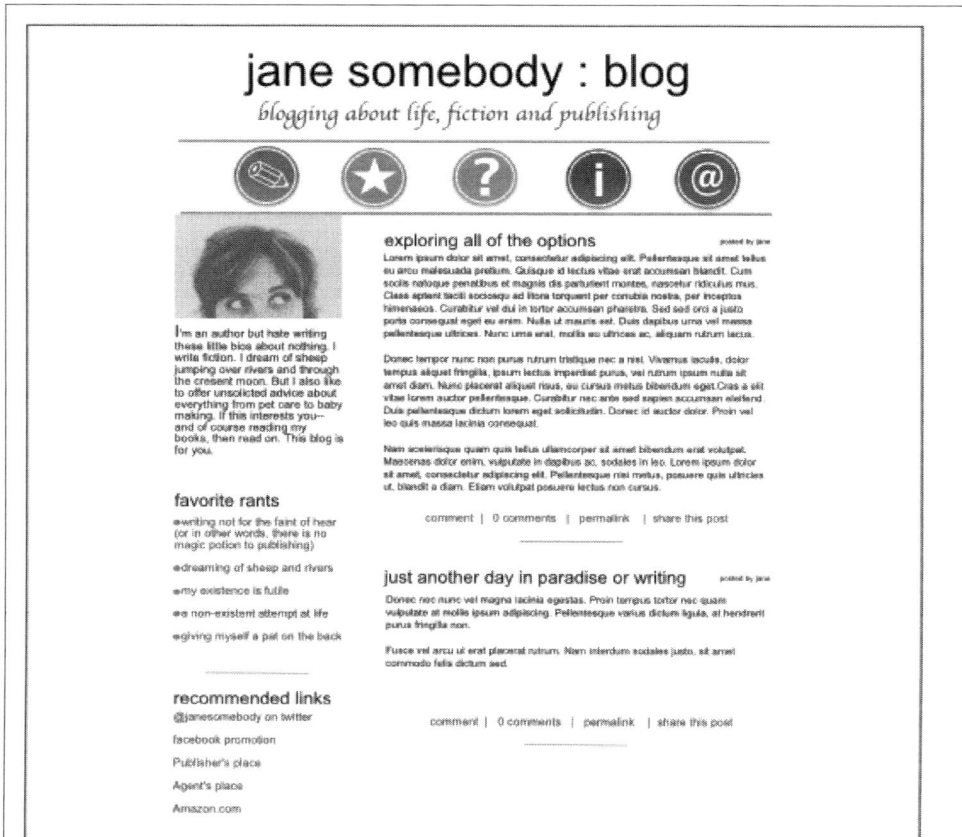

46. There will likely also be a sub-page of this content that will show an individual blog post. We can design that page, based on how we want it to look here—watch for it in the next section.

47. Finally, for this page, let's add blog footer with some copyright information to see a completed blog design. Create a new layer (*Shift + Ctrl + N*) called Footer.

48. Select the horizontal bar under the navigation icon. From the main menu select **Edit** and then **Duplicate**.

49. Select the duplicate rectangle and use the guides to place it at the footer area of your web page.

50. Select the Create and Edit text tool and type a copyright attribution statement. In the following example we entered: © **2010 Jane Somebody | All rights reserved**.

51. Select both the rectangle in the footer and the copyright text and open the Align and Distribute dialog (*Shift + Ctrl + A*). Click the Center on Vertical Axis button to center the footer content.

jane somebody : blog

blogging about life, fiction and publishing

exploring all of the options

posted by jane

Lorem ipsum dolor sit amet, consectetur adipiscing elit. Pellentesque sit amet tellus eu arcu malesuada pretium. Quisque id lectus vitae erat accumsan blandit. Cum sociis natoque penatibus et magnis dis parturient montes, nascetur ridiculus mus. Class aptent taciti sociosqu ad litora torquent per conubia nostra, per inceptos himenaeos. Curabitur vel dui in tortor accumsan pharetra. Sed sed orci a justo porta consequat eget eu enim. Nulla ut mauris est. Duis dapibus urna vel massa pellentesque ultrices. Nunc urna erat, mollis eu ultrices ac, aliquam rutrum lacus.

Donec tempor nunc non purus rutrum tristique nec a nisl. Vivamus iaculis, dolor tempus aliquet fringilla, ipsum lectus imperdiet purus, vel rutrum ipsum nulla sit amet diam. Nunc placerat aliquet risus, eu cursus metus bibendum eget.Cras a elit vitae lorem auctor pellentesque. Curabitur nec ante sed sapien accumsan eleifend. Duis pellentesque dictum lorem eget sollicitudin. Donec id auctor dolor. Proin vel leo quis massa lacinia consequat.

Nam scelerisque quam quis tellus ullamcorper sit amet bibendum erat volutpat. Maecenas dolor enim, vulputate in dapibus ac, sodales in leo. Lorem ipsum dolor sit amet, consectetur adipiscing elit. Pellentesque nisi metus, posuere quis ultricies ut, blandit a diam. Etiam volutpat posuere lectus non cursus.

comment | 0 comments | permalink | share this post

just another day in paradise or writing

posted by jane

Donec nec nunc vel magna lacinia egestas. Proin tempus tortor nec quam vulputate at mollis ipsum adipiscing. Pellentesque varius dictum ligula, at hendrerit purus fringilla non.

Fusce vel arcu ut erat placerat rutrum. Nam interdum sodales justo, sit amet commodo felis dictum sed.

comment | 0 comments | permalink | share this post

deadlines and other book nonesense

posted by jane

Vivamus tempor tincidunt elementum. Donec ut sapien sit amet lorem mollis viverra. Duis aliquam fermentum ultrices. Etiam porta sem id nisl laoreet dapibus. Phasellus tincidunt eros sed odio eleifend quis iaculis erat vulputate. Mauris sed interdum quam.

Fusce ipsum nisl, scelerisque ut dignissim eu, sagittis et nulla. Maecenas sodales neque sed ante vehicula fermentum. Pellentesque eu neque eget ipsum condimentum suscipit. Nullam sit amet nulla augue, quis luctus urna. Vivamus mollis imperdiet cursus.

Praesent consequat, augue quis malesuada cursus, purus eros tempus quam, sed volutpat turpis ipsum a sem. Vivamus ac metus vitae nisl tristique porttitor. Fusce gravida consectetur condimentum. Cras sit amet arcu eget nulla bibendum aliquam. Maecenas dictum orci vel arcu luctus nec imperdiet erat tempor.Fusce bibendum ornare sagittis. Nunc ultricies dui a massa blandit bibendum. Aliquam tempus vulputate sem, sed pellentesque neque pharetra nec. Phasellus at velit non velit auctor porttitor a at sapien. Nam consectetur erat nec eros vestibulum porta. Proin sit amet purus eget nisl euismod ultrices eget hendrerit ipsum. Curabitur consectetur suscipit tincidunt. Nulla dignissim justo at lacus lobortis fringilla sodales lorem accumsan.

Vivamus convallis dictum felis ut aliquet. Cras eros mi, iaculis eu imperdiet vitae, faucibus sed eros. Mauris et augue risus.Nam ut risus vitae ipsum consectetur cursus quis ac velit. Vestibulum malesuada iaculis est pellentesque dapibus. Fusce sapien sapien, iaculis eget viverra rhoncus, vestibulum a sem. Ut tempus odio eu nunc tincidunt ut gravida nunc iaculis. Pellentesque habitant morbi tristique senectus et netus et malesuada fames ac turpis egestas.

comment | 0 comments | permalink | share this post

I'm an author but hate writing these little bios about nothing. I write fiction. I dream of sheep jumping over rivers and through the cresent moon. But I also like to offer unsolicted advice about everything from pet care to baby making. If this interests you—and of course reading my books, then read on. This blog is for you.

favorite rants

- writing not for the faint of hear (or in other words, there is no magic potion to publishing)
- dreaming of sheep and rivers
- my existence is futile
- a non-existent attempt at life
- giving myself a pat on the back

recommended links

@janesomebody on twitter

facebook promotion

Publisher's place

Agent's place

Amazon.com

As stated in Step 46, there will also likely be a "sub-page" used in a blog to show each individual post as it's unique web address (if you want to link to the one blog post instead of the dynamic stream posts). Here's what this page would look like:

jane somebody : blog

blogging about life, fiction and publishing

exploring all of the options posted by jane

I'm an author but hate writing these little bios about nothing. I write fiction. I dream of sheep jumping over rivers and through the cresent moon. But I also like to offer unsolicted advice about everything from pet care to baby making. If this interests you—and of course reading my books, then read on. This blog is for you.

Lorem ipsum dolor sit amet, consectetur adipiscing elit. Pellentesque sit amet tellus eu arcu malesuada pretium. Quisque id lectus vitae erat accumsan blandit. Cum sociisnatoque penatibus et magnis dis parturient montes, nascetur ridiculus mus. Classaaptent taciti sociosqu ad litora torquent per conubia nostra, per inceptos himenaeos. Curabitur vel dui in tortor accumsan pharetra. Sed sed orci a justo porta consequat eget eu enim. Nulla ut mauris est. Duis dapibus urna vel massa pellentesque ultrices. Nunc urna erat, mollis eu ultrices ac, aliquam rutrum lacus.

Donec tempor nunc non purus rutrum tristique nec a nisl. Vivamus iaculis, dolor tempus aliquet fringilla, ipsum lectus imperdiet purus, vel rutrum ipsum nulla sit amet diam. Nunc placerat aliquet risus, eu cursus metus bibendum eget.Cras a elit vitae lorem auctor pellentesque. Curabitur nec ante sed sapien accumsan eleifend. Duis pellentesque dictum lorem eget sollicitudin. Donec id auctor dolor. Proin vel leo quis massa lacinia consequat.

Nam scelerisque quam quis tellus ullamcorper sit amet bibendum erat volutpat. Maecenas dolor enim, vulputate in dapibus ac, sodales in leo. Lorem ipsum dolor sit amet, consectetur adipiscing elit. Pellentesque nisi metus, posuere quis ultricies ut, blandit a diam. Etiam volutpat posuere lectus non cursus.

favorite rants

●writing not for the faint of hear (or in other words, there is no magic potion to publishing)

●dreaming of sheep and rivers

●my existence is futile

●a non-existent attempt at life

●giving myself a pat on the back

comment | 2 comments | permalink | share this post

comments

posted by **writerwannabe** at 12:04am 01 june 2010

Nunc placerat aliquet risus, eu cursus metus bibendum eget.Cras a elit vitae lorem auctor pellentesque. Curabitur nec ante sed sapien accumsan eleifend. Duis pellentesque dictum lorem eget sollicitudin. Donec id auctor dolor. Proin vel leo quis massa lacinia consequat.

posted by **miss_WRITE** at 2:47pm 01 june 2010

Curabitur nec ante sed sapien accumsan eleifend. Duis pellentesque dictum lorem eget sollicitudin. Donec id auctor dolor. Proin vel leo quis massa lacinia consequat.

recommended links

@janesomebody on twitter

facebook promotion

Publisher's place

Agent's place

Amazon.com

As you can see, it looks very much like the main blog page, just without any posts before it, or after it. And in this case, we display the comments on this post directly instead of just making it a link.

To modify the existing web page file to match the previous image, you would:

1. Open the existing file in Inkscape.

2. From the main menu select **File** and then **Save a Copy**. Give this a new file name.

3. Delete any sample blog posts below the first one.

4. Use the Create and Edit text tool to create the comments, headings, and text.

5. Re-align all text appropriately with guides and the Align and Distribute dialog (*Shift + Ctrl + A*).

6. Save the file again to save your work.

Designing a storefront and merchandise pages

As discussed, when creating item pages for an online store, you often use a grid system to show off items that your store is selling in sort of a catalog fashion. These pages would also include prices, brief descriptions, a way to add them to the shopping cart, a link to a return, or purchasing policies. Below is a wireframe on how you could design a merchant store based on a grid. We'll keep this example to wireframes (black and white drawings) to show that elements are based on a grid, and as an example of a fast and easy mock up to start. But remember header graphics, shopping cart graphics, product pictures, and more are always added into a design mock up at the next phase to get approvals and "test" the design.

1. Again, let's start with a basic area layout in a new document in Inkscape. Open Inkscape, and create a new document. From the file menu, select **File**, **New**, and **Desktop_800x600**.

2. When open, create a new layer (*Shift + Ctrl + N*) and call it Background.

3. Use the rectangle tool to draw a background that fills the entire canvas. Use the control bar to set the width to 800 and height to 600.

4. Use the Color Palette to choose a fill color of white.

5. In the Status bar, right-click the Stroke setting and select **Remove Stroke**.

6. Create a new layer (*Shift + Ctrl + N*) called Header.

7. Use the **Rectangle Tool** to draw a rectangle for the background of your header area. Use the control panel to make sure the width is exactly 800 pixels.

8. Use the Color Palette to choose a fill color of gray.

9. Next use the **Rectangle Tool** to draw a rectangle as a placeholder for the company logo. Place it in the left side of the header. Use the Color Palette to choose a fill color of gray and keep a stroke of 1.

10. Use the text tool to put in a placeholder company name and some navigational elements. Remember to use the Align and Distribute dialog (*Shift + Ctrl + A*) to adjust for spacing, alignment, and centering.

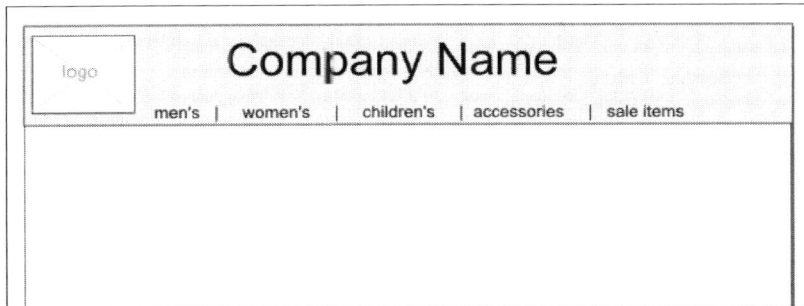

11. Next let's add in the header and footer locations. Create a new layer (*Shift + Ctrl + N*) called Footer.

12. Use the rectangle tool to create a rectangle along the bottom of the page. Use the Color Palette to choose a fill color of gray.

13. In the control bar, make sure the width of this rectangle is exactly 800 pixels.

14. Select the Create and Edit text tool and type some footer text. Since this is placeholder text, just make sure it looks about the same length as a copyright attribution.

15. Select the text and open the Align and Distribute dialog (*Shift + Ctrl + A*). Click the Center on the Horizontal Axis icon to center the text.

16. Now we can add in the "grid" of products to give it a catalog feel. Create a new layer (*Shift + Ctrl + N*) called product display.

17. Use the rectangle tool to create a square. Use the Color Palette to choose a fill color of gray.

18. Use the Bezier tool to create two lines to make a cross in the middle of the square.

19. Then use the Create and Edit text tool to type: Product Photography. Use the color palette to change the text color to a gray color.

20. Select the square and the text, then open the Align and Distribute dialog (*Shift + Ctrl + A*). In the relative to drop down, choose first selected, and then click the Center on the Vertical Axis icon to center the textbox.

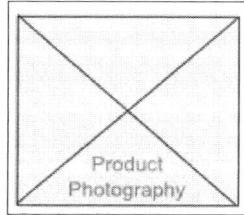

21. Below this square, let's add some placeholder product information. Select the Create and Edit text tool and create a textbox (click, hold, drag, and then let go of mouse).

    Type: Product Name

    Price: $12.99

22. Using the control bar, adjust font and size.

23. Now select the square, the two lines, Product Photography text and product information text. Select the first item, then use *Shift* + Click to select multiple items.

24. Press *Ctrl + G* (or from the main menu select **Object,** then **Group**) to group the items so they can be treated as a single object.

25. With this group object selected, from the main menu select **Edit, Clone,** and then **Create Tiled Clone**.

26. Select the *Shift* tab, and set **Shift X**, per column and **Shift Y**, per row to 15%. Also set **Rows, columns** to **2 x 4**.

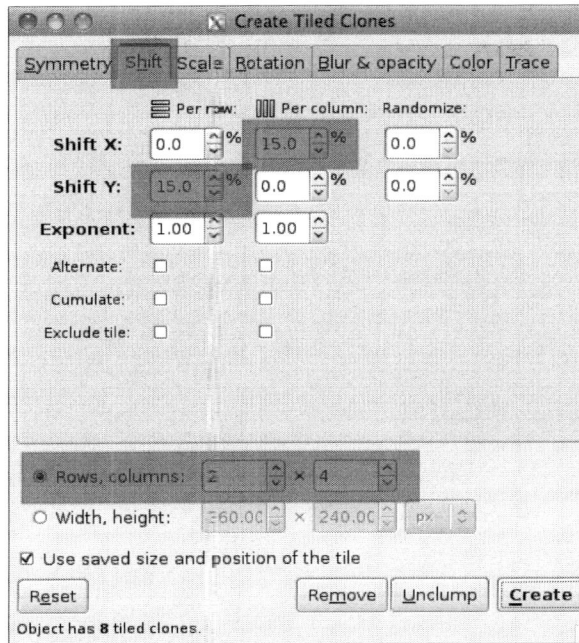

27. Click **Create**.

    Your product image and information is replicated into a 2 x 4 grid, spaced evenly on the canvas.

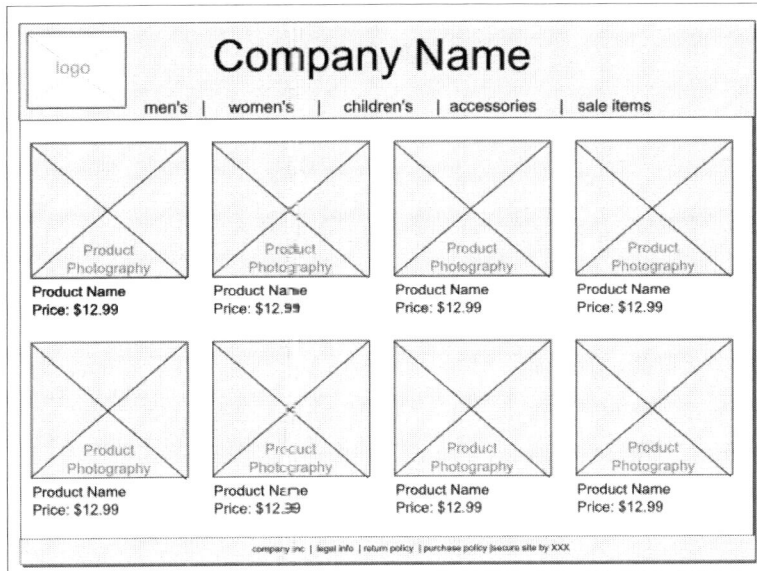

28. Let's add in a shopping cart area that shows what has been added into the cart, a link to checkout, and a link to the returning user account. First find a shopping cart image (from `http://www.openclipart.org/`) or use the client's desired design.

29. Select the Header layer.

30. From the main menu, select **File** and then **Import** and select the shopping cart image.

31. Place the image on the right side of the header.

32. If needed use the Create and Edit text tool to add in some additional text and cart information to the graphic to illustrate how the shopping cart will function and look on the web page. Your page should now look similar to the following screenshot:

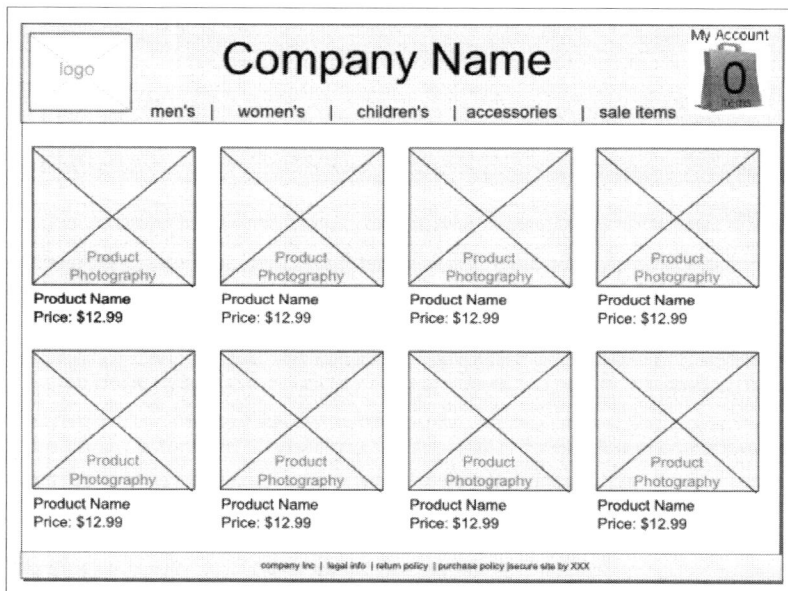

You can also use a template to create the product details pages for each individual item in your store. These pages contain more detailed descriptions of items, the price, specifications (if applicable), and at least one picture of an item. Let's look at how this could look.

Start with the simple product page layout, but keep the same header, footer, and shopping cart as the main catalog page. Add in photography for different angles or sizes and content for product specifications and details and links to add it to the shopping cart and/or return to the catalog. A mock up of that page might look like the following:

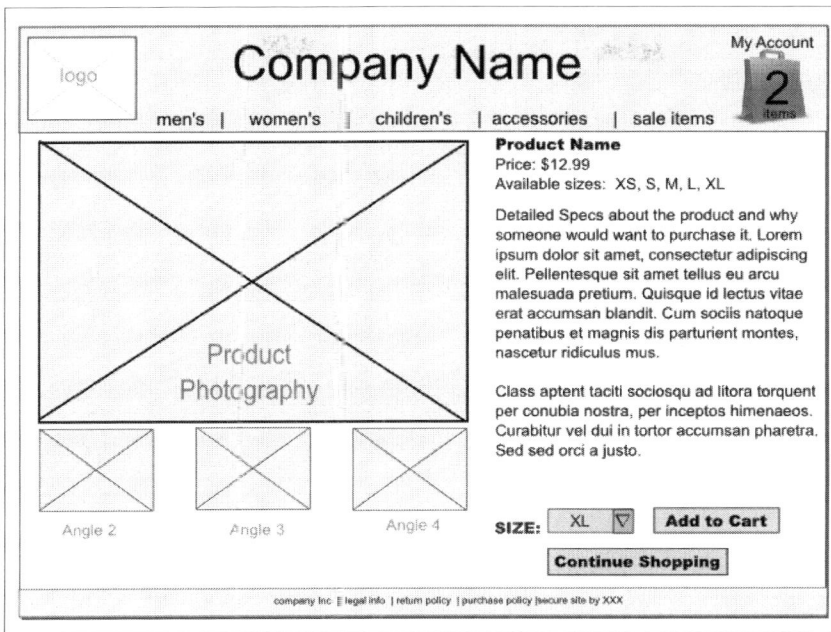

To create the mock up, you would use the rectangle, Bezier, create and edit and alignment tools—just like the previous example.

Even just using wireframe boxes to indicate pictures (as we did in both examples), it gives a clear idea of the design. It is one of the fastest ways to create mock-up designs of these pages, but still provide enough information to a client and/or programming team to help create the site.

Also, within this scenario you'll need to design forms for checking out, collecting credit card and/or PayPal information, and more. But from the perspective of templates and creating similar catalogue and product details web pages, you've seen a couple wireframe examples to start.

Grids and Cascading Style Sheets (CSS)

In all of our examples, our designs have been based on rectangles, turned, and varying width/height rectangles, but all rectangles nonetheless. That being said, then, all of your designs can also be the same—and essentially designed using Inkscape's Grid and Guideline features. Using this method would allow you to use tables to design your site. But a cleaner approach would be to use Cascading Style Sheets or CSS.

As a refresher, CSS are used with the HTML/XML coding to define the look and formatting of an entire website. One style sheet can be created that determines fonts, colors, spacing, placement, and more. And they are based on grids to determine the exact placements of areas within the site. What this means is if you decide to change the colors of your fonts, or spacing within an area on the site, you can do it in one file—and changes will happen throughout the site.

How best can you implement a CSS? If you make the areas of your site (as we did in each initial step of the template designs) the exact sizes of your CSS "areas" then dropping in the content and/or graphics into those areas will be easier from a programming standpoint.

There are online tools or CSS frameworks that also help with the Inkscape XML/SVG and CSS creation. All of the mentioned systems, give you common layouts based on grid sizes and then let you customize them. Here's an overview of a few of these CSS systems below:

- **960 Grid System** (http://960.gs/): This framework uses a width of 960 pixels and creates CSS based on 12 and/or 16 columns, which can be used separately or together.

- **Blueprint** (http://www.blueprintcss.org/): This is a bit more flexible framework that let's you determine how many columns you want, how wide they should be, and how much space you want between them. It has some pre-loaded cross-browser support, some built-in fonts and styles and plugin support.

- **YUI Grids** (http://developer.yahoo.com/yui/grids/): Offers six templates as a base, with four page widths. You can also stack next regions of 2, 3, or 4 columns—all in all about 1000 page layout combinations.

Using a framework to help you create your CSS, or working with a programmer to help create one for larger websites, CSS creation helps keep blogs, storefronts, and catalogues consistent in look and feel as the content for these types of sites are driven by dynamic content that is pulled from a content management system to display it on the web.

As with all the other designs—template, grid, and/or CSS-based—you export all of your graphics for the programmers to work their magic as they implement the blog or the store you designed.

To export in PNG—as you have many times—follow the instructions we've always reviewed, but this time use the design areas to help you export in a batch form:

1. Make sure you select all the rectangles of the Basic Layout areas selected (even if you have made them "invisible" you should be able to select them). Use the select tool and select each of them while pressing the *Shift* key to multi-select.

2. Once they are all selected, from the main menu select **File** and then **Export Bitmap**. The Export Area screen is displayed.

3. Make sure the **Batch export selected objects** is checked.

4. Click **Export**. Inkscape will automatically save the Background Areas— as you defined in the ID fields (right-click an object and select Object Properties)—as PNG image files in the export location in the Filename field.

Now you're ready to hand your graphic files to the team that will create the HTML for the web pages. As always, when providing files to programmers include:

- The PNG image files which you just exported from your design
- The source Inkscape SVG file of the page you designed and all other elements on the page like buttons, logos, and headings

Summary

We spent most of this chapter learning about designing for blogs and online merchant stores. We walked through simple designs for each, defining common elements for each website type and even some sub-level pages to help keep the designs consistent. At a more technical level we also looked at creating templates so that you can create the design and each part of the web page faster so it can be pushed into development, including using grids and CSS. A few CSS framework tools were also given as options to help create the CSS or at least give you a place to start if you want design with these tools in mind. Of course we also reviewed exporting all of your work in Inkscape to hand off to a programming team.

Up next we'll be learning how to use the built-in XML editor.

Using the XML Editor 9

Now we're ready to dig into some code. We're going to learn about the XML editor that is included within Inkscape. This is a cool trick that can help for global changes and when working with a programming team that can also create scripts to automatically make some changes. The goals of this chapter are to:

- Learn how to access the XML editor
- Understand the basics of the SVG coding language Inkscape uses (which is an iteration of XML)
- Learn how to edit some of the object XML code
- Review the essentials for handling off files to make sure the XML/SVG code can be fully functional and usable for any backend programming that needs to be done

Let's first learn a bit about the editor.

What is Inkscape's XML Editor

One of the features that sets Inkscape apart from other vector graphics programs is the XML editor. The XML editor is a code-based version of your canvas, all objects, properties, and more. Within the XML editor you can change any aspect of the document and see it immediately reflected on your canvas.

The catch here is you need to learn of a bit of SVG code in order to be able to do this fun editing. And, if you learn it, you can do *even more* within the XML interface than you can via the main Inkscape interface as it stands today. But, again, it takes a bit of learning on your part to learn SVG attributes and how best to edit them for your needs.

To start, you can view the W3C website directly from Inkscape at any time to see the SVG specifications. From the main menu select **Help** and then **SVG 1.1 Specification**. Understanding and using the SVG code allows you to create consistent shadows for objects in your web page design without having to fiddle in a number of menus and settings; or, create rectangles that always have the same rounded corners — again, without menus and fields and settings. However, let's just start at the beginning and open the XML editor.

Accessing the XML Editor

Accessing the XML editor is the easy part. From any open Inkscape document, on the main menu, select **Edit** and then **XML Editor**.

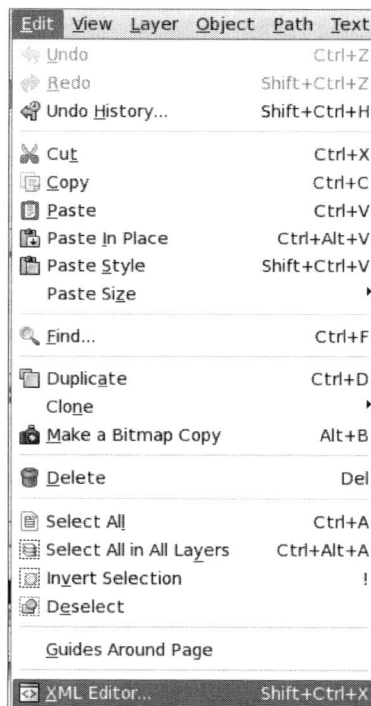

[💡 You can also open the XML editor using the keyboard shortcut *Shift+Ctrl+X*.]

The XML window opens — and if your Inkscape canvas is blank — it will look something like this:

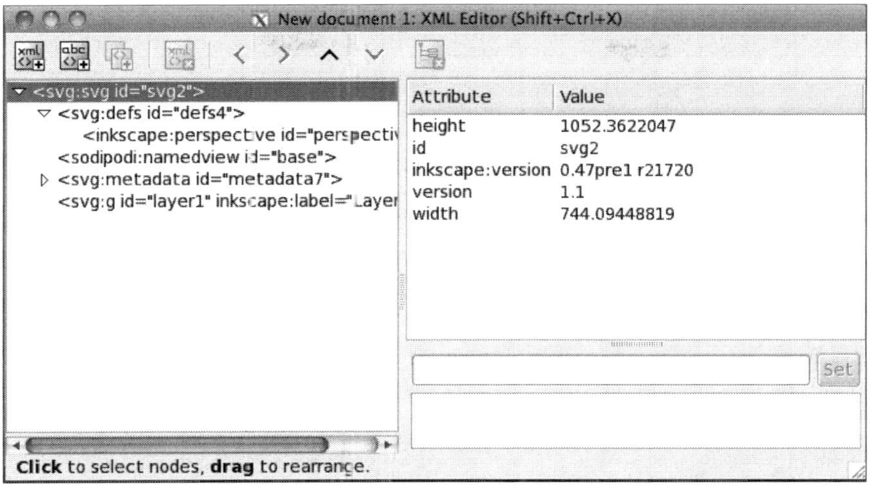

But let's look at a more complicated Inkscape document that is populated with a web design. Then we can discuss the screen basics, the SVG code and understand how we might be able to edit it for our use. We'll use our blog design from the last chapter and its corresponding SVG code. The following screenshot shows an open Inkscape document and the associated SVG code that you would see side by side.

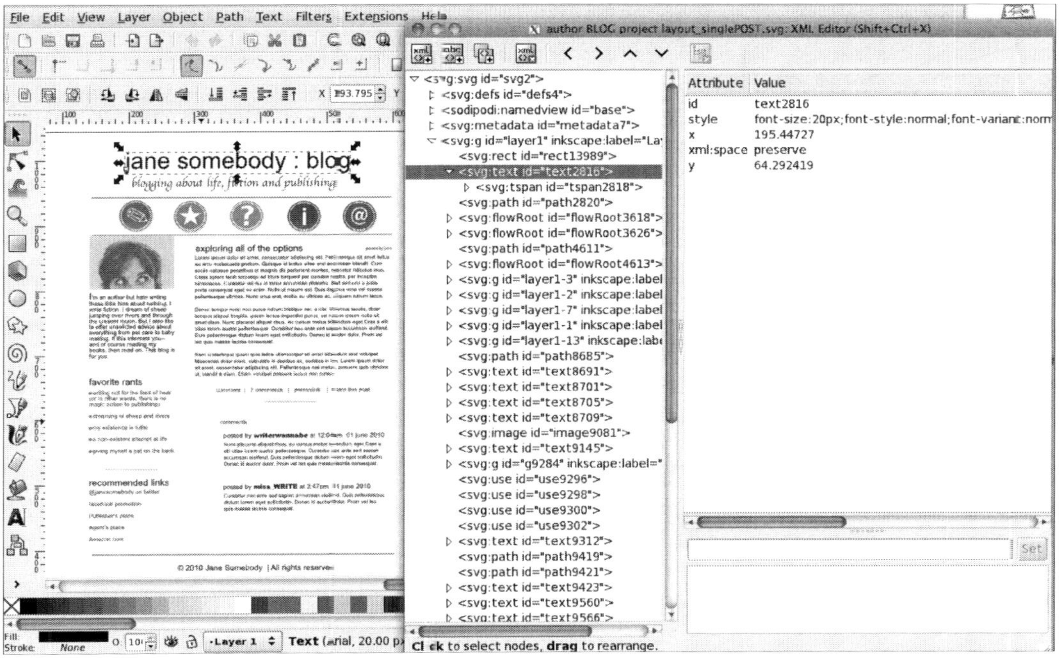

As you select items in the SVG code, you will see that it selects the items in the design (and vice versa). Also, if you were to edit any of the object properties, all changes would happen in real time on the canvas. But let's not get ahead of ourselves. First we need to understand the basics of the XML editor screen:

- The **structure** or **tree** of the XML is the portion of the screen where basically the entire canvas is shown in SVG code.

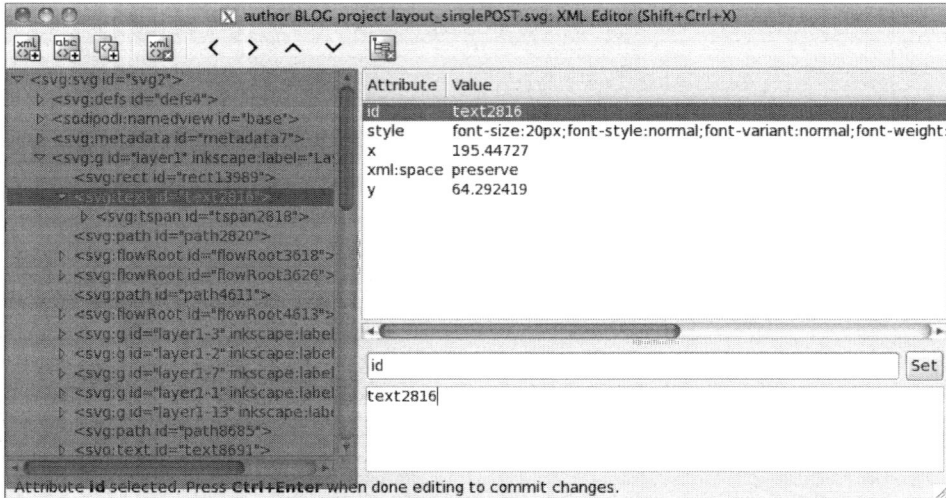

- A **layer** is essentially a "node" in the tree. If the layer contains objects, then they would be represented by nodes under the layer's node.

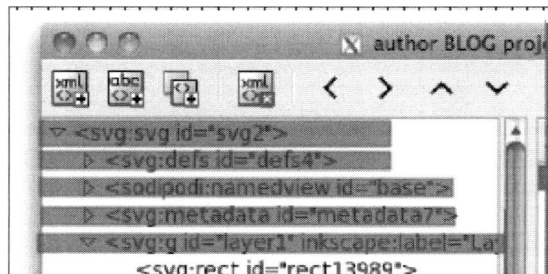

These are expandable by clicking the arrow on the left side. When pointing down, all objects are viewable (and editable). When the arrow is sideways, the objects are hidden.

- The **attributes** or **properties** of a selected object are on the left side of the screen. This is where you would edit the properties.

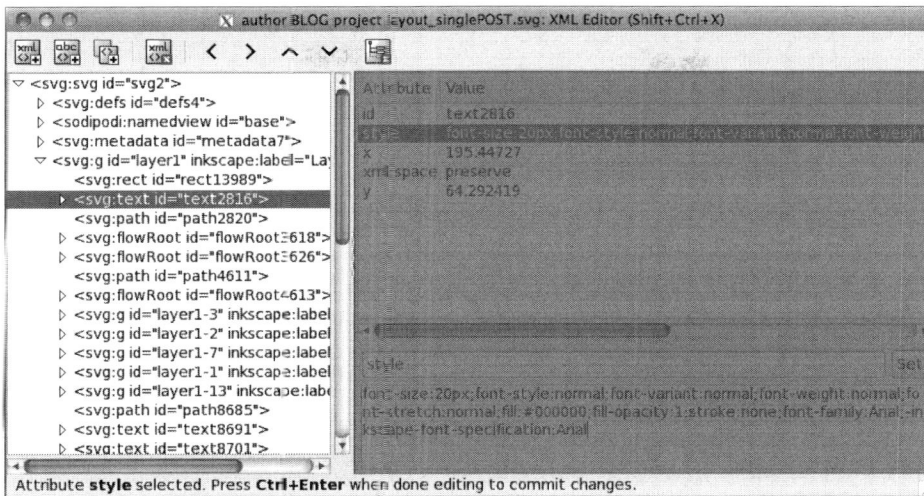

You select an attribute of the object to edit, and then at the bottom portion of the screen, you make your changes and click the **Set** button to commit to the change (as shown below).

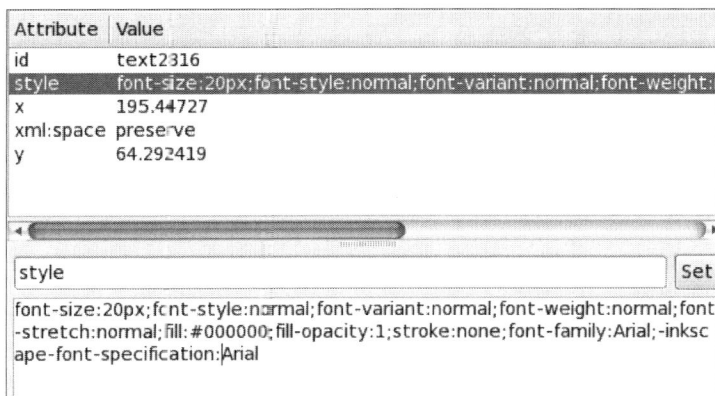

SVG basics

Let's take a step back for a moment and understand the attributes—or the SVG code found in the XML editor. We'll still keep it in the context of the Inkscape XML editor window, so you won't have to know all of the SVG syntax code. But it is enough to understand the common attributes and what they mean to your web designs.

Attribute types

First, attributes fall into two categories. Those that are SVG standard and then those that can only be found in Inkscape. For those that fall within the SVG standards, they will be recognized by other SVG rendering programs, and thus can be edited by them as well. However the others—the Inkscape-only attributes—are only recognized in Inkscape. What does this mean if you do export and use them in other SVG rendering programs? Not much, they'll just be ignored. Or you can also export the drawing in a way that will not even include these elements.

Thus, when you are saving a document in Inkscape, you are given the option to save as Inkscape SVG or plain SVG.

Inkscape SVG (*.svg)

Plain SVG (*.svg)

Compressed Inkscape SVG (*.svgz)

Compressed plain SVG (*.svgz)

To maintain editability, we recommend saving in Inkscape SVG.

How can you tell which attributes are Inkscape-only and which are SVG standard? The answer is the **sodipodi** tag. This tag is only on attributes that are Inkscape-only. In the following example, you can see that the icons width (sodipodi: rx) and height (sodipodi: ry) are both Inkscape-native SVG code, along with the circle attributes cx that give the exact location of the Circle's Height Transform's Node and cy that gives the position of the Circle's Width Transformation node.

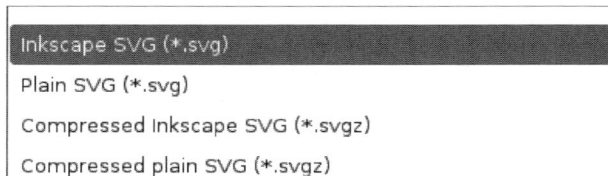

Basic attributes

There are books that can explain how best to code and script using SVG. Here, is a brief overview of the code and how you can "read" it and the attribute properties.

This isn't intended to show you how to "hand–code" the SVG data. As it is rarely done that way. As with Inkscape, you would use a SVG authoring environment with a graphical interface that creates most of the code and then will go in later and edit the attribute information. But even with this, it helps to understand the very basics of the attribute properties and how they are structured.

To start we will discuss objects. SVG offers four data types to work with: paths, shapes, images, and text. For each of these objects you have a number of attributes you define to actually create, define, and position the images you see on the canvas.

Paths

In SVG (and Inkscape), paths are outlines of shapes. These paths can be filled (add color) and/or have a stroke associated with them—and thus paths are a critical object to create shapes and other items in Inkscape.

How does SVG allow you to create us all these "pictures"? Well each object is made up of a number of shapes. And thus, SVG also uses six predefined shape "elements" within its code for you to manipulate. These basic shape elements are:

- rectangle (rect)
- circle
- ellipse
- line
- polyline
- polygon

Each SVG shape has a number of attributes associated with it, and once those attributes are defined, the code can be made into an actual shape. Let's go through each of these as an example.

Rectangles have four attributes—x, y, width, and height—which explain the placement and dimensions of the rectangle. The **x** attribute is the distance from the left side of the canvas; the **y** is the distance from the top of the canvas. Using the 'x' and 'y' together you are defining the top-left cover of the rectangle. Then the **width** and **height** attributes as expected, define exactly what you would assume. The dimensions of the two-dimensional object.

Here's how you would see the code in the XML editor:

Notice that the rect ID **<svg:rect id=rect2816>** is the object information, and is shown on the left side, while all of the attributes (x, y, height, and width) are shown on the right side. There is also an ID and style attribute which is common to all objects. The ID attribute is either automatically assigned in Inkscape or set when making the object in the graphical interface in **Object Properties.** The style attribute captures all of the color, stroke, opacity, fill, and more information. As you can see above, when you select any attribute, you can see all the details at the bottom of the screen (this is where you would edit that information also).

What would this rectangle as seen in this SVG code look like? See the following screenshot:

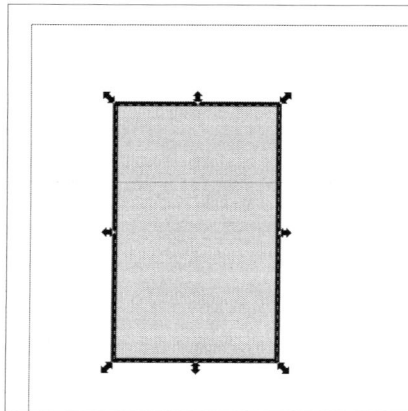

Next let's discuss a circle. It uses the path ID to create it and has four attributes: **cx**, **cy**, **rx**, and **ry**. The cx and cy define the exact center of the circle (placement), while the rx and ry value is the radius of the circle. An example of the SVG code would look like this in the XML editor:

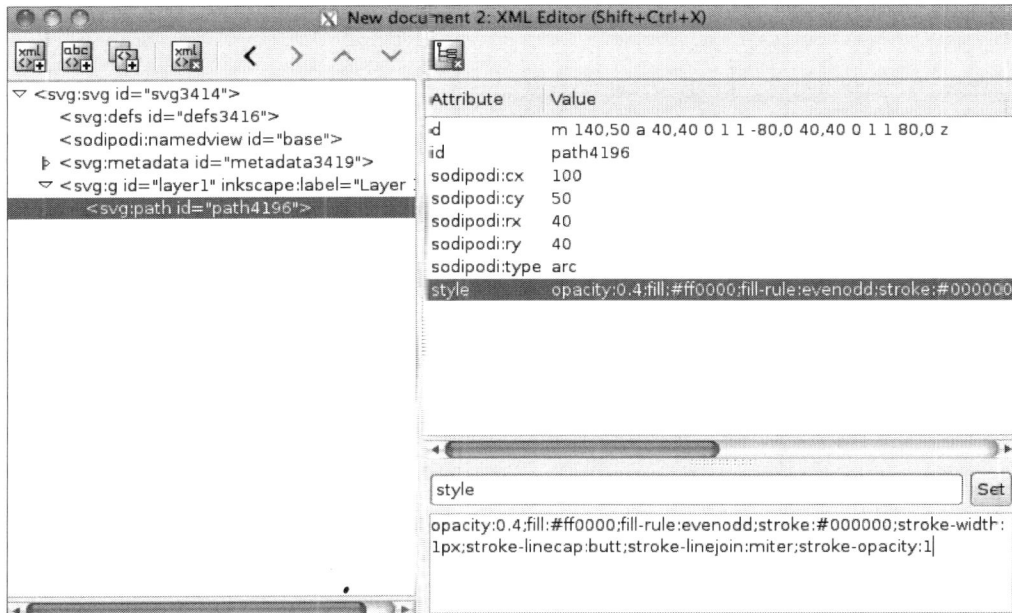

From this code we see that the center of the circle is at 100, 50 and the circle would have a radius of 40. We can also see from the `style` attribute that there is color in the circle, but it is at 40 percent capacity and a stroke outline that is two pixels thick.

On the canvas this all translates into looking like this:

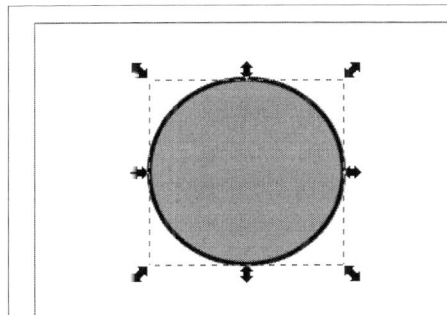

The ellipse is similar to the circle, except that it has four path ID attributes in Inkscape: **cx**, **cy**, **rx** and **ry**. Again cx and cy specify the center of the ellipse. The r attributes—rx and ry—give the x-axis and y-axis radius of the ellipse. Again, unless geometry is a favorite past time, typically you would create this object using the graphical interface and then refine in the XML editor code. So, let's see what the code would look like:

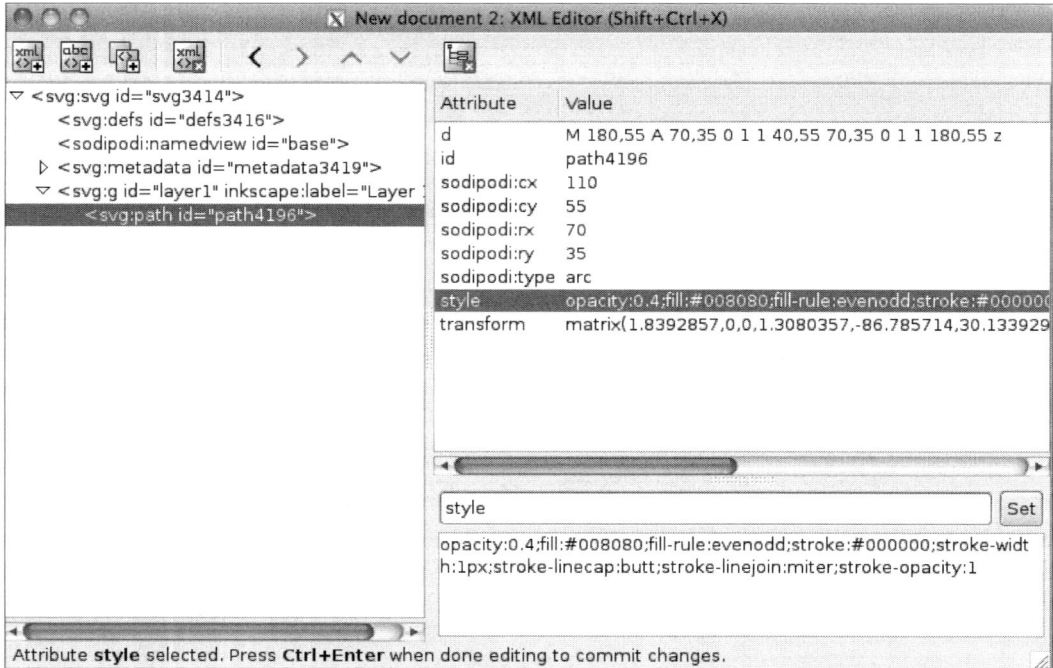

We see here, for this example, the center of the circle is at 110, 55 and it has an x-axis radius of 70 and y-axis radius of 35.

The ellipse would look like this on the canvas:

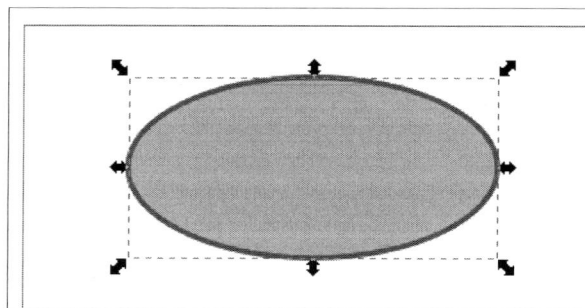

Next up, we will learn about the path object. Essentially, you will map every 'point' or node on the object. That means you will have many x and y coordinate pairs in the code for these types of objects. Here's a sample of the code in the XML editor:

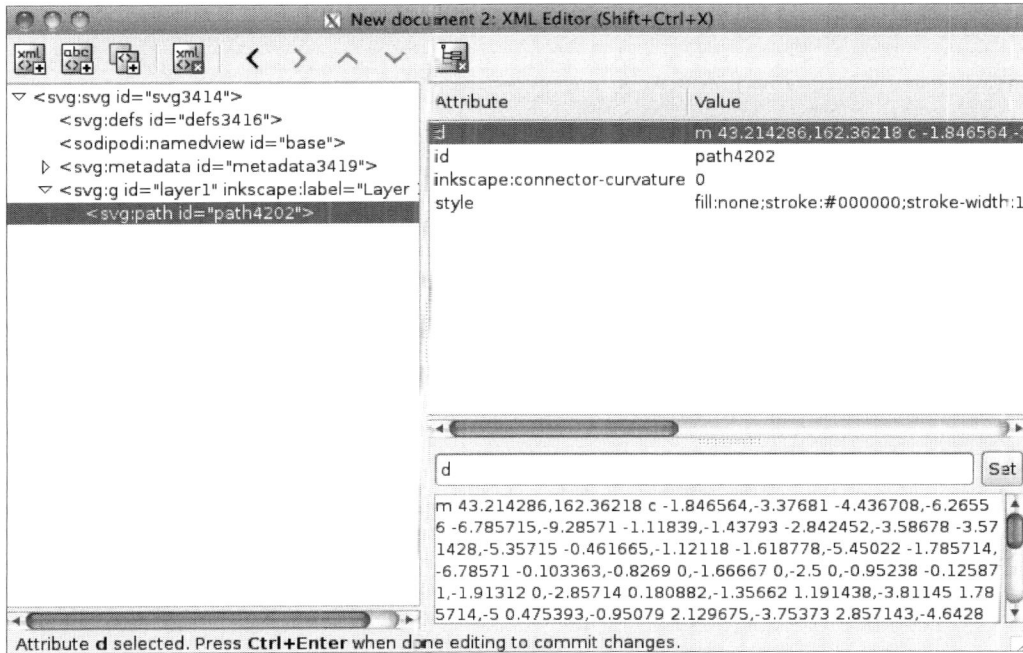

And the corresponding line on the canvas:

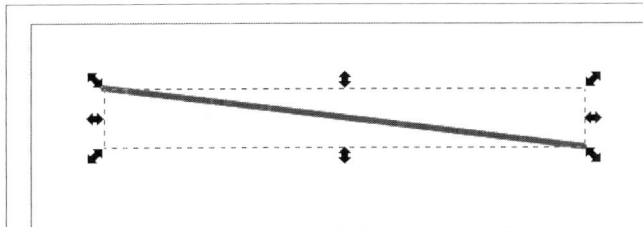

Now for the details about polylines and polygons the attributes are the same as those of the path object. Every 'point' or node on the object is mapped with x and y coordinates pairs in the code for these types of objects.

But what is the difference between polygons and polylines if the attributes are the same (an x and y value for every node of the shape)? It's the stroke outline—for polylines, it doesn't automatically close the shape as the 'polygon' element automatically does.

Here's a simple code example for a polyline (again, this would be the same for a polygon, except the stroke would "close" the shape).

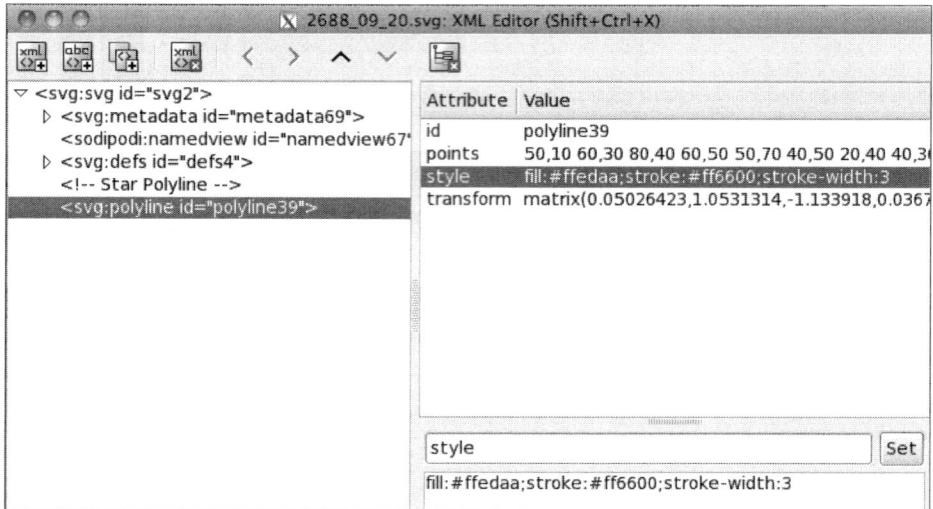

And it would look like this on the canvas:

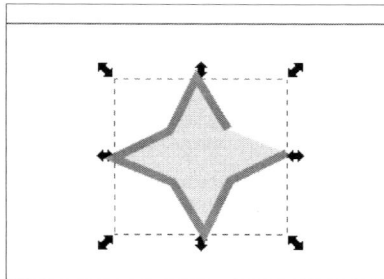

With this example you can see how difficult it would be to hand-code all of the nodes of the star to make the image. In fact you would likely spend more time trying to find coordinates and mapping them, instead of actually drawing the shapes. Thus, Inkscape's interface is best for drawing, and use the XML to edit or manage some settings, which we'll talk about next.

> You always have to make sure you have an even number of coordinate values. Meaning, for every x value you have, specify a corresponding y coordinate. SVG coding programs will prompt you for this and in Inkscape it is recommended you "draw" the graphics using the interface. Then go into the XML editor to change any specific settings.

Images

As you have seen, SVG files that are considered the source files for Inkscape are graphic images themselves. But they can also contain other graphic formats (like PNG, JPG, or other SVG files). You can even transform and animate those graphics as well (and even use some scripting to work with them).

In order to do all of that, there is also an 'image' object in Inkscape. The attributes for it are: x and y which again define the top-left corner of the image, 'width' and 'height' attributes that give measurements, and the `'xlink:href'` attribute. This defines the actual path or location of the original image. Think of it as the 'link' to the original image file, like in the HTML code.

Let's look at a code sample in the XML editor:

Text

Lastly, as you know from the many examples we have created so far, you can create text in your images. Much like the image attribute there are x and y values that set the top-left/starting point for your text and then the actual text that is displayed. Here's a sample of what that looks like in the XML Editor as well:

Using the XML Editor to change characteristics

Now, suppose you have created a mock website using the graphical interface of Inkscape and you have handed off all of your files to the programming team. Suddenly, your client decides that they want all heading text to be a specific color of gray (4d4d4d).

Do you have to open each graphic file and make this change? Maybe! But you can also change it right in the XML editor (and if your programmers are using your SVG files directly, they might even be able to make the change). Here's how you would do it:

1. Open up the XML editor (or an SVG authoring tool) and open your website file.

2. Find the headings you want to change. To do this, find text objects that match what you are looking for. Programmers may have named all of these as **HeadingXX**, where XX is a number to identify each of them.

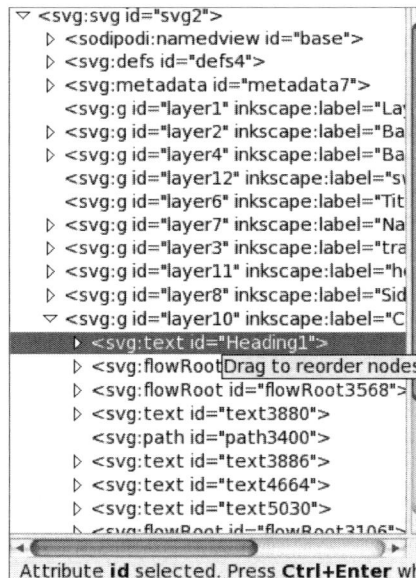

```
▽ <svg:svg id="svg2">
    ▷ <sodipodi:namedview id="base">
    ▷ <svg:defs id="defs4">
    ▷ <svg:metadata id="metadata7">
      <svg:g id="layer1" inkscape:label="La
    ▷ <svg:g id="layer2" inkscape:label="Ba
    ▷ <svg:g id="layer4" inkscape:label="Ba
      <svg:g id="layer12" inkscape:label="s\
      <svg:g id="layer6" inkscape:label="Tit
    ▷ <svg:g id="layer7" inkscape:label="Na
    ▷ <svg:g id="layer3" inkscape:label="tra
    ▷ <svg:g id="layer11" inkscape:label="h(
    ▷ <svg:g id="layer8" inkscape:label="Sid
    ▽ <svg:g id="layer10" inkscape:label="C
      ▶ <svg:text id="Heading1">
    ▷ <svg:flowRoot Drag to reorder node:
    ▷ <svg:flowRoot id="flowRoot3568">
    ▷ <svg:text id="text3880">
      <svg:path id="path3400">
    ▷ <svg:text id="text3886">
    ▷ <svg:text id="text4664">
    ▷ <svg:text id="text5030">
      ▷ <svg:flowRoot id="flowRoot3106">
Attribute id selected. Press Ctrl+Enter wl
```

3. Expand the object and find the `style` attribute.

Attribute	Value
id	Heading1
sodipodi:linespacing	125%
style	font-size:24px;font-style:normal;font-variant:
x	23.384617
xml:space	preserve
y	203.85915

4. Then look for the Fill information and change that web color to the new gray one: 4d4d4d.

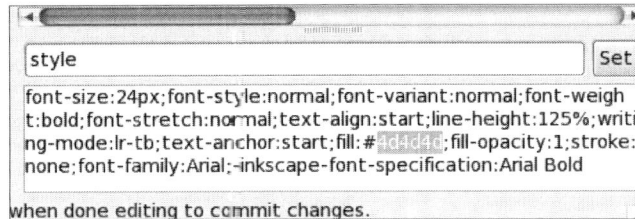

style | Set

font-size:24px;font-style:normal;font-variant:normal;font-weigh
t:bold;font-stretch:normal;text-align:start;line-height:125%;writi
ng-mode:lr-tb;text-anchor:start;fill:#4d4d4d;fill-opacity:1;stroke:
none;font-family:Arial;-inkscape-font-specification:Arial Bold

when done editing to commit changes.

5. Click **Set**, and voila! The heading will be changed just like that.

Travel your way through retirement

Lorem ipsum dolor sit amet, consectetuer adipiscing elit. Suspendisse venenatis. Nunc in turpis ac lacus eleifend sagitis. Suspendisse molestie sem. Sed dolor.

Lorem ipsum dolor sit amet, consectetuer adipiscing elit. Donec at diam a tellus dignissim vestibulum. Quisque facilisis, urna sit amet pulvinar mollis, purus arcu adipiscing velit, non condimentum diam purus eu massa.

Phasellus at purus sed purus cursus iaculis.

You can even write scripts that would be able to automatically search and find all Heading IDs (as described in Step 2) and change them! Work with your programming team if you want to learn how to do this (or search the web). Lots of tools can help you learn the XML/SVG code side of this.

Using XML and graphics with programmers

XML, the SVG code, and scripting typically land in the laps of those that actually code the web page. Sometimes that can be the same person — but in larger corporate or consulting groups, it is a split responsibility. And the one major point to remember and we have reviewed it in every chapter, is that when you hand over your design mock-up files: include everything!

That is, all SVG source files, all output PNG files, every graphic you used to create the mock up and more. And in fact, if you created object properties (names) for your layers and objects—give the programming team a cheat sheet of that information as well. All of this will make the transition from web design mock up to real web page easier, cleaner, and more efficient.

Summary

This chapter was full of the technical XML and SVG code, objects, attributes, x and y values, and more. First we learned how to open the XML editor. Then we took a step back and learned about SVG coding: all about the shape, image, text attributes, and more. We even dug further into the code a bit to edit some text. There, of course, is a bunch more that can be done with the code version of your graphics—but we left most of that to a programming team. Or more investigative work on your part! With all the files at your (and a team's) disposal, there are endless possibilities for coding an efficient and effective website.

Next up is building simple animations using Inkscape.

10
Creating Simple Animations

Inkscape has limited capabilities for creating animations. However, using raster graphics you can export graphic file formats — like PNG — and use these individual animation frames to create simple animations called, appropriately, **animated GIFs**.

In this chapter we'll discuss:

- Animation in web design. Pros, cons, and then some general guidelines so your animations work well in your overall design
- How to create animation frames and then compile them using GIMP (another open-source software program)
- How to create scrolling text and an animated banner

Animations in web design

If you've sat in a web design class recently, it is likely that animated GIFs (or a lack thereof) formed part of the discussion. In the past few years, animation on the web has taken on a more "elegant" approach. Five years ago, almost any web page had some sort of animated GIF rotating, spinning, or flashing items to a user. Now, this trend has changed for a cleaner design feel — as it should. Animation can be eye-catching and also very distracting.

However, this is not to say that simple animations do not have their place online. They do, especially, when you might want to convey simple movement or draw attention to one portion of your design. That being said, here are some simple design guidelines related to adding animation (or not) to your web design:

- Animations can be added to web page load time. A good application of this rule is adding animation to your site. Sure, animation looks "cool" and does initially catch your eye, but animation graphics tend to be large files. Test the download time of your pages first. If the download time of your page is relatively short and the addition of animation does not unreasonably increase the download time of your page, then and ONLY then should animation be a consideration. Do not have more than two or three animations in view at any one time.

  Animation CAN be good for:

  ° Showing change over time. Meaning—showing a weather front moving across a region or the growing population of butterflies in the midwest.

  ° Turning an object and showing its 3D form. This doesn't always mean a full 360 degree turn either. Sometimes just a quick look from a corner angle is all that is needed to illustrate the full 3D aspects of a drawing.

- Show animated text once. Meaning, if you have scrolling text that is more than a few words long, it might be best to show the animation once and then stop it. It is harder to read moving text and you don't want the viewer to become annoyed (or distracted by the movement).

There may also be instances when you will be asked to create a banner add or logo thumbnail that is animated so that it can be part of a promotional campaign. Again, the sample principles apply for creating these items (banners or thumbnails) as you just export to the specific size requirements given to you when creating the design.

Basic techniques to animate

We use Inkscape to create each animation frame and save it in a PNG format. Then we use Gimp, another open-source program, to tie all of the images together and create the animation.

Installing Gimp

Since we can rely on Gimp to pull all of our frame images together and animate it, let's install it before we begin. Then, when we're ready to see the animation in action—we'll be ready to go.

1. Open a browser window and go to http://www.gimp.org/.
2. Find the Download area to download and install the appropriate version of Gimp for your computer system using the instructions provided.

No need to open Gimp yet. Let's get started by creating the object(s), which we will later use Gimp to animate.

Creating the animation

It isn't on a whim you've decided to create an animation. Therefore, it is also likely you have planned (at least roughly) what you are going to draw and how you want it to move. These can be paper sketches so that you know "where to start" with your first image.

For our example, we are going to use a boat image from the Open Clip Art library and show it sailing across a horizon. Here's how to make this happen:

1. Open Inkscape and draw your beginning or starting point of the animation. We do this by importing (**File** and then **Import**) our clip art, make modifications, and place the boat at the far left side of the canvas.

> Remember you can download free clip art for these sample projects from http://www.openclipart.org/.

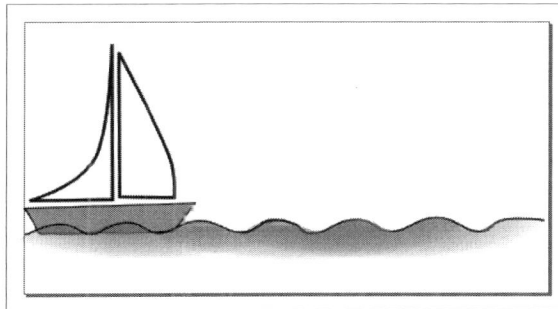

2. Once the boat is in the starting position, export (**File** and then **Export Bitmap**) the entire canvas as a PNG file—saving it specifically in a directory that can hold many frames of an animation. For an easy animation sequence, name this 1.png.

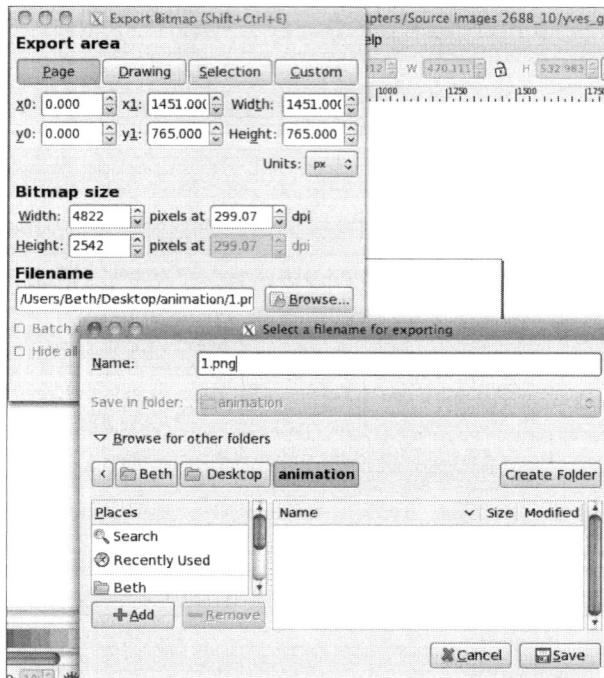

3. Move the boat slightly to the right—so it can be the next bit of movement for the boat and save this as the second frame. Select **File** and then **Export Bitmap** and name the file 2.png.

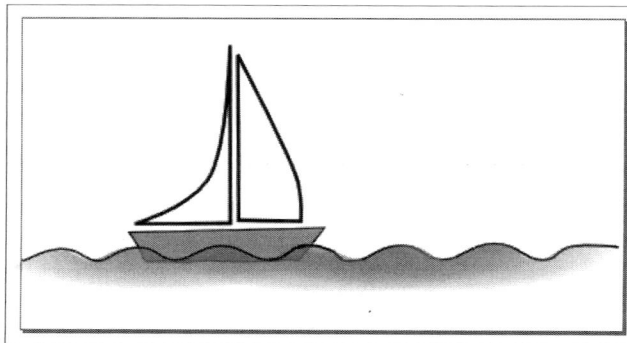

4. Continue moving the boat to the right little-by-little, saving each sequential frame.

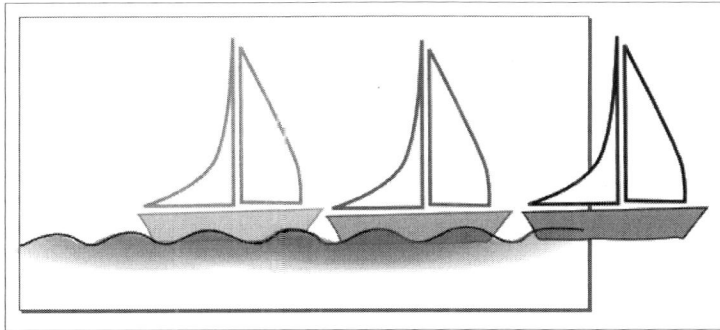

5. We're going to have the boat sail right "off the page". The last frame will only show the ocean and the sun. Again, export this canvas as a PNG and save it in the directory where your animation frames are located.

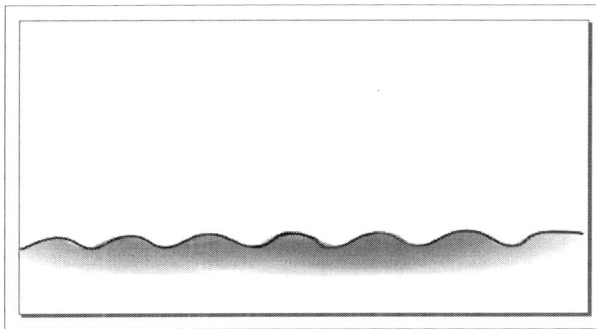

Now, we are ready to take each of these frames, and tie them together into an animation sequence.

Bringing the animation together

Since Inkscape doesn't have full animation capabilities, we use Gimp to create our animation sequence based on the frames created in the last section.

1. Open Gimp and then open the `1.png` file created in the last section. It will be the first frame of the animation.

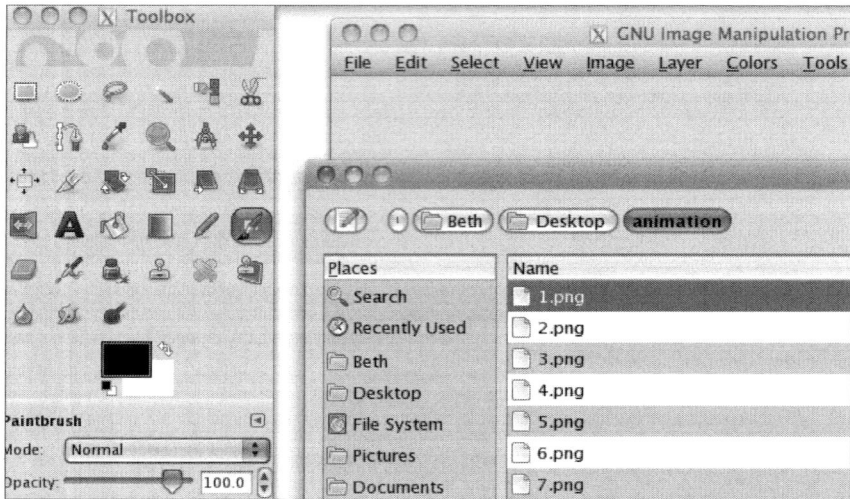

2. By default, Gimp should have placed this image onto the first layer, but let's make sure. If your Layers dialog is not open, open it. From the main menu select **File**, **Dialogs**, and then **Layers**.

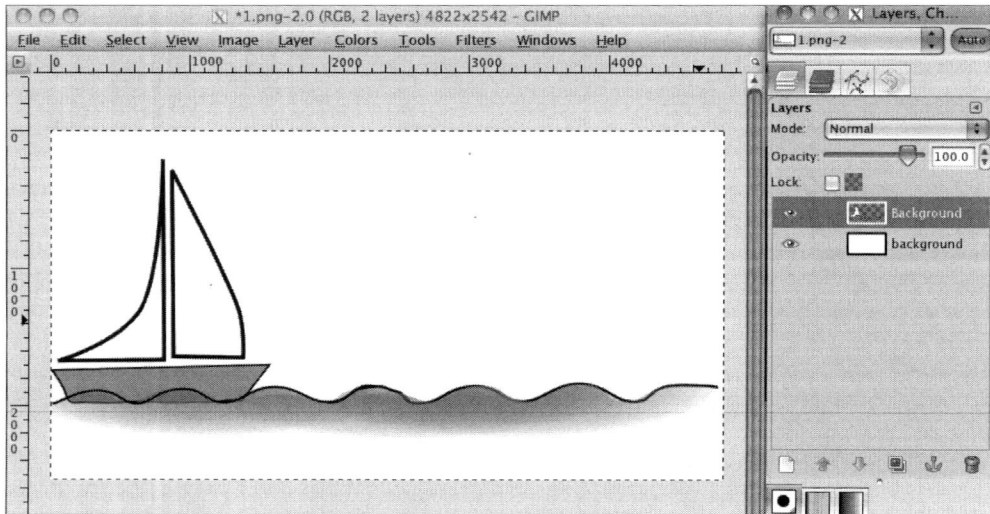

3. You should see the dialog open on the right side of the screen.

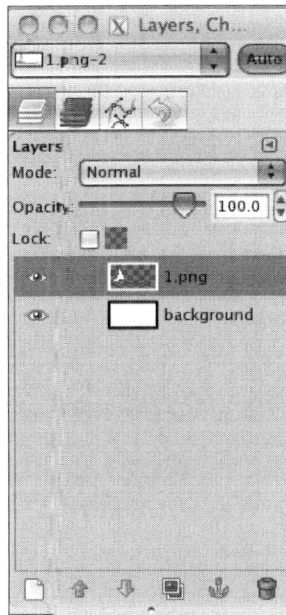

4. Open the next frame, file 2.png. From the main menu select **File**, **Open as Layers**, and select file **2.png**. It should appear "on top" of the first frame in the Layers dialog.

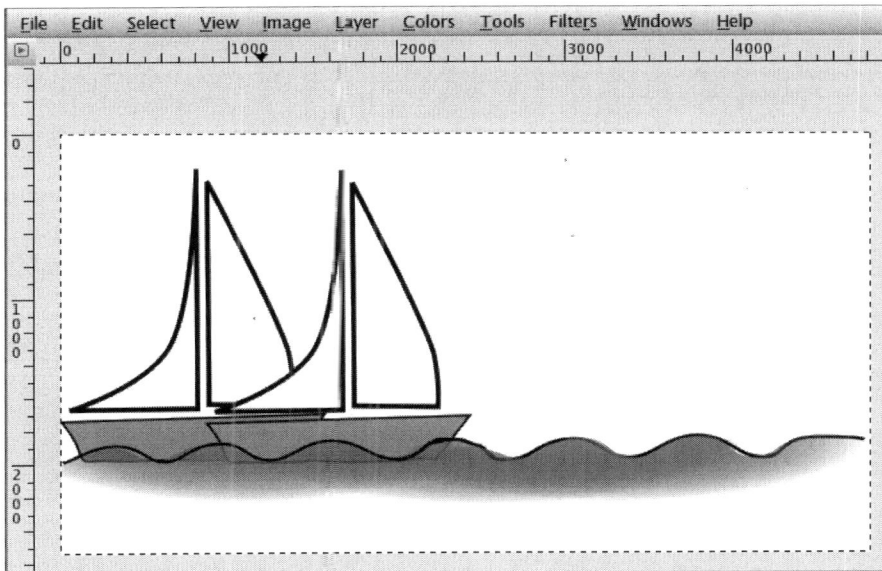

5. Repeat this step, placing all of the frames onto the Gimp canvas, making sure each frame appears on top of the last one in the Layers dialog.

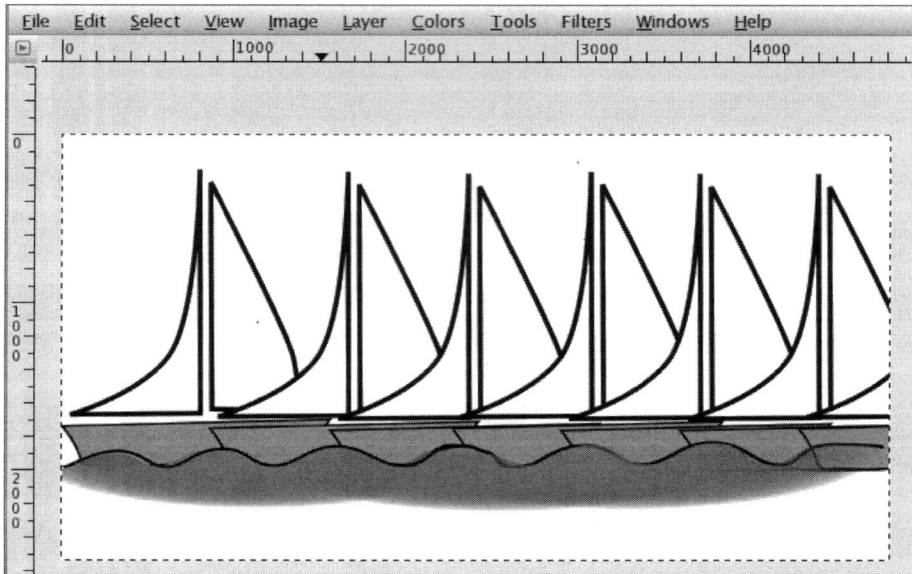

6. When the final frame is placed, save the file. From the main menu select **File** and then **Save as**.

7. Enter a filename. Then choose the file format as **GIF image** and press **Save**.

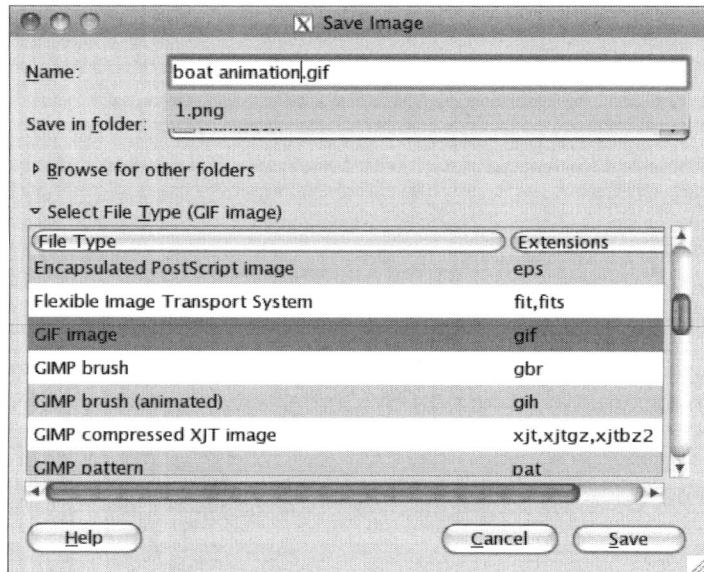

8. The **Export File** window appears–choose **Save as Animation** and **Convert to indexed using default settings,** then click **Export**.

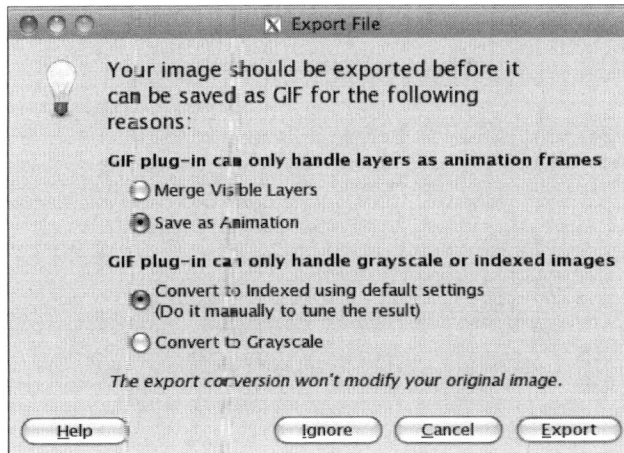

9. A **Save as GIF** window appears asking for additional animation information. Uncheck **Loop forever,** and then change the **Delay between frames where unspecified** to **200 ms** (milliseconds). Once you have entered the information, press **Save**.

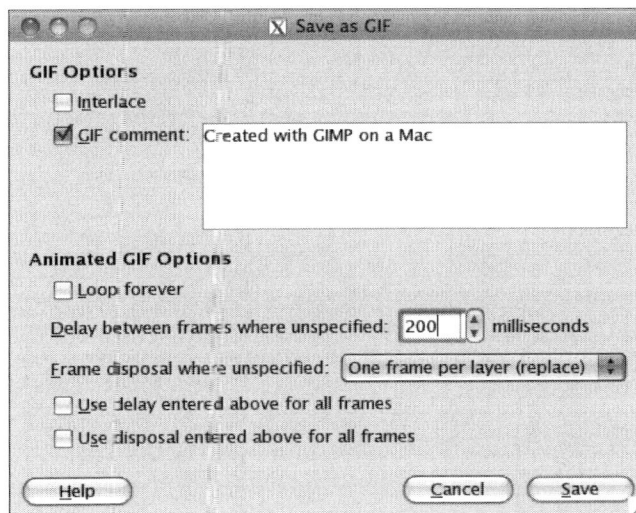

Voila, your animated GIF is now saved. In a browser window, open the file you just created and you'll see your new animation in action.

The more frames you have in an animated GIF, the larger the file size and thus larger the load times. Testing the file (and animation) before delivery is recommended.

Creating scrolling text

The essentials for creating scrolling text are very much like how we created the animation of the boat. Have your text scroll, one character movement to the right (or left) at a time. To create the "scrolling" feel—have the text start "off the page" and move on, through and then off again.

1. Open Inkscape and create a new document to the size of the animation you would like to create. Our example will be in a banner of size 468px x 60px, which is a pre-set size offered by Inkscape. From the main menu select **File**, **New**, and then **web_banner_468x60**.

2. Start with a blank canvas, and export the entire page as **1.png**. From the main menu select **File** and then **Export Bitmap**. Choose a save location such as a specific project folder to save all the animations.

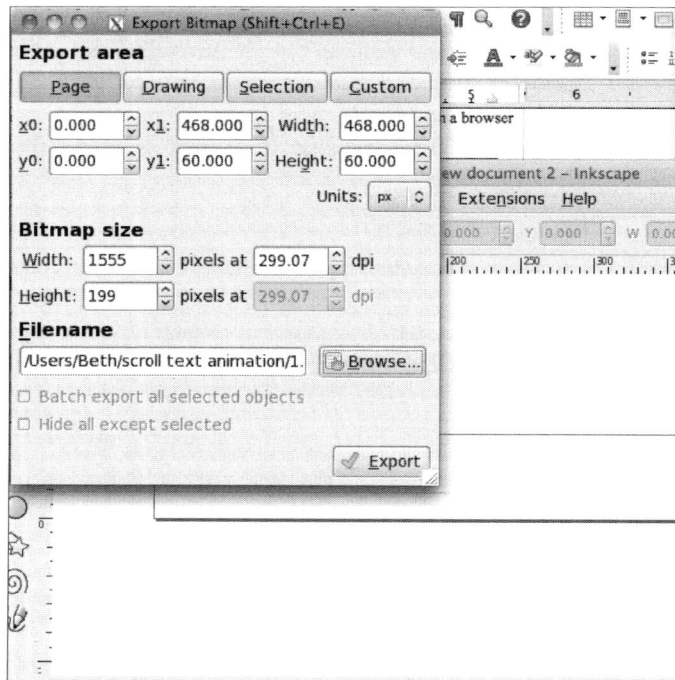

3. Show the last letter of the scrolling text on the screen. Select **File** and then **Export** and name the file 2.png.

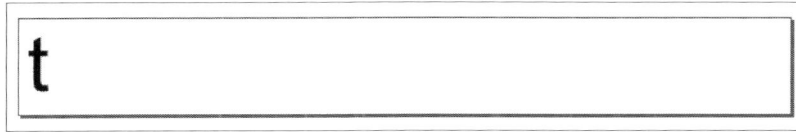

> t

4. Move that letter over one spot to the right and add in the next to the last letter. Export this as 3.png.

> xt

5. Move both of those letters over one character placement to the right and add another letter—the third from last letter, and save this as 4.png.

> ext

6. Continue this pattern until you have all of your words on the page (and spaces). And then—keep moving one character space to the right and saving.

> Scrolling Text

7. Do this until you have the words almost off the page. The last letter in this sequence should be the very first letter of your text on the far right side of the canvas. Save this file as the last frame.

> S

8. Open Gimp and from the main menu select **File** and then **Open as Layers...**.

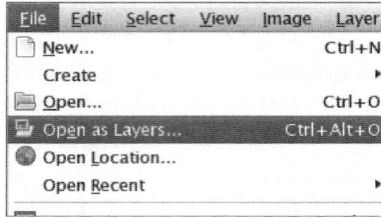

9. As this animation may have many frames to import, try importing all of the frames at one time. To do this, select all of the frames for this animation and click **Open**.

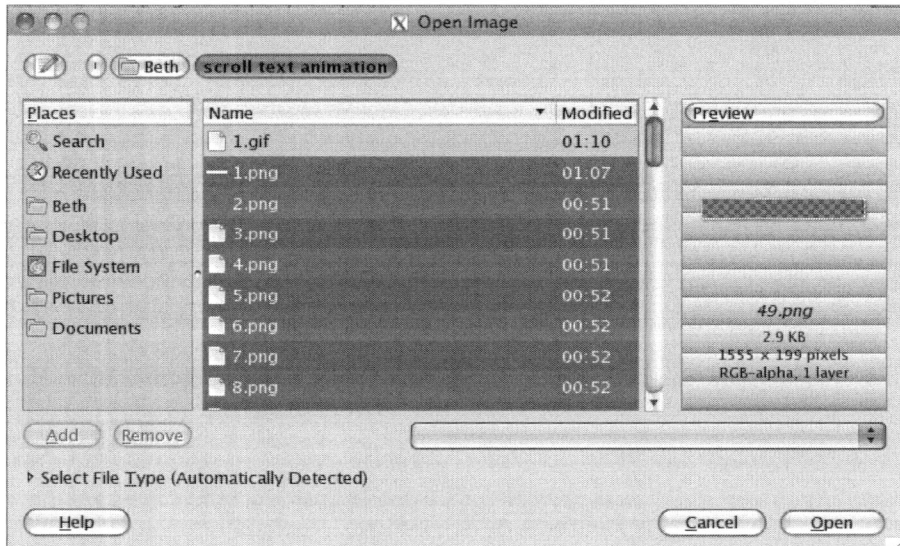

All of the images will open on top of one another.

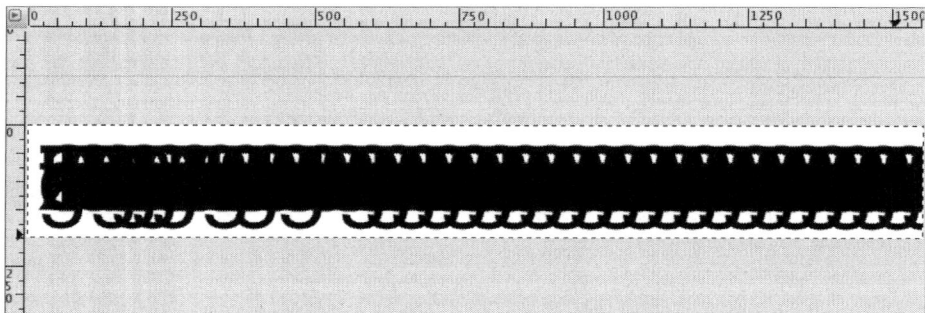

> Importing all of the frames at one time will work correctly only if you have numbered the frame files in sequential order.

1. Enter a filename, and then select a file format of **GIF Image** and press **Save**.
2. An Export file window appears. Choose **Save as Animation** and **Convert to indexed**, then click **Export**.
3. A **Save as Gif** window displays and asks for additional animation information. Choose a filename. Then check the **Loop forever** and the **Delay between frames where unspecified** to **150ms** (milliseconds) between frames. Once you have entered the information, press **Save**.

Voila, your animated GIF is now saved. Open the new file you just created in a web browser and you'll see your new animation in action.

Exporting animations

To deliver your animation to the web team, just deliver the final GIF file with instructions on where you need the file to be placed. It is easier to integrate an animation into a web interface than it is to integrate a web page because the animation is just one self-contained file.

If the animation is part of a larger design—or within a web page you are creating—then just as with the delivery of the web page, include the GIF file in the bundle of SVG, image files (PNG) so they can use it to re-create your entire web page as designed.

Creating animating banners or advertisements

Using the techniques and the graphics presented in this chapter, we've created a web page or an advertisement. Banners or advertisements are a form of advertising on the web. They are embedded in a web page to attract and entice the visitor to click on the banner and go to the web site it represents. One of the main purposes of a banner is to drive traffic to a site to gain more viewers, and potentially more customers. Here's an example of a small banner ad. There are no restrictions on the size or shape of such an ad. It depends on the web site that is hosting or sponsoring the ad.

And here is how it is seen on the Inkscape forums at `http://www.inkscapeforum.com/`:

We won't go through the detailed steps on creating the animated GIF — as animation is not essential in a banner ad — but instead focus on how you deliver a banner ad to be placed on another web site after it is created.

A banner ad is much like the other files we discussed in previous chapters — first export the banner ad. If it is animated, export as an animated GIF from Gimp as described in the section *Bringing the animation together*. If it is a static file that will just become a link, then it is exported as a PNG — as with other images.

1. Select all elements of the banner ad and then from the main menu select **File** and then **Export Bitmap**. The Export Area screen is displayed.

2. Make sure **Selection** is checked.

3. Choose a save location and name.

4. Click **Export**. Inkscape will automatically save the banner as PNG image files in the export location in the Filename field.

Now you're ready to hand off your graphic files to the team that will create the HTML for the web pages. As always, when providing files to programmers include:

- The PNG image files you just exported from your design

- The original Inkscape SVG file you created for the banner ad and/or the web page as a whole

- And all other elements that you used or created like buttons, logos, and headings

The programming team will then reconstruct your web page into a working web site.

Summary

Inkscape has limited capabilities for creating animations — but with a little help from another open source tool like Gimp, you can still create animations. To do this, we learned how animations might work in a web design and then started creating our own. We broke down an animation into individual animation frames and created each one that would then be brought together using Gimp to complete a full animation sequence. We then used the same animation principles and created a scrolling text animation. To wrap up, we also discussed exporting an animated GIF as one self-contained file for a web development team to incorporate into a web interface.

Finally we discussed how animations (or not) could create banner ads. We defined them, looked at an example and then discussed how we can export these graphics for use in a full web design.

Next up is our final chapter, which discusses Inkscape templates and plug-ins.

11
Plugins, Scripts, and Templates

Templates can make a web designer's life easier—or at least preparation time when starting a new mock-up. This chapter will discuss in detail templates and then plugins and scripts. Specifically it:

- Looks at what templates are available within Inkscape
- How to install new templates
- How to create custom templates
- Defining plugins, scripts, and extensions
- Requirements for installing each online resources that might be useful for web designers

Templates in Inkscape

Inkscape has some pre-defined templates that you can use to start your development To access these templates, go to the main menu select **File** and then **New**. A pop-up menu appears showing a number of default page (or canvas) sizes to choose from.

Installing and using templates

Most templates are pre-loaded into the Inkscape release and installation. However, if you find additional Inkscape templates you want to use, they can be easily installed. Follow these steps:

1. Download the new template file. If it is in a compressed format (ZIP, RAR, and so on), uncompress or extract the SVG template file.

2. Open the SVG file itself in Inkscape to view the template to make sure it fits your needs.

3. From the main menu, select **File** and then **Save As**.

4. Choose a save location in your computer operating system's Inkscape template directory.

   For Windows, that directory is within the **C:\Program Files\Inkscape\ share\templates** folder. For Mac OS the directory is **/Applications/Inkscape/ Contents/Resources/Templates/**. For Linux the directory is typically **/usr/lo-cal/share/inkscape/templates/**

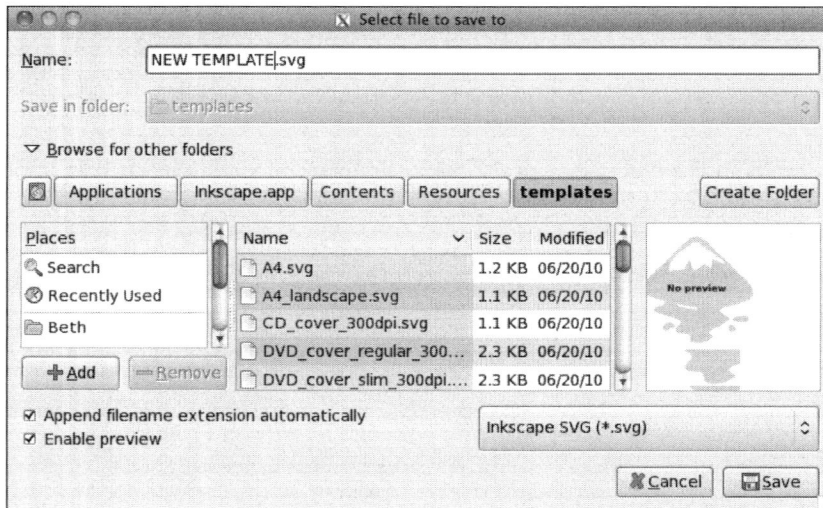

5. Click **Save**.

6. If you restart Inkscape and go to the main menu and select **File** and then **New**, then the new custom template should be in the submenu.

Creating your own custom templates

If you need to create your own template, or modify one of these existing options—there are a few ways you could do this.

To modify an existing template:

1. Open the template that most resembles the new one you would like to create.

2. Modify the **Document Properties** (choose **File** and then **Document Properties** or use the *Shift + Ctrl/Option + D* keyboard shortcut) or other settings applicable to the template you want to create.

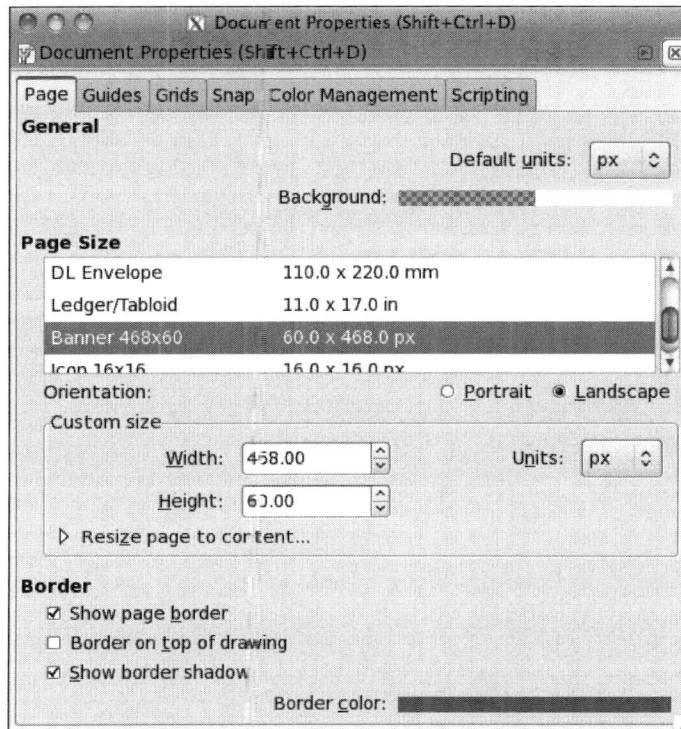

3. From the main menu choose **File** and then **Save As**.

4. Choose a save location in your computer operating system's Inkscape template directory.

    For Windows, that directory is located within the **C:\Program Files\Inkscape\share\templates** folder. For Mac OS it is in **/Applications/Inkscape/Contents/Resources/Templates/**. For Linux the directory typically is: **/usr/local/share/inkscape/templates/**. Use a descriptive template name to describe your new custom template.

5. Once saved, restart Inkscape and go to the main menu and select **File** and then **New** — and the new custom template should be in the submenu.

If you want to create a new template from scratch, that is almost as easy. You just create the file specifications and properties as you need them to be, and start with Step 3 above to complete and save your new template.

Plugins, scripts, and extensions

Let's first understand what plugins, scripts, and extensions are in Inkscape. **Plugins** add new capabilities to software programs—thus customizing what you want them to do for you. More common plugins are those that you use with your web browser. Adobe Flash players, Quicktime video players, and similar plugins allow you to view certain file types from within your browser.

When you use scripts with Inkscape, you essentially add new features to the existing software. A script takes control of the Inkscape software to perform a certain feature. Scripts themselves differ from plugins in that they are usually written in a different programming language than the main program (Inkscape in this case) and can be modified any time.

Extensions are a lot like scripts—and in the world of Inkscape are thought to be the same. They are created to be incorporated into Inkscape itself to "extend" the software's features or functionality and on their own outside of their use in Inkscape, wouldn't work correctly. An example of an extension for Inkscape is the one that allows importing and exporting of non-SVG file types into the program.

Inkscape plugins are available here: `http://wiki.inkscape.org/wiki/index.php/Tools`. You can also find common extensions here: `http://wiki.inkscape.org/wiki/index.php/ExtensionsRepository#Extensions`. Although they are not all-inclusive lists of what is available, they give a healthy start in your search for customizing Inkscape.

Installation

The procedures for installing plug-ins vary because there are some dependencies on your computer's operating system and on what software you already have installed on your computer. The best rule of thumb is to read the plug in installation instructions.

Script installation is a bit easier—it requires the script code file itself and an INX file. It is as simple as copying both files and placing them into the extension folder directly. In Windows, this directory is **C:\Program Files\Inkscape\share\ extensions**. In the Mac OS and Linux, this is typically in the **home/.inkscape/ extensions** directory.

Always be sure to read script installation instructions because they often have dependencies. For example, they may require additional programs to be installed before they can work. If you don't know these dependencies up front, you can try an install and then read the error message after you run the script from a command line interface.

Common extras for web design

The common extras for web design are:

- **Agave:** In web design, colors can be key. You can use Agave, a color scheme tool, to help create pleasing color palettes based on standard color composition rules. Once you create the palette, you can export it for use in Inkscape. Here's where you can find more information: `http://home.gna.org/colorscheme/`.

- **Export to PDF CMYK**: CMYK (Cyan/Magenta/Yellow/ Black) is a critical color separation in the print design. Unfortunately, Inkscape does not support it. The Export to PDF CMYK extension generates a vector PDF file using the color system CMYK. For more information about this extension go to: `http://wiki.softwarelivre.org/InkscapeBrasil/ExportarPDFCMYK` (you may need to use browser translation from Portuguese).

Summary

We dug right in at the start of this chapter and reviewed how to access the pre-installed templates in Inkscape. Then we took a look and how to install new templates that one might find online. We discussed in detail how to modify a standard template and save it as a custom one and how to start from scratch and save a custom template. We also jumped into learning about plugins, scripts, and extensions. Specifically we learned what each of those items are in terms of Inkscape, where you can find more information to search through, as well as how to install and use them within your projects. We even defined a few "web favorites" that might help make your life easier with future projects.

From web design basics through the intricacies of Inkscape, we've learned a lot. From text styling, creating complex shapes, backgrounds, and tracing tools to working with images, designing for blogs or storefronts and using plugins we've kept centered on learning how best to use Inkscape for web design. Add in all the practical, detailed examples and we've had enough hands-on experience to tackle almost any web design project.

A
Keyboard Shortcuts

The following are the basic keyboard shortcuts for Inkscape .48 release of software.

[*(notes)* If you are using the Windows operating system, all instances of Command (*Cmd*) should be replaced with the Control (*Ctrl*) key.]

You can also download and use a graphical version of the Inkscape Keyboard Layout from: http://www.openclipart.org/detail/81331.

Keyboard shortcut	Feature function
File menu shortcuts	
Cmd+N	create new document
Cmd+O	open an SVG document
Shift+Cmd+E	export to PNG
Cmd+I	import bitmap or SVG
Cmd+P	print document
Cmd+S	save document
Shift+Cmd+S	save under a new name
Shift+Cmd+Alt+S	save a copy
Cmd+Q	exit Inkscape

Keyboard shortcut	Feature function
Tools shortcuts	
F1, s	Selector
Space	Switch to the Selector tool temporarily; another Space switches back
Shift+F2, w	Tweak tool
F3, z	Zoom tool
F4, r	Rectangle tool
Shift+F4, x	3D box tool
F5, e	Ellipse/arc tool
F6, p	Freehand (Pencil) tool
Shift+F6, b	Bezier (Pen) tool
Cmd+F6, c	Calligraphy tool
Shift+F7, u	Paint Bucket tool
Cmd+F1, g	Gradient tool
F7, d	Dropper tool
F8, t	Text tool
F9, i	Spiral tool
Shift+F9,	Star tool
Cmd+F2, o	Connector tool
Dialog windows	
Shift+Cmd+F	Fill and Stroke
Shift+Cmd+W	Swatches
Shift+Cmd+T	Text and Font
Shift+Cmd+M	Transform
Shift+Cmd+L	Layers
Shift+Cmd+A	Align and Distribute
Shift+Cmd+O	Object Properties
Shift+Cmd+H	Undo History
Shift+Cmd+X	XML Editor
Shift+Cmd+D	Document Preferences
Shift+Cmd+P	Inkscape Preferences
Shift+Cmd+E	Export to PNG
Cmd+F	Find
Shift+Alt+B	Trace Bitmap
Shift+Cmd+7	Path Effects

Keyboard shortcut	Feature function
Basic object shortcuts	
Shift+Cmd+Y, Cmd+Z	Undo
Shift+Cmd+Z, Cmd+Y	Redo
Cmd+C	Copy selection
Cmd+X	Cut selection
Cmd+V	Paste clipboard
Cmd+Alt+V	Paste in place
Shift+Cmd+V	Paste style
Cmd+7	Paste path effect
Cmd+D	Duplicate selection
Alt+D	Clone object
Shift+Alt+D	Unlink clone
Shift+D	Select original
Alt+B	Create a bitmap copy
Shift+Alt+B	Trace bitmap
Alt+I	Object(s) to pattern
Shift+Alt+I	Pattern to object(s)
Shift+Cmd+U, Cmd+G	Group selected objects
Shift+Cmd+G, Cmd+U	Ungroup selected group(s)
Home	Raise selection to top
End	Lower selection to bottom
PgUp	Raise selection one step
PgDn	Lower selection one step

B

Glossary of Terms

Alignment: Lines up all the elements, horizontally or vertically, upon the screen. Use natural alignments within an entire web space when you use more than one graphical element such as photos, graphics, and/or text.

Animated GIFs: In Inkscape, you can create vector graphics and export them as PNG files. Then you can use those individual PNG files and create individual animation frames that can be used in other open source programs like Gimp to create animated GIFs.

Attributes: It is the properties of an object as seen in the Inkscape XML Editor. Selecting an attribute (like stroke or fill) will then let you see the detailed properties (such as color codes and line thicknesses).

Backgrounds: These are "behind" the overall design of a web page. Can be of any design, shape, size or color but, as a rule of thumb, a background should not distract from the overall design of a web page.

Blogs: Now commonplace on the web, these are web sites or portions of websites that offer commentary on personal events, politics, videos, pictures, and anything else that can be "posted" online. Blogs are structured around posts that are published in reverse-chronological order and allow readers to provide comments and sometime ratings.

Buttons: Used on forms and other forms of web pages where a user needs to "submit" information that will be stored.

Canvas: The page or document in Inkscape where your objects and shapes are created.

Cascading Style Sheet (CSS): Used with the HTML/XML coding to define the look and formatting of an entire web site. One style sheet determines fonts, colors, spacing, placement, and more—reducing complexity and repetition in the coding of the pages themselves.

Contrast: A design principle that can help create effective and pleasant web pages. Contrast uses abstractly different sizes, colors, directions, shapes and fonts (mixing modern with old style), font weights, and more.

Diagram: A graphical representation of information that uses shapes, images, and more to create a cohesive thought. There are a number of diagram types such as Venn, Activity, Tree, Network, and more.

Dialogs: Windows or portions of screens that appear in response to a user action and invite the user to select from a set of options in the window to or make a decision. Often, the user must click OK to confirm the decision.

Extensions: Inkscape scripts that, when installed, "extend" the features or functionality of the software.

Fill: Terminology to describe the color of an object or shape.

Font: A certain size and style of type in text fields.

Flow chart: One of the most common types of diagrams. It shows the general process for completing a task or decision. It shows each step, decision, and option as a particular box/option/connector. And in general it represents a step-by-step solution to a given problem.

Gimp: An open-source photo manipulation software tool. It is used in this book for the process of creating an animated GIF. More information can be found at: http://www.gimp.org.

Grids: A tool in Inkscape to help align and measure objects. Can be particularly useful in creating web page designs because there are "snap to grid" options to help with exact alignment.

Guides: Another tool in Inkscape that can be user-generated. You can create guides on your canvas to help with align and place objects.

Handle: Small squares or circles at edges of an object in Inkscape. Handles are often used to change the size of an object or change the shape of a path.

Icons: Usually smaller objects that represent a certain feature or function on a web page. However, they can be completely graphical or a combination of graphics and text.

Layers: A feature of Inkscape software that allows multiple "layers" on a canvas for easier creation. Each layer can be locked, viewed, moved, and more. You must select a layer before you can start manipulating objects within that layer. This selected layer, is then termed the drawing layer.

Lock: Objects, shapes, text, and layers can all be locked in Inkscape. Once this setting is in place, these objects cannot be edited until they are unlocked.

Logos: A visual representation of a company or brand.

Lorem Ipsum: A text effect that displays a pseudo-Latin form of text that is used as a "placeholder" in the larger context of the web page design. Allows visual correlation of text content, without having to create actual text for that space in the design.

Open Clipart Library: An open-source, free clip art image library that you can search directly from Inkscape.

Organizational chart: Or "org chart" shows the structure of an organization. It also details roles, job titles, and sometimes the relationships between the jobs.

Panning: Moving left, right, or up and down on the Inkscape main screen.

Paths: Lines that have a start and end point, curves, angles, and points that are calculated with a mathematical equation. However paths are not limited to being straight—they can be of any shape, size, and even encompass any number of curves. When you combine them, they create drawings, diagrams, and can even help create certain fonts.

Plugins: Additional software you install to add new capabilities to Inkscape.

Properties: Attributes/details of an object created in Inkscape. These are typically editable and can be changed with the software interface or within the XML editor.

Proximity: A grouping of similar information together on a web page.

Rasterized images: Images that are created by tiny rectangular dots which we call pixels. File types like JPG, FIG, and BMP are all rasterized images.

Repetition: The idea of repeating elements such as buttons, shapes (graphical or just placement), or colors in a design to make a pleasing impact.

RSS (Really Simple Syndication) feeds: A basic way to continually broadcast (or publish) blog entries. These feeds are in a standardized XML format and pull the metadata tags you assigned when publishing your blog post and display them in "readers" for others to automatically receive.

Scalable Vector Graphics or SVG: An OASIS standard vector-based drawing language that uses some basic principles: it can be scalable to any size without losing detail and a drawing can use an unlimited number of smaller drawings used in any number of ways (and reused) and still be a part of a larger whole.

Scans: A process Inkscape uses to describe a "pass" over a bitmap image in order to create a trace of the image. Single scans are done with a single pass (or scan) to create the paths. Multiple scans, in turn, use multiple passes with different settings each time to create different paths that are then stored and displayed in a group to create the trace.

Scripts: Add new features to Inkscape. They must be installed after the initial Inkscape installation and are typically written in a different programming language than the main program (Inkscape in this case) and can be modified at any time.

Shapes: In Inkscape and SVG there are basic shape elements that include rectangles, circles, ellipses, straight lines, polylines, and polygons. They have different attributes than paths, and can have fill and stroke information edited via the software interface as well as with the XML editor directly.

SIOX Simple Interactive Object Extraction: A process of separating an object from the background in a bitmap image.

Site tree/Site map: A list of all the individual pages of a web site. Typically the site map outlines how each page is linked to the others. It can be used for web site planning, but also as a user interface aide to help web site users find where they need to be on the site.

Storefronts: Any web site that sells a commodity. They often allow you to search through products and then purchase a product through a "shopping cart".

Stroke: The border of an object or shape. You can often change the stroke color and thickness.

Template: A base document that has been created to simplify the design process. Basic settings like canvas size, fonts, colors, and placement have already been pre-defined and set in the document.

Text styling: Manipulating text so that it creates a certain feel when seen in an overall design. Sometimes it is also called typography or typesetting.

Tracing: The process of creating paths (and nodes) to represent an underlying bitmap image and then using those paths to create a vector based image.

Vector graphics: The use of points, lines, curves, and shapes or polygon(s), which are all based on mathematical equations, to represent images in computer graphics.

Wallpapers: Images used as desktop backgrounds. These are also commonly used (and downloaded) with cell phones and other electronic devices.

XML Editor: Code-based version of objects and drawings on your Inkscape canvas. Within the XML editor you can change any aspect of the document and see it immediately reflected on your canvas.

Zoom: A function that magnifies your canvas to see more detail (zoomed in) or displays the entire canvas at a glance (zoomed out).

C
Fonts

A font is a character set that has the same style and size of a particular typeface. For example, a character set of 10 point, Times New Roman typeface would be a font as would the character set of the 9 point, Times New Roman normal. Within the context of Inkscape, fonts and text/letters can become confusing. You have a Create and Edit text tool—that relies on your computer systems and the installed fonts—and the ability to use these same letters and words to create vector-based objects, as seen in *Chapter 4, Styling Text*. There is second text tool labeled **T** in the command bar. It is the Text and Font Tool and is used after the text has been created on the canvas. This tool allows you to View and Select the installed Font Families, Size, Styling, and Spacing. What is critical is that the text appears as designed across web browsers, even when the "end viewer" doesn't have the fonts installed on their computers.

SVG fonts and Inkscape

SVG uses WebFonts, as defined in the Cascading Style Sheets, level 2 specifications (http://www.w3.org/TR/2008/REC-CSS2-20080411/ section 15.1) to deliver font data via a browser. Generally this means that an SVG application creates a graphic, and any text element that uses fonts in its creation gets categorized as WebFonts and is given a SVG document fragment. Then the WebFonts are saved in a location relative to the referencing document.

When you deliver the SVG file to a programming team, you must send them the SVG file, source graphics, and, if you want to edit the text, the font files. However, for a display—the only type of environment allowing someone to view the page, but not edit it—you can deliver the SVG file without the font. The display-only environment allows two or more parties to view the file, even comment on it, but only the creator of the file can then edit it.

Inkscape automatically embeds Type 1 fonts and subsets all fonts used in the document when exporting PS, EPS, or PDF. This preserves the files for editing and allows it to look as it is designed when opening on any computer system.

When we created bitmaps of text objects in *Chapter 4*, *Styling Text*, no font embedding was necessary. The files are exported and cannot be edited. They essentially become graphics themselves. The source Inkscape SVG file is required in order to edit the text.

Using common web browser fonts

In web design, it is critical to consider the availability of fonts on a viewer's computer. For example, if you set some of your heading fonts on your web page to be **Wide Latin**, but the visitor to your site does not have this font, the browser will just use the default font. The result will be a design effect much different than you intended, and probably not the best design effect.

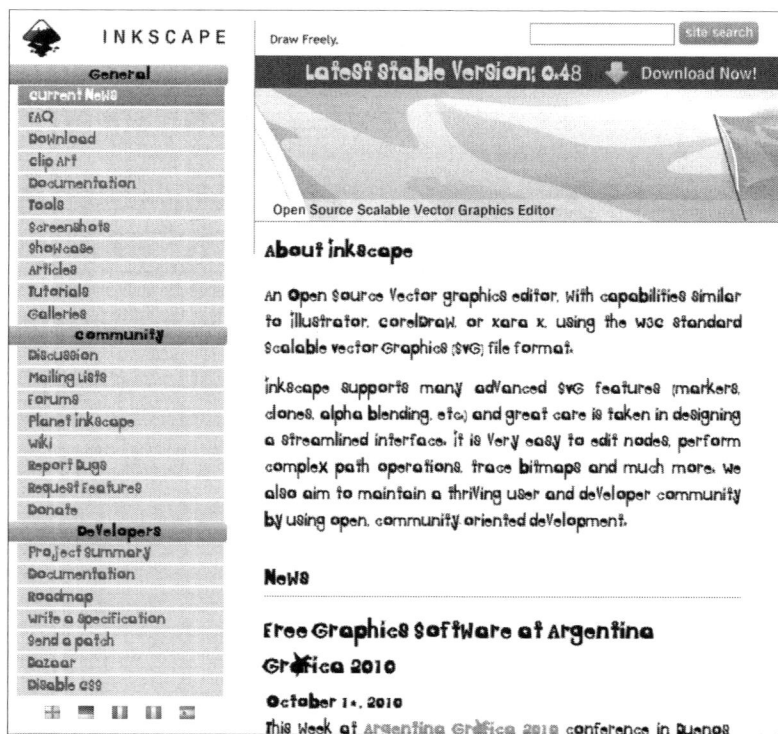

As seen above, the wrong font can cause the page alignment to be awkward as well as the overall look of the web page to be skewed compared to how it is was designed to look (see the following image).

To work around this issue, use fonts that are commonly available across browsers (and computers), particularly for websites that will use a lot of body text. Here's a list of the most common:

- The Sans-serif font family: Arial, Verdana, Geneva, Helvetica, sans-serif
- The Serif font family: Georgia, Times New Roman, Times, serif
- The Monospace font family: Courier New, Courier, monospace

For key headings or select text pieces, you can also create bitmap graphics of text items. This book presents some unique ways to do this in *Chapter 4, Styling Text*. One word of caution! The more graphics provided at a given site, the greater the potential for long load times. So any graphic versions of text should be used sparingly and only when it will provide the most design impact.

If you are using a CSS, however, then there are a few CSS image replacement techniques that can be used as well instead of graphics. It lets you replace a text element with an image and vice versa. For example, you might want a company logo on the web page, but still use an `<h1>` or other text tags for text for the accessibility and SEO benefits.

For some additional font choices when creating text stylings, you can visit websites like `Dafont.com` and `Fontfreak.com`. These sites, and similar ones, provide free fonts if the design is for non-commercial use. Check the legal disclaimers before using these on client websites. Or also look at alternative techniques for creating a similar look to a custom font by investigating: Cufon (a JavaScript option, `http://cufon.shoqolate.com/generate/`), sIFR (a Flash/JavaScript option, `http://www.mikeindustries.com/blog/sifr`), or @font-face (a CSS option, `http://www.css3.info/preview/web-fonts-with-font-face/`).

Index

O

P

R

S

Thank you for buying
Inkscape 0.48 Essentials for Web Designers

About Packt Publishing

Packt, pronounced 'packed', published its first book "*Mastering phpMyAdmin for Effective MySQL Management*" in April 2004 and subsequently continued to specialize in publishing highly focused books on specific technologies and solutions.

Our books and publications share the experiences of your fellow IT professionals in adapting and customizing today's systems, applications, and frameworks. Our solution based books give you the knowledge and power to customize the software and technologies you're using to get the job done. Packt books are more specific and less general than the IT books you have seen in the past. Our unique business model allows us to bring you more focused information, giving you more of what you need to know, and less of what you don't.

Packt is a modern, yet unique publishing company, which focuses on producing quality, cutting-edge books for communities of developers, administrators, and newbies alike. For more information, please visit our website: www.packtpub.com.

About Packt Open Source

In 2010, Packt launched two new brands, Packt Open Source and Packt Enterprise, in order to continue its focus on specialization. This book is part of the Packt Open Source brand, home to books published on software built around Open Source licences, and offering information to anybody from advanced developers to budding web designers. The Open Source brand also runs Packt's Open Source Royalty Scheme, by which Packt gives a royalty to each Open Source project about whose software a book is sold.

Writing for Packt

We welcome all inquiries from people who are interested in authoring. Book proposals should be sent to author@packtpub.com. If your book idea is still at an early stage and you would like to discuss it first before writing a formal book proposal, contact us; one of our commissioning editors will get in touch with you.

We're not just looking for published authors; if you have strong technical skills but no writing experience, our experienced editors can help you develop a writing career, or simply get some additional reward for your expertise.

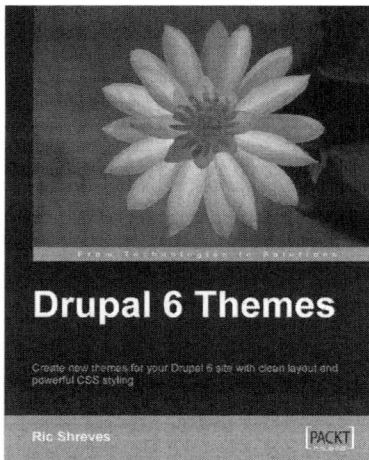

Drupal 6 Themes

ISBN: 978-1-847195-66-1   Paperback: 312 pages

Create new themes for your Drupal 6 site with clean layout and powerful CSS styling

1. Learn to create new Drupal 6 themes

2. No experience of Drupal theming required

3. Techniques and tools for creating and modifying themes

4. A complete guide to the system's themable elements

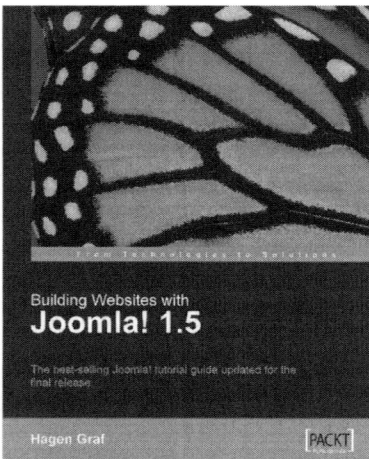

Building Websites with Joomla! 1.5

ISBN: 978-1-847195-30-2   Paperback: 384 pages

The best-selling Joomla! tutorial guide updated for the latest 1.5 release

1. Learn Joomla! 1.5 features

2. Install and customize Joomla! 1.5

3. Configure Joomla! administration

4. Create your own Joomla! templates

5. Extend Joomla! with new components, modules, and plug-ins

Please check **www.PacktPub.com** for information on our titles

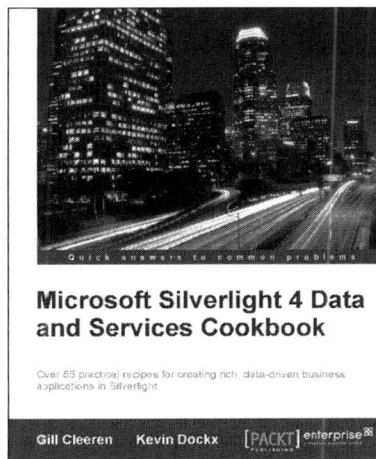

Microsoft Silverlight 4 Data and Services Cookbook

ISBN: 978-1-847199-84-3   Paperback: 476 pages

Over 80 practical recipes for creating rich, data-driven business applications in Silverlight

1. Design and develop rich data-driven business applications in Silverlight

2. Rapidly interact with and handle multiple sources of data and services within Silverlight business applications

3. Packed with practical, hands-on cookbook recipes, illustrating the techniques to solve particular data problems effectively within your Silverlight business applications

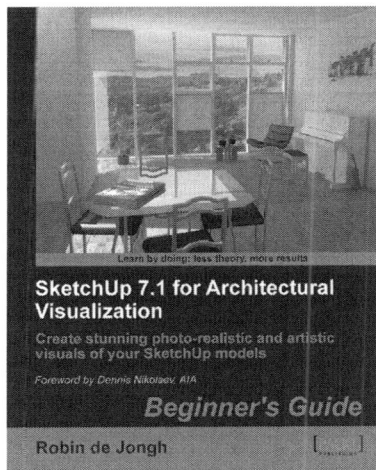

SketchUp 7.1 for Architectural Visualization: Beginner's Guide

ISBN: 978-1-847199-46-1   Paperback: 408 pages

Create stunning photo-realistic and artistic visuals for your SketchUp models

1. Create picture-perfect photo-realistic 3D architectural renders for your SketchUp models

2. Post-process SketchUp output to create digital watercolor and pencil art

3. Follow a professional visualization studio workflow

Please check **www.PacktPub.com** for information on our titles

Printed in Great Britain by
Amazon.co.uk, Ltd.,
Marston Gate.